TOP TRAILS™
Northern California's Redwood Coast

TOP TRAILS™

Northern California's Redwood Coast

MUST-DO HIKES FOR EVERYONE

Written by

Mike White

 WILDERNESS PRESS ... *on the trail since 1967*

To the Pneuma Project—thanks for a family of love, acceptance, and kindness.

Top Trails Northern California's Redwood Coast: Must-Do Hikes for Everyone

1st EDITION 2014, 4th printing 2019

Copyright © 2014 by Mike White
Cover and interior photos copyright © 2014 by Mike White
Maps: Mike White
Cover design: Frances Baca Design and Scott McGrew
Interior design: Frances Baca Design
Production: Annie Long
Copyeditor: Laura Shauger
Indexer: Rich Carlson

ISBN 978-0-89997-751-5; eISBN 978-0-89997-752-2
Manufactured in the United States of America

Published by: **Wilderness Press**
                An imprint of AdventureKEEN
                2204 First Avenue South, Suite 102
                Birmingham, AL 35233
                (800) 443-7227
                info@wildernesspress.com
                www.wildernesspress.com

Visit our website for a complete listing of our books and for ordering information.

Distributed by Publishers Group West

Cover photo: Visitors admire the coast redwoods in the Stout Grove (Trail 54)

SAFETY NOTICE: Although Wilderness Press and the author have made every attempt to ensure that the information in this book is accurate at press time, they are not responsible for any loss, damage, injury, or inconvenience that may occur to anyone while using this book. You are responsible for your own safety and health while in the wilderness. The fact that a trail is described in this book does not mean that it will be safe for you. Be aware that trail conditions can change from day to day. Always check local conditions, know your own limitations, and consult a map.

The Top Trails™ Series

Wilderness Press

When Wilderness Press published *Sierra North* in 1967, no other trail guide like it existed for the Sierra backcountry. The first run of 2,800 copies sold out in less than two months and its success heralded the beginning of Wilderness Press. Since we were founded more than 40 years ago, we have expanded our territories to cover California, Alaska, Hawaii, the U.S. Southwest, the Pacific Northwest, New England, and Canada.

Wilderness Press continues to publish comprehensive, accurate, and readable outdoor books. Hikers, backpackers, kayakers, skiers, snowshoers, climbers, cyclists, and trail runners rely on Wilderness Press for accurate outdoor adventure information.

Top Trails

In its Top Trails guides, Wilderness Press has paid special attention to organization so that you can find the perfect hike each and every time. Whether you're looking for a steep trail to test yourself on or a walk in the park, a romantic waterfall or a city view, Top Trails will lead you there.

Each Top Trails guide contains trails for everyone. The trails selected provide a sampling of the best that the region has to offer. These are the "must-do" hikes, walks, runs, and bike rides, with every feature of the area represented.

Every book in the Top Trails series offers:

- The Wilderness Press commitment to accuracy and reliability
- Ratings and rankings for each trail
- Distances and approximate times
- Easy-to-follow trail notes
- Map and permit information

Northern California's Redwood Coast Trails

TRAIL NUMBER AND NAME	Page	Difficulty -12345+	Length in Miles	Type	Dayhiking	Backpacking	Running	Biking	Dogs Allowed	Handicapped Access	Child-Friendly
1. Mendocino											
1 Big Hendy Loop	25	1	1.4	●	●		●				●
2 Montgomery Woods Trail	30	2	1.5	●	●		●				●
3 Fern Canyon & Pygmy Forest Loop	35	3	9.0	●	●	●	●	●			
4 Chapman Point & Spring Ranch Headlands	41	2	2.9	●	●		●		●		
5 Big River Haul Road	46	2	9.0	●	●		●	●	●		
6 Mendocino Headlands	50	1	3.2	●	●		●		●		
7 Forest History Trail	55	3	4.1	●	●		●	●	●		
8 Russian Gulch Loop	60	3	7.1	●	●		●	●		●	
9 Point Cabrillo Light Station	66	1	2.3	●	●		●		●	●	●
10 Ecological Staircase Trail	71	3	4.7	●	●		●				
11 Chamberlain Creek Falls Loop	76	3	2.9	●	●		●		●		
12 Ten Mile Beach	81	3	11.0	●	●		●		●		
2. King Range & Sinkyone											
13 Lost Coast Trail: North Section	93	3	24.8	●		●					
14 Lightning Trail to King Peak	103	4	5.4	●	●	●	●				
15 Lost Coast Trail: South Section	108	5	28.7	●		●					
3. Humboldt											
16 Franklin K. Lane Loop	129	1	0.5	●	●						●
17 Stephens Grove Loop	133	1	0.7	●	●						●
18 Nature Trail Loop	136	1	0.7	●	●					●	●
19 Founders Grove & Mahan Loop	140	1	1.3	●	●						●
20 Rockefeller Grove Loop	145	1	0.6	●	●						●
21 Big Tree Loop	149	1	0.6	●	●						●
22 Big Tree & Homestead Loop	153	2	2.5	●	●		●				
23 Bull Creek Flats & Big Tree Loop	158	3	9.4	●	●		●				
24 Allens Trail	164	4	2.6	●	●		●				
25 High Rock River Trail	168	3	2.0	●	●		●				
26 Grieg, French & Bell Groves Loop	172	1	0.6	●	●						●
27 Drury-Chaney Loop	176	1	2.2	●	●						
28 Cheatham Grove	180	1	0.7	●	●						●
29 Elk River Trail	184	3	10.0	●	●		●	●	●	●	●

Refer to the Trail Table Legend on page xviii.

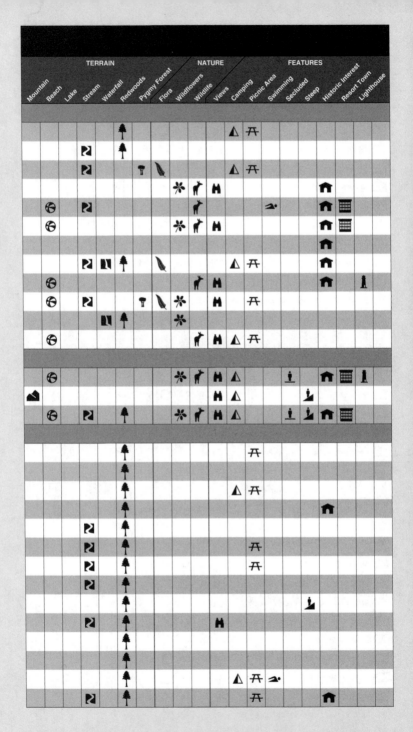

Northern California's Redwood Coast Trails

TRAIL NUMBER AND NAME	Page	Difficulty 1 2 3 4 5+	Length in Miles	Type	Dayhiking	Backpacking	Running	Biking	Dogs Allowed	Handicapped Access	Child-Friendly
4. Redwood National Park & Vicinity											
30 Trinidad Head Loop	198	3	1.4	loop	hiking		running		dogs		
31 Agate Beach & Rim Trails	203	3	0.6 or 4.2	out & back	hiking		running				
32 Stone Lagoon	210	2	8.0	out & back	hiking		running				
33 Redwood Creek Trail	215	3	16.4	out & back	hiking	backpacking	running				
34 Lady Bird Johnson Grove	221	1	1.4	loop	hiking					handicapped	child
35 Tall Trees Grove	225	3	3.2	loop	hiking		running				
36 Emerald Ridge Loop	230	4	5.2	loop	hiking		running				
37 Dolason Prairie Trail	236	3	10.4	out & back	hiking		running				
38 Lyons Ranch Loop	241	3	4.5	loop	hiking		running				
39 Coastal Trail: Skunk Cabbage Section	246	4	8.0	out & back	hiking		running				
40 Trillium Falls Loop	251	2	2.6	loop	hiking		running				child
5. Prairie Creek											
41 Fern Canyon Loop	263	2	1.6	loop	hiking		running				
42 Irvine & Miners Loop	268	3	7.5	loop	hiking		running				
43 Big Tree Loop	274	2	3.0	loop	hiking		running				child
44 Brown Creek Loop	279	3	3.6	loop	hiking		running				
45 West Ridge & Prairie Creek Loop	283	3	5.9	loop	hiking		running				
46 Hope Creek & Ten Taypo Creek Loop	288	3	3.5	loop	hiking		running				
47 Ossagon Trail	292	4	4.2	out & back	hiking		running	biking			
6. Del Norte Coast Redwoods											
48 Yurok Loop & Hidden Beach	303	1	2.3	loop	hiking		running				child
49 Klamath Overlook	307	3	8.2	out & back	hiking		running				
50 Damnation Creek Trail	312	4	3.8	out & back	hiking						
51 Coastal Trail: Enderts Beach	316	2	1.5	out & back	hiking		running				
52 Coastal Trail: Crescent Beach	319	2	4.0	out & back	hiking		running				
7. Jedediah Smith Redwoods											
53 Boy Scout Tree Trail	331	3	5.4	out & back	hiking		running				
54 Stout Grove Loop	335	1	0.6	loop	hiking						child
55 Leiffer & Ellsworth Loops	339	2	1.9	loop	hiking						
56 Simpson-Reed & Peterson Loop	343	1	0.8	loop	hiking					handicapped	
57 Myrtle Creek Trail	347	2	2.0	out & back	hiking		running				

Refer to the Trail Table Legend on page xviii.

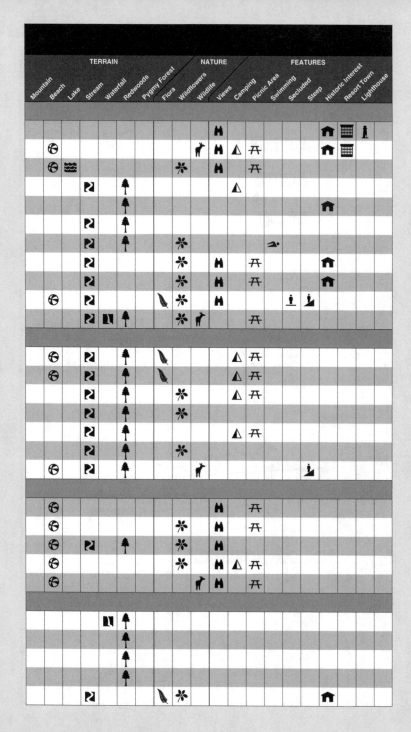

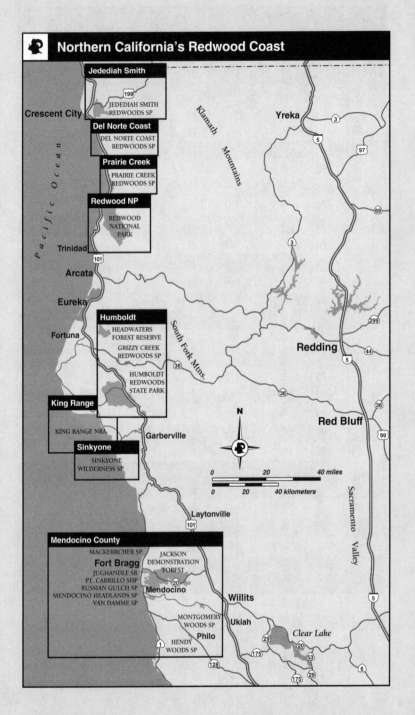

Northern California's Redwood Coast

Jedediah Smith

199

JEDEDIAH SMITH
REDWOODS SP

Crescent City

Del Norte Coast

DEL NORTE COAST
REDWOODS SP

Prairie Creek

PRAIRIE CREEK
REDWOODS SP

Redwood NP

REDWOOD
NATIONAL
PARK

Trinidad

101

Arcata

Eureka

Fortuna

Humboldt

HEADWATERS
FOREST RESERVE

GRIZZY CREEK
REDWOODS SP

HUMBOLDT
REDWOODS
STATE PARK

King Range

KING RANGE NRA

Sinkyone

SINKYONE
WILDERNESS SP

Garberville

Pacific Ocean

Klamath Mountains

Yreka

3

97

5

89

3

299

Redding

44

5

36

36

36

Red Bluff

99

South Fork Mtns.

N

0   20   40 miles

0   20   40 kilometers

Laytonville

101

Mendocino County

MACKERRCHER SP

Fort Bragg

JUGHANDLE SR
PT. CABRILLO SHP
RUSSIAN GULCH SP
MENDOCINO HEADLANDS SP
VAN DAMME SP

JACKSON
DEMONSTRATION
FOREST

20

Mendocino

MONTGOMERY
WOODS SP

Philo

1

HENDY
WOODS SP

128

Willits

Ukiah

175

29

20

53

Clear Lake

Sacramento Valley

5

6

175

29

Contents

CHAPTER 1

Mendocino 17

Using Top Trails™

Organization of Top Trails

Top Trails is designed to make identifying the perfect trail easy and enjoyable, and to make every outing a success and a pleasure. With this book, you'll find it's a snap to find the right trail, whether you're planning a major hike or just a sociable stroll with friends.

The Region

Top Trails guide begins with the **regional map** (page x), displaying the entire area covered by the guide and providing an overview of the geography. The map is clearly marked to show which area is covered by each chapter.

In addition to the regional map, refer to the **master trail table** (pages vi–ix), which lists every trail covered in the guide. Here you'll find a concise description, basic information, and highlighted features, all indispensable when planning an outing. A quick reading of the regional map and the master trail table will give you a good overview of the entire region covered by the book.

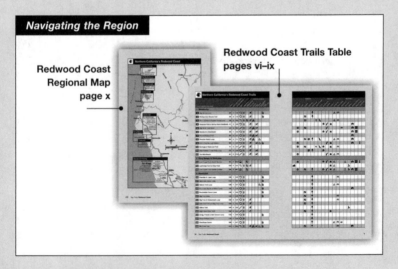

Navigating the Region

Redwood Coast
Regional Map
page x

Redwood Coast Trails Table
pages vi–ix

The Areas

The region covered in each book is divided into areas, with each chapter corresponding to one area in the region. Each area chapter introduction contains information to help you choose and enjoy a trail every time out. Use the table of contents or the regional map to identify an area of interest, then turn to the area chapter to find the following:

- An overview of the area, including park and permit information
- An area map with all trails clearly marked
- A trail features table providing trail-by-trail details
- Trail summaries, written in a lively, accessible style

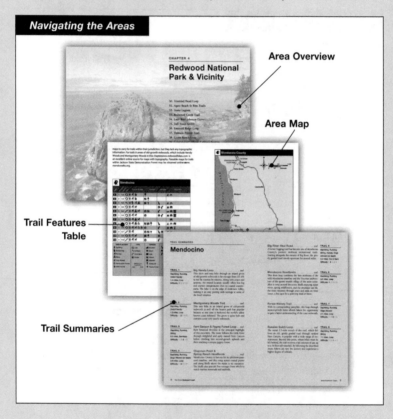

The Trails

The basic building block of each Top Trails guide is the **trail entry**. Each one is laid out to make finding and following the trail as simple as possible, with all pertinent information presented in this easy-to-follow format:

- A detailed trail map
- Trail descriptors for trail use and type, length, difficulty level, GPS coordinates, and other at-a-glance information in the margin of each entry's opening page
- The main trail text
- Trail milestones providing easy-to-follow, turn-by-turn trail directions

Some trail descriptions offer additional information:
- An elevation profile
- Trail options
- Trail highlights (shown by labeled icons)

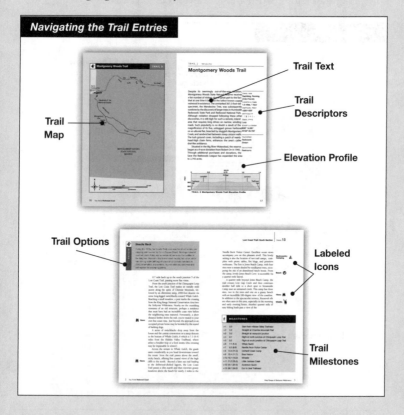

Navigating the Trail Entries

Trail Map

Trail Text

Trail Descriptors

Elevation Profile

Trail Options

Labeled Icons

Trail Milestones

Choosing a Trail

Top Trails provides several different ways of choosing a trail, using easy-to-read tables and maps.

Location

If you know in general where you want to go, Top Trails makes it easy to find the right trail in the right place. Each chapter begins with a large-scale map showing the starting point of every trail in that area.

Features

This guide describes the top trails of Northern California's Redwood Coast, and each trail is chosen because it offers one or more features that make it appealing. Using the trail descriptors, summaries, and tables, you can quickly examine all the trails for the features they offer or seek a particular feature among the list of trails.

Season & Condition

Time of year and current conditions can be important factors in selecting the best trail. For example, an exposed, low-elevation trail may be a riot of color in early spring, but an oven-baked taste of hell in midsummer. Wherever relevant, Top Trails identifies the best and worst conditions for the trails you plan to hike. Where relevant, Top Trails identifies the best and worst conditions for the trails you plan to hike.

Difficulty

Every trail has an overall difficulty rating on a scale of 1 to 5, which takes into consideration length, elevation change, exposure, trail quality, etc., to create one (admittedly subjective) rating. The ratings assume you are an

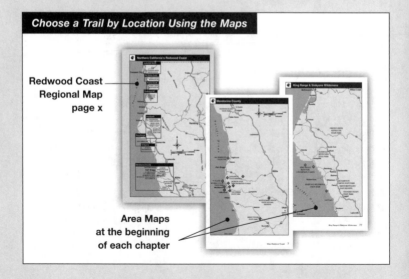

Choose a Trail by Location Using the Maps

Redwood Coast Regional Map page x

Area Maps at the beginning of each chapter

able-bodied adult in reasonably good shape, using the trail for hiking. The ratings also assume normal weather conditions—clear and dry.

Readers should make an honest assessment of their own abilities and adjust time estimates accordingly. Also, rain, snow, heat, wind, and poor visibility can all affect the pace on even the easiest of trails.

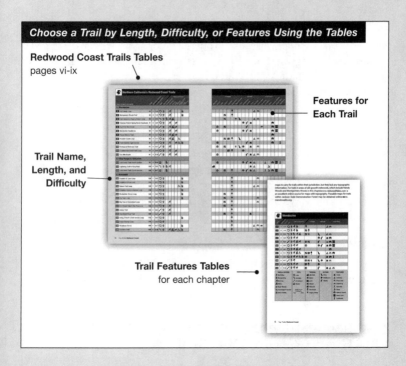

Choose a Trail by Length, Difficulty, or Features Using the Tables

Redwood Coast Trails Tables
pages vi–ix

Features for Each Trail

Trail Name, Length, and Difficulty

Trail Features Tables
for each chapter

Trail Table Legend

USES & ACCESS	TYPE	TERRAIN	NATURE	FEATURES
🥾 Dayhiking	🔄 Loop	⛰️ Mountain	🌿 Flora	🎯 Views
🎒 Backpacking	🔁 Semiloop	🏖️ Beach	🌼 Wildflowers	⛺ Camping
🏃 Running	↗️ Out & Back	🌊 Lake	🦌 Wildlife	🪵 Picnic Area
🚴 Biking	🚌 Shuttle	💧 Stream		🏊 Swimming
🐕 Dogs Allowed		💦 Waterfall		🏕️ Secluded
♿ Handicapped Access	DIFFICULTY	🌲 Redwoods		🪜 Steep
👫 Child-Friendly	- 1 2 3 4 5 +	🌳 Pygmy Forest		🏛️ Historic Interest
	less more			🏨 Resort town
				🗼 Lighthouse

Top Trails Difficulty Ratings

1 A short trail, generally level, which can be completed in one hour or less.

2 A route of 1 to 3 miles, with some ups and downs, which can be completed in one to two hours.

3 A longer route, up to 5 miles, with uphill and/or downhill sections.

4 A long or steep route, perhaps more than 5 miles or with climbs of more than 1,000 vertical feet.

5 The most severe route, both long and steep, more than 5 miles long with climbs of more than 1,000 vertical feet.

Vertical Feet

Every trail description contains the approximate trail length and the overall elevation gain and loss over the course of the trail. It's important to use both figures when considering a hike; on average plan to hike about one hour for every 2 miles, and add an hour for every 1,000 feet you climb.

Hikers often underestimate this important measurement when gauging the difficulty of a trail. The Top Trails measurement accounts for all elevation change, not simply the difference between the highest and lowest points, so that rolling terrain with lots of ups and downs will be identifiable.

The calculation of vertical feet in the Top Trails books is accomplished by a combination of trail measurement and computer-aided estimation. For routes that begin and end at the same spot—i.e., loop or out-and-back trips—the vertical gain exactly matches the vertical descent. With a point-to-point route, the vertical gain and loss will most likely differ, and both figures will be provided in the text.

Finally, all trail entries with at least 250 feet of elevation gain include an **elevation profile**, an easy means for visualizing the topography of the route. These profiles graphically depict the elevation throughout the length of the trail.

TOP TRAILS™

Northern California's Redwood Coast

Fog-filtered *sunlight in Patrick's Point State Park*

Introduction to the Redwood Coast

The rugged Northern California coast of Mendocino, Humboldt, and Del Norte Counties is one of the most dramatic stretches of coastline in North America. Unlike the sandy beaches typically associated with Hollywood visions of Southern California, steep bluffs, rocky beaches, and offshore rocks combine to create the classic portrait of the Golden State's far northern coastline. Above this stunning seascape resides a forest containing the world's tallest trees. Protected in pockets of national and state parks, old-growth redwoods soar skyward to heights approaching 400 feet, the tallest trees on earth. Throw in tall mountains occasionally sliced by ocean-bound rivers, and the portrait of the landscape is nearly complete.

Few experiences in the natural world can match the transcendence of standing in a grove of straight and tall old-growth coast redwoods, gazing skyward through the dappled sunlight for a seemingly endless distance toward the forest canopy. Standing on a bluff at the edge of the continent to watch an endless parade of Pacific waves crash into craggy sea-stacks is an equally stunning moment. Northern California's Redwood Coast offers these opportunities and much more. Welcome to paradise.

Geography & Topography

The waves of the Pacific Ocean crash onto the beaches, rocks, and headlands of Northern California's picturesque shoreline, a rugged coastline that allows few significant harbors of any size from Mendocino County north to the Oregon border. The difficult terrain posed significant challenges for ships loading and transporting the region's redwood lumber during the reconstruction of San Francisco following the fires of the Great Earthquake of 1906.

Not far beyond the coast, mountains rose steeply for thousands of feet. For example, the sudden relief between the ocean and the top of the King Range on the Lost Coast in a mere few miles is rarely duplicated anywhere on the globe. The hillsides of these mountains were carpeted with a dense forest of tall redwoods and nearly as tall Sitka spruces, Douglas firs, grand firs, and western hemlocks. Before settlement, rivers were the only things

Pacific Vista

to slice through this otherwise impenetrable wall of forest. At one time, what is now referred to as Northern California's Redwood Coast was a vast, unbroken, inhospitable wilderness.

Once the impressive coast redwoods were discovered for their high-quality lumber, the terrain of the area changed dramatically. Towns sprang up, relatively flat areas were cleared for farm and ranch land, sawmills appeared, and railroads and doghole ports were developed to transport the lumber. Beginning in the mid-1800s and continuing almost to the end of the next century, all but 5% of the old-growth coast redwoods in existence were chopped down. If it were not for the efforts of conservationists, such as the Save the Redwoods League and others, perhaps none of the tall trees would've been spared.

What we are left with along the Redwood Coast, much of which is still picturesque and impressive, is a fraction of the majestic landscape that once existed, especially in relation to the coast redwoods. Nowadays, old-growth redwood trees are isolated in a number of groves within the several state parks and one national park in the area. While admiring some of the tallest redwoods in existence is a straightforward exercise requiring little physical effort in many spots, a true wilderness experience among the tall trees proves to be an elusive goal. For the average visitor to Northern California's Redwood Coast, however, there's still plenty to see and enjoy.

Flora

The most distinct plant of Northern California's Redwood Coast is the namesake evergreen tree. The coast redwood *(Sequoia sempervirens)* is one of three remaining redwood species still in existence, along with the Sierra Nevada's giant sequoia and China's dawn redwood. Once carpeting a swath of coastal real estate from the southwestern corner of Oregon to central California, old-growth coast redwoods have been limited by excessive logging to pockets of forest, mainly in far northwestern California. Estimates conclude that 95% of the old-growth trees of the former range have been harvested, with logging beginning in the mid-1800s and extending all the way to the 1990s, when the last old-growth timber was felled on privately held land. Although some of the former redwoods were estimated to have topped out at more than 400 feet, the current record holder, Hyperion, is listed at just shy of 380 feet.

The coast redwood, although growing quite tall, has a very shallow root system, which typically extends outward a good distance from the base and often intertwines with the roots of neighboring redwoods. This root network gives individual trees a more secure foundation, but mature redwoods usually meet their demise by simply toppling over. As you might imagine, the

Tangle of ferns

toppling of such a tall tree can create quite a disturbance in the otherwise serene forest. A falling redwood might also knock down or weaken its neighbors. Redwoods on the perimeter of a grove are more susceptible to damage from high winds and flooding.

Coast redwoods require certain conditions to thrive. Although they can tolerate varied conditions of sedimentary soils, the tallest trees usually occur on or near alluvial flats along the area's rivers and streams. Abundant moisture is essential to the tree's growth, with heavy seasonal rains, cool coastal air, and fog drip contributing to the damp environment. However, redwoods do not tolerate salt air, which is why they are absent from the immediate coastline, where Sitka spruce is the dominant conifer.

Evergreen associates of the coast redwood commonly include Douglas fir and western hemlock, with grand fir, Coulter pine, Monterey pine, Port Orford cedar, Sitka spruce, and western red cedar playing lesser roles. Bigleaf maple, California bay, canyon live oak, coast live oak, golden chinquapin, madrone, and tanoak are familiar hardwood associates. Ground-cover associates most often include carpets of redwood sorrel, vanilla leaf, false lily-of-the-valley, and several varieties of ferns. In elevations above the redwood forest, Douglas fir becomes the dominant conifer.

Where more sunlight penetrates the forest along river and stream corridors, a lush riparian area thrives. Here, bigleaf maple and red alder intermix with berry brambles and western azalea. Skunk cabbage, cow parsnip, and giant horsetails bloom in late spring and early summer.

Other plant communities common on Northern California's Redwood Coast include coastal prairie, windswept grasslands occupying marine terraces above coastal cliffs. Much of the native vegetation was cleared in these areas for farming and ranching purposes and replaced mostly by nonnative grasses. Coastal prairies are typically havens for a wide variety of colorful wildflowers in spring and early summer. The open topography allows for beautiful views of the rugged Northern California coastline.

Oftentimes separating the grasslands above the ocean beach from the redwood forest beyond is a strip of coastal scrub, a zone filled with shrubs and grasses, including such plants as berry brambles, California sagebrush, coyote bush, thimbleberry, and poison oak. Seasonal wildflowers are also common in this zone.

The dry upper slopes of the mountains above the redwood forest are often carpeted with chaparral, Spanish for dwarf or scrub oak. Typical members of this shrubby community include ceanothus, chamise, manzanita, mountain mahogany, and toyon. The Bald Hills above Redwood National Park represent an example of another plant community, the upland prairie, where tall fescue and oat grass carpet hillsides amid widely scattered white oak trees.

Fauna

That such a rich environment supports a wide variety of animals should come as no surprise to first-time visitors. From tidepools teeming with marine life to upland forests harboring numerous species of birds and wildlife, the area is swarming with fauna. Perhaps no other critter is more identified with Northern California's Redwood Coast than the slow-moving banana slug *(Ariolimax columbianus)*. Hikers in damp, forested environments are likely to see these yellow-colored slugs inching their way across trails throughout the region. On the opposite end of the size scale, Roosevelt elk are also commonly seen members of the Redwood Coast community, especially along the Lost Coast, near Elk Prairie in Prairie Redwoods State Park, and near Elk Meadow in Redwood National Park. These animals, which range in weight from 575 to 1,100 pounds, tolerate the presence of humans quite well, but should always be viewed from a safe distance.

Along with the Roosevelt elk, several varieties of mammal live in the area. You may see a harbor seal or sea lion lounging on beaches or on nearby

Elk *near Carothers Cove*

Banana Slug

rocks. Farther offshore, migrating whales are prevalent at certain times of the year. Mule deer are fairly common in the forest and along streams. While black bear and mountain lion inhabit the region, they are seldom seen. Smaller mammals of the Redwood Coast include badgers, chipmunks, coyotes, foxes, otters, skunks, squirrels, raccoons, and ringtails.

An abundance of bird species, including cormorants, egrets, herons, gulls, oystercatchers, pelicans, and sandpipers, fill the skies and dot the beaches along the coastline. Bald eagles, ospreys, and kingfishers inhabit the coastal river corridors. Birds seen in the forest include sparrows, wrens, thrushes, and woodpeckers, although the most commonly noticed member might be the squawking black crow. The marbled murrelet and spotted owl are two of the most threatened species of birds in the redwood forest.

Wet and damp areas of the redwood forest are rich in amphibian life, including frogs, toads, and salamanders. Reptiles are less well represented, but some varieties of snakes and lizards inhabit the region.

When to Go

One of the main advantages of Northern California's Redwood Coast is its temperate climate, which allows recreationists the opportunity to hike many of the area's trails year-round. Except for periods of heavy rain during the occasional winter storm, the weather is usually mild enough to allow for pleasant hiking conditions. Following such storms, some trails may become muddy enough to make hiking undesirable. Extended rainy periods may produce flooding, making access roads and trails impassable and causing some parks to close temporarily. Otherwise, hiking in the redwoods is an all-year activity.

During summer, the coastline is often blanketed with a layer of marine fog, which obscures ocean views and may create chilly, humid conditions for hikers. The fog typically diminishes the farther inland you travel, although rivers provide an easy thoroughfare for tentacles of fog to stretch a good distance upstream. Humboldt Redwoods State Park is a classic example of such occurrences, where fog travels up the Eel River a considerable distance from the ocean, providing the moisture and cool temperatures necessary for the continued survival of the coastal redwood species. When summer temperatures in inland California often spike above 100°F, the north coast may experience temperatures 40° cooler.

Autumn is often an excellent season for a visit to the redwoods, when periods of fog are minimal, temperatures are moderate, and storms are few and far between. Also, the number of tourists declines dramatically after Labor Day weekend. Much the same is true for spring once the rainy season has passed. Spring, along with early summer, has the added bonus of wildflowers.

Trail Selection

Several criteria were employed to arrange this collection of the area's best trails. Only the premier paths were included, based upon beautiful scenery, ease of access, quality of trail, and diversity of experience. Many of the selected trails are highly popular, while others may see infrequent use. Anyone fortunate to complete all the trips in this guide would have a comprehensive appreciation for the natural beauty of one of the West's most scenic recreational havens.

Due in large part to the timing of the discovery of the coast redwoods and their subsequent commercial logging, many of the region's trails are fairly short, relatively flat, and within close proximity to major highways. The opportunity to enjoy a wilderness backpacking experience far from the tentacles of development is extremely limited (the Lost Coast being the obvious exception). However, the area offers lots of short and easy hikes, many of them loops, to sandy beaches, stunning vista points, and stately old-growth redwood groves—a virtual dayhikers' paradise.

Key Features

Top Trails guides contain information about "features" for each trail. Northern California's Redwood Coast encompasses a diverse cross section of topography, so much so that many different features are highlighted. From walks along the beach within a stone's throw of the crashing surf to grand vistas atop a mountain peak, this area boasts a wide variety of hiking opportunities. Lush vegetation along a tumbling stream contrasts vividly with the tall grasses and wildflowers of an upland prairie. The region is also steeped in interesting human history. In the midst of all of these attributes is the mighty coast redwood, whose towering groves have lured countless visitors to this rugged land.

Trail Safety

Aside from the usual concerns regarding hiking in the backcountry, California's Redwood Coast poses some unique challenges. Beach hikes require walking across sand or rocks. Trudging across the dry sand above the water line can be extremely tiring. Walking on wet sand provides a firmer surface and better footing, which should prove to be less tiring. Rocky sections of beach can be equally challenging, especially over long distances. In either case, avoid the tendency to underestimate the time required to traverse these landscapes. Beach hikes also necessitate keeping a wary eye on the ocean to avoid being swept away by a sneaker wave. On certain trails, such as the north section of the Lost Coast, sections of shoreline are impassable during high tide. Hikers must pay attention to tide charts on such routes to avoid an untimely end.

Ticks and rattlesnakes are both members of the coastal community, although most visitors to the area probably won't have to deal with either of them. Ticks are most commonly seen in the spring. Hikers should wear light-colored clothing to make it easier to spot the dark-colored pests and use an insect repellent in tick-infested areas. Some hikers tuck their pant legs into their socks to make access to their skin more difficult. Thoroughly inspect your body and clothing for ticks at least once a day.

If you are bitten, firmly grasp the pest with a pair of tweezers and use gentle traction for its removal, making sure none of the head is left behind. Wash the affected area with antibacterial soap and water, and apply an antibiotic ointment. Contact a medical professional if you develop flulike symptoms, such as a headache, rash, joint pain, or fever, as they could be the first signs of Lyme disease or Rocky Mountain spotted fever. Hearing the rattle of a rattlesnake is fairly uncommon, seeing the creature even more so, and being bitten is extremely rare. If you are so unlucky, seek medical attention immediately.

Black bears, mountain lions, and Roosevelt elk are large animals that call the Redwood Coast home. Of the three, you are most likely to see elk on the trail. While many individuals appear to be well adapted to the presence of humans, they are very large animals with more than enough power to injure or kill a person who approaches too closely. Always maintain a safe distance, and never get between a mother and its offspring—a good rule for all wildlife interactions. If you are backpacking, bear canisters are required in some areas and highly recommended otherwise. In addition to using bear canisters to store all food and scented items, maintain a clean camp and pack out all trash.

If you happen upon a mountain lion, don't run—stand your ground and make yourself appear to be as large as possible by raising your arms above your head. Never leave small children unattended; mountain lions see them as prey.

A number of trails may support thickets of poison oak, a three-leaved plant that may produce a rash after contact. Learning to identify the plant will help you avoid it. People susceptible to the rash should wear long-sleeved shirts and long-legged pants in areas where poison oak is prevalent. If you suspect contact between your skin and the leaves or stems of poison oak, rinse the affected area thoroughly in a nearby stream, and bathe or shower as soon as possible. Thoroughly wash your clothes as well because the plant oil can transfer easily from clothing to your skin. If you develop a rash, consult a medical professional.

Fees, Camping & Permits

Entrance into the parks and forests containing trails described in this guide within Mendocino County is generally free of charge. The exceptions are Hendy Woods, Van Damme, and Russian Gulch State Parks, where visitors must purchase a day-use pass. Along the Lost Coast, King Range National Conservation Area and Sinkyone Wilderness State Park do not charge entrance fees. Humboldt Redwoods State Park does not charge any entrance fees, but it does charge a user fee at the Williams Grove Day Use Area.

Since US 101 is the principal thoroughfare of northbound and south-bound motorists traveling through northwestern California, there are no entrance stations or fees charged to pass through Redwood National Park. Other than a fee station at Gold Bluffs Beach, Prairie Creek Redwoods State Park also has free access along the Newton B. Drury Scenic Parkway. Both Del Norte Coast Redwoods and Jedediah Smith Redwoods State Parks do not charge an entrance fee.

Northern California's Redwood Coast offers abundant camping opportunities for tent and recreational vehicle camping, principally within the area's numerous state parks. All of the parks charge fees for overnight camping at their developed campgrounds. Information about the campgrounds nearest a particular trailhead is included near the end of each trail's Finding the Trail section. Most of the campgrounds can be reserved at **reserve america.com** for overnight stays during the summer season. At other times of the year, campsites are available on a first-come, first-served basis.

In addition to the public campgrounds within the parks, many private campgrounds are strung along the roads and highways of the redwood coast. Several resort communities offer a wide range of lodging as well, from modest cabins to upscale resorts and bed-and-breakfasts.

Trail *through living Sequoia*

Overnight users traveling within the King Range National Conservation Area are required to self-register at trailheads for a backcountry permit. Backpackers overnighting within Sinkyone Wilderness State Park also need to self-register and pay a fee at the Needle Rock Visitor Center for a backcountry permit.

On the Trail

Every outing should begin with proper preparation, which usually takes only a few minutes. Even the easiest trail can turn up unexpected surprises. People seldom think about getting lost or injured, but unexpected things can and do happen. Simple precautions can make the difference between a good story and a dangerous situation. Use the Top Trails ratings and descriptions to determine if a particular trail is a good match with your fitness and energy level, given current conditions and time of year.

Have a Plan

Choose Wisely The first step to enjoying any trail is to match the trail to your abilities. It's no use overestimating your experience or fitness—know your abilities and limitations, and use the Top Trails difficulty rating that accompanies each trail.

Leave Word about Your Plans The most basic of precautions is leaving word of your intentions with friends or family. Many people will hike the backcountry their entire lives without ever relying on this safety net, but establishing this simple habit is free insurance.

It's best to leave specific information—location, trail name, and intended time of travel—with a responsible person. However, if this is not possible or if your plans change at the last minute, you should still leave word somewhere with someone. If there is a registration process available, make use of it. If there is a ranger station, trail register, or visitor center, check in.

Review the Route Before embarking on any hike, read the entire description and study the map. It isn't necessary to memorize every detail, but it is worthwhile to have a clear mental picture of the trail and the general area.

Prepare and Plan

- Know your abilities and your limitations.
- Leave word about your plans.
- Know the area and the route.

If the trail or terrain is complex, augment the trail guide with a topo-graphic map. Contact local ranger stations and park offices for maps and current weather and trail-condition information.

Carry the Essentials

Proper preparation for any type of trail use includes gathering certain essential items to carry. Trip checklists will vary tremendously by trail and conditions.

Clothing When the weather is agreeable, light, comfortable clothing is the obvious choice. It's easy to believe that very little spare clothing is needed, but a prepared hiker has something tucked away for any emergency from a surprise shower to an unexpected night in a remote area.

Clothing includes proper footwear, essential for hiking and running trails. On more demanding trails, you need footwear that performs. Running shoes are fine for many trails, and footwear choices are based partly on a hiker's preference and experience. If you will be carrying substantial weight or encountering sustained rugged terrain, step up to hiking boots.

In hot, sunny weather, proper clothing includes a hat, sunglasses, a long-sleeved shirt, and sunscreen. In cooler weather, particularly when it's wet, carry waterproof outer garments and quick-drying undergarments (avoid cotton). As general rule, whatever the conditions, bring layers that can be combined or removed to provide comfort and protection from the elements in a wide variety of conditions.

Water and Treatment Never embark on a trail without carrying water. At all times, particularly in warm weather, adequate water is of key importance. Experts recommend at least two quarts of water per day, and when hiking in heat, a gallon or more may be more appropriate. At the extreme, dehydration can be life threatening. More commonly, inadequate water brings fatigue and muscle aches.

For most outings, unless the day is very hot or the trail very long, you should plan to carry sufficient water for the entire trail. Unfortunately, in North America natural water sources are questionable and generally loaded with various risks, such as bacteria, viruses, and fertilizers.

Trail Essentials

- Dress to keep cool, but be ready for cold.

- Bring plenty of water and adequate food.

If you must make use of trailside water, filter, treat it, or boil it. Boiling is best, but often impractical because it requires a heat source, a pot, and time. Chemical treatments, available in sporting goods stores, handle some problems, including the troublesome *Giardia* parasite, but they do not combat many man-made chemical pollutants. The preferred method is filtration, which removes parasites and other contaminants and doesn't leave an unpleasant aftertaste.

If this advice hasn't convinced you to carry all the water you need, one final admonishment: be prepared for surprises. Water sources described in the text or on maps can change course or dry up completely. Never run your water bottle dry in expectation of the next source; fill up when water is available, and always keep a little in reserve.

Food While not as critical as water, food is energy; its importance shouldn't be underestimated. Avoid foods that are hard to digest, such as candy bars and potato chips. Carry high energy, fast-digesting foods: nutrition bars, dehydrated fruit, gorp, and jerky, for instance. Bring a little extra food—it's good protection against an outing that turns unexpectedly long, perhaps due to weather or losing your way.

Other Useful Items

Map & Compass (& the Know-How to Use Them) Many trails don't require much navigation, meaning a map and compass aren't always as essential as water or food, but it can be a close call. If the trail is remote or infrequently visited, a map and compass should be considered necessities.

A hand-held GPS receiver is also a useful trail companion, but it is really no substitute for a map and compass. Knowing your longitude and latitude is not much help without a map.

Cell Phone Most parts of the country, even remote destinations, have some level of cellular coverage. In extreme circumstances, a cell phone can be a lifesaver. But don't depend on it; coverage is unpredictable and batteries fail. And be sure that the occasion warrants the phone call—a blister doesn't justify a call to search and rescue.

Gear Depending on the remoteness and rigor of the trail, you may consider bringing many additional useful items: a pocketknife, flashlight, fire source (waterproof matches, a lighter, or a flint), and first-aid kit.

Every member of your party should carry the appropriate essential items described above; groups often split up or get separated along the trail. Solo hikers should be even more disciplined about preparation and should carry more gear because traveling solo is inherently more risky.

Trail Etiquette

- Leave no trace. Never litter.
- Stay on the trail. Never cut switchbacks.
- Share the trail. Use courtesy and common sense.
- Leave it there. Don't disturb wildlife.

Trail Etiquette

The overriding rule on the trail is "Leave No Trace." Interest in visiting natural areas continues to increase in North America, even as the quantity of unspoiled natural areas continues to shrink. These pressures make it ever more critical that we leave no trace of our visits.

Never Litter If you carried it in, it's easy enough to carry it out. Leave the trail in the same, if not better, condition than you found it. Try picking up any litter you encounter and packing it out—it's a great feeling! Just one piece of garbage and you've made a difference.

Stay on the Trail Paths have been created, sometimes over many years, for many purposes: to protect the surrounding natural areas, to avoid dangers, and to provide the best route. Leaving the trail can cause damage that takes years to undo. Never cut switchbacks. Shortcutting rarely saves energy or time, and it takes a terrible toll on the land, trampling plant life and hastening erosion. Moreover, safety and consideration intersect on the trail. It's hard to get truly lost if you stay on the trail.

Share the Trail The best trails attract many visitors and you should be prepared to share the trail with others. Do your part to minimize impact.

Commonly accepted trail etiquette dictates that bike riders yield to both hikers and equestrians, hikers yield to horseback riders, downhill hikers yield to uphill hikers, and everyone stays to the right. Not everyone knows these rules of the road, so let common sense and good humor be the final guide.

Leave It There Destruction or removal of plants and animals or historical, prehistoric, or geological items is certainly unethical and almost always illegal.

Getting Lost If you become lost on the trail, stay on the trail. Stop and take stock of the situation. In many cases, a few minutes of calm reflection will yield a solution. Consider all the clues available; use the sun to identify directions if you don't have a compass. If you determine that you are indeed lost, stay put. You are more likely to encounter other people if you stay in one place.

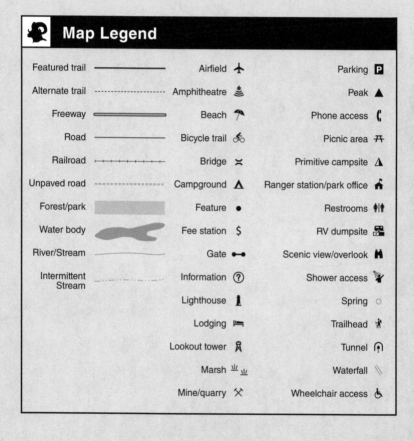

Map Legend

Featured trail	Airfield ✈	Parking 🅿
Alternate trail	Amphitheatre ♨	Peak ▲
Freeway	Beach 🏖	Phone access ☎
Road	Bicycle trail 🚲	Picnic area 🛱
Railroad	Bridge ✕	Primitive campsite △
Unpaved road	Campground ⛺	Ranger station/park office ⌂
Forest/park	Feature ●	Restrooms ♦♦
Water body	Fee station $	RV dumpsite 🚐
River/Stream	Gate ●—●	Scenic view/overlook M
Intermittent Stream	Information ⑦	Shower access 🚿
	Lighthouse 🗼	Spring ○
	Lodging 🛏	Trailhead 🚶
	Lookout tower ⚑	Tunnel ⌒
	Marsh ⧫	Waterfall \\
	Mine/quarry ✕	Wheelchair access ♿

Mendocino

Mendocino

F amous for its picturesque coastline of high bluffs, rocky sea-stacks, tidepools, and strips of sandy beach, Mendocino County is also home to a lesser-known inland forest with isolated pockets of old-growth redwoods, rugged stream canyons, and a few waterfalls. Most of these features are protected within a number of state parks or reserves, providing the public with straightforward access to some of the area's best scenery.

California Highway 1 (CA 1), also known as the Shoreline Highway, provides the principal access to these lands, with many of the state parks located directly adjacent to this scenic highway. Inland trails in Hendy Woods State Park (Trail 1), Montgomery Woods State Natural Reserve (Trail 2), and Jackson State Demonstration Forest (Trails 7 and 11), which are accessible via state and county roads, are the exceptions.

Visitors to Mendocino County, which is situated a good distance from major population centers, are rarely just passing through. Fortunately, several of the state parks have campgrounds, and the resort communities strung out along CA 1 offer numerous lodging options, spanning the range from private campgrounds to high-end bed-and-breakfasts.

Permits

Permits are not required for the dayhikes or backpacking trips profiled in this area. Some California state parks require entrance fees, which in this chapter include Hendy Woods, Van Damme, and Russian Gulch.

Maps

There are virtually no up-to-date topographic maps covering the trails in this chapter. The USGS 7.5-minute quadrangles, the standard for backcountry travel in most other areas, typically do not show the hiking trails described in this chapter. Park brochures from California State Parks are usually the

Overleaf and opposite: *Coastline of Mendocino Headlands*

best maps to carry for trails within their jurisdiction, but they lack any topographic information. For trails in areas of old-growth redwoods, which include Hendy Woods and Montgomery Woods in this chapter, **redwood hikes.com** is an excellent online source for maps with topography. Passable maps for trails within Jackson State Demonstration Forest may be obtained online at **mendowalks.org.**

Mendocino

TRAIL	DIFFICULTY	LENGTH	TYPE	USES & ACCESS	TERRAIN	NATURE	FEATURES
1	1	1.4	Loop	Dayhiking, Running, Child-Friendly	Redwoods		Camping, Picnic Area
2	2	1.5	Loop	Dayhiking, Running, Child-Friendly	Stream, Redwoods		
3	3	9.0	Semiloop	Dayhiking, Backpacking, Running, Biking	Stream, Pygmy Forest	Flora	Camping, Picnic Area
4	2	2.9	Loop	Dayhiking, Running, Dogs Allowed		Wildflowers, Wildlife	Views, Historic Interest
5	2	9.0	Out & Back	Dayhiking, Running, Biking, Dogs Allowed	Beach, Stream	Wildlife	Swimming, Historic Interest, Resort town
6	1	3.2	Loop	Dayhiking, Running, Dogs Allowed	Beach	Wildflowers, Wildlife	Views, Historic Interest, Resort town
7	3	4.1	Loop	Dayhiking, Running, Biking, Dogs Allowed			Historic Interest
8	3	7.1	Loop	Dayhiking, Running, Biking, Handicapped Access	Stream, Waterfall, Redwoods	Flora	Camping, Picnic Area, Historic Interest
9	1	2.3	Loop	Dayhiking, Running, Dogs Allowed, Handicapped Access, Child-Friendly	Beach	Wildlife	Views, Historic Interest, Lighthouse
10	3	4.7	Out & Back	Dayhiking, Running	Beach, Stream, Pygmy Forest	Flora, Wildflowers	Views, Picnic Area
11	3	2.9	Loop	Dayhiking, Running, Dogs Allowed	Waterfall, Redwoods	Wildflowers	
12	3	11.0	Out & Back	Dayhiking, Running, Dogs Allowed	Beach	Wildlife	Views, Camping, Picnic Area

USES & ACCESS	TYPE	TERRAIN	NATURE	FEATURES
Dayhiking	Loop	Mountain	Flora	Views
Backpacking	Semiloop	Beach	Wildflowers	Camping
Running	Out & Back	Lake	Wildlife	Picnic Area
Biking	Shuttle	Stream		Swimming
Dogs Allowed		Waterfall		Secluded
Handicapped Access	DIFFICULTY	Redwoods		Steep
Child-Friendly	- 1 2 3 4 5 +	Pygmy Forest		Historic Interest
	less more			Resort town
				Lighthouse

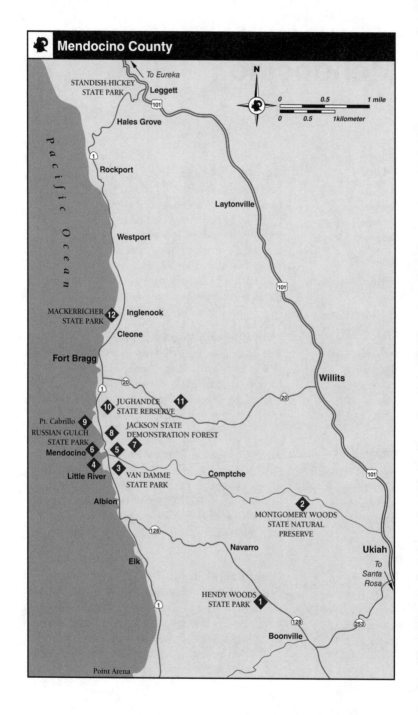

Mendocino County

STANDISH-HICKEY
STATE PARK

To Eureka

Leggett

N

0   0.5   1 mile
0   0.5   1kilometer

Hales Grove

Pacific Ocean

Rockport

Laytonville

Westport

MACKERRICHER
STATE PARK

12 Inglenook

Cleone

Fort Bragg

Willits

JUGHANDLE
STATE RERSERVE

10

11

Pt. Cabrillo 9
RUSSIAN GULCH
STATE PARK

8

JACKSON STATE
DEMONSTRATION FOREST

6

5

7

Mendocino

4

3

Little River

VAN DAMME
STATE PARK

Comptche

Albion

2

MONTGOMERY WOODS
STATE NATURAL
PRESERVE

Ukiah

Navarro

To
Santa
Rosa

Elk

HENDY WOODS
STATE PARK

1

Boonville

253

128

Point Arena

Mendocino

TRAIL 1

Dayhiking, Running,
Child-Friendly

1.4 miles, Loop

Difficulty: **1** 2 3 4 5

Big Hendy Loop 25

This short and easy hike through an inland grove of old-growth redwoods is far enough from US 101 to not be overrun by tourists. Along with peace and serenity, the inland location usually offers less fog and warmer temperatures than its coastal counterparts. The hike is on the edge of Anderson Valley, making it an easy pairing with tastings at some of the local wineries.

TRAIL 2

Dayhiking, Running,
Child-Friendly

1.5 miles, Loop

Difficulty: 1 **2** 3 4 5

Montgomery Woods Trail 30

This easy hike in an inland grove of old-growth redwoods is well off the beaten path but popular because at one time it harbored the world's tallest known coast redwood. The grove is quite lush and contains some very stately redwoods.

TRAIL 3

Dayhiking, Running,
Biking, Backpacking

9.0 miles, Semiloop

Difficulty: 1 2 **3** 4 5

Fern Canyon & Pygmy Forest Loop . . . 35

Rich botanical diversity is the principal highlight of this excursion. The route follows the Little River through delightful and aptly named Fern Canyon before climbing into second-growth uplands and then reaching a unique pygmy forest.

TRAIL 4

Dayhiking, Running,
Dogs Allowed (on leash)

2.9 miles, Loop

Difficulty: 1 **2** 3 4 5

**Chapman Point &
Spring Ranch Headlands** 41

Mendocino County is famous for its picture-postcard coastline, and this romp across coastal prairie and along bluffs above the ocean is no exception. The bluffs also provide fine vantages from which to watch marine mammals and seabirds.

Big River Haul Road 48

A former logging road has become one of Mendocino County's premier multiuse recreational trails. Starting alongside the estuary of Big River, the gently graded road travels upstream for several miles.

TRAIL 5

Dayhiking, Running, Biking, Horses, Dogs Allowed (on leash)

9.0 miles, Out & Back

Difficulty:1 **2** 3 4 5

Mendocino Headlands 50

This short loop combines the best attributes of the wild Mendocino coastline and the Victorian architecture of the quaint seaside village of the same name. After a romp around the scenic bluffs enjoying ocean views, spring wildflowers, and the abundant sea life, the route traverses through town and ends on Main Street, a fine spot for a post-trip meal or brew.

TRAIL 6

Dayhiking, Running, Dogs Allowed (on leash)

3.2 miles, Loop

Difficulty: **1** 2 3 4 5

Forest History Trail 55

With its corresponding pamphlet, this loop through second-growth forest affords hikers the opportunity to gain a better understanding of the coast redwoods.

TRAIL 7

Dayhiking, Running, Dogs Allowed

4.1 miles, Loop

Difficulty: 1 2 **3** 4 5

Russian Gulch Loop 60

The initial 1.5-mile stretch of this trail, which follows an old, gently graded road through verdant Fern Canyon, is popular with a wide range of recreationists. Beyond this point, where bikes must be left behind, the trail receives a fair amount of use up to a 36-foot-tall waterfall. By following the described route, hikers can vary the scenery and experience a higher degree of solitude.

TRAIL 8

Dayhiking, Running, Biking, Handicapped Access

7.1 miles, Loop

Difficulty: 1 2 **3** 4 5

Big Hendy Loop

Near the fringe of bucolic Anderson Valley, Hendy Woods State Park is a fine spot for enjoying some magnificently tall, old-growth redwoods without the crush of tourists common to the more popular parks along US 101. Farther inland, Hendy Woods is not as foggy as parks closer to the ocean, typically experiencing warmer temperatures as well.

The tall trees, some more than 16 feet in diameter and more than 300 feet tall, are found within two areas of the park, both of which occupy a floodplain alongside the meandering Navarro River. The premier site, Big Hendy Grove is an 80-acre parcel with numerous old-growth specimens. For a park of this size (600 acres), there is an extensive network of hiking trails, offering numerous extensions to the short trip described here.

Although not as famous as Napa and Sonoma, Anderson Valley is a fine wine region in its own right, specializing in cool grape varietals, such as Rieslings, Gewürztraminers, chenin blancs, and pinot noirs. There are several wineries within a few miles of Hendy Woods; wine tasting and a picnic lunch at one of the local wineries would be a lovely pairing with your hike.

TRAIL USE
Dayhiking, Running, Child-Friendly

LENGTH & TIME
1.4 miles, 1 hour

VERTICAL FEET
Nominal

DIFFICULTY
- **1** 2 3 4 5 +

TRAIL TYPE
Loop

START & FINISH
N39° 04.454'
W123° 27.969'

FEATURES
Redwoods

FACILITIES
Campgrounds
Picnic Area
Restrooms
Visitor Center
Wineries Nearby

Best Time

As with most coast redwood groves, Hendy Woods is open all year. Summer is the busiest season. The park is oftentimes deserted in the winter, even during periods of good weather. Spring and fall are perhaps the optimum time to enjoy the redwoods, when temperatures are cool and visitation is low.

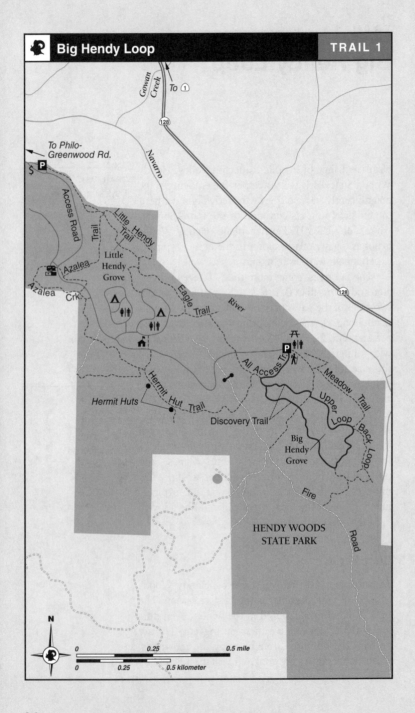

Big Hendy Loop

TRAIL 1

Gowan Creek

To ①

128

To Philo-
Greenwood Rd.

S

Access Road

Little Hendy Trail

Trail

Azalea

Little Hendy Grove

Azalea

Azalea Crk.

Eagle Trail

Navarro

River

128

All Access Tr.

Meadow Trail

Hermit Hut Trail

Hermit Huts

Discovery Trail

Upper Loop

Big Hendy Grove

Back Loop

Fire

HENDY WOODS
STATE PARK

Road

N

0   0.25   0.5 mile
0   0.25   0.5 kilometer

Finding the Trail

Drive on CA 128 to a junction with Philo-Greenwood Road, 6 miles west of Boonville and 17 miles east of CA 1. Follow Philo-Greenwood Road for 0.6 mile to the signed entrance for Hendy Woods State Park, which is just past a bridge over the Navarro River. Turn left and follow the park road for 2 miles to the end at the day-use parking lot, which has picnic tables and vault toilets). The park has two campgrounds: Azalea and Wildcat.

Trail Description

A large sign and trail map mark the start of the hike, ▶1 initially following the wide track of the All Access Trail into the deep shade of an old-growth redwood forest. A box nearby contains interpretive pamphlets loaded with interesting botanical information about the redwood forest corresponding to 13 numbered posts along the way (the pamphlet is also available at the park's website, **www.parks .ca.gov/?page_id=438**). You don't have to wait long at all to stand beneath some impressive specimens, as the Big Hendy Grove harbors quite a number of very old and very tall redwoods. Soon after crossing a run-down footbridge, turn left at a junction ▶2 with the Discovery Trail.

Redwoods

Follow a counterclockwise route on the Discovery Trail to match the sequence of the numbered posts, reaching a junction ▶3 with the Upper Loop section after 0.2 mile. Continue straight ahead onto the Upper Loop, walking through a ground cover of redwood sorrel and sword and bracken ferns. In springtime you may see beautiful trilliums scattered about the forest floor.

Wildflowers

Reach the next junction after 0.3 mile, where the trail ahead is the Back Loop. You could add an extra 0.4 mile to this rather short hike by following the Back Loop, but since doing so would take you

A visitor admires *the old-growth redwoods in Hendy Woods State Park*

away from the most magnificent redwoods in the Big Hendy Grove, which occur on the northeast leg of the Upper Loop, turn left at the junction. ▶4 The farther you progress on the Upper Loop, the more magnificent the redwoods become, towering over an unbroken swath of redwood sorrel. After 0.2 mile of splendid redwoods, you reach the second junction ▶5 with the Back Loop.

Turn left at the junction, and follow the east leg of the Upper Loop through shady forest for another 0.3 mile to junctions ▶6 with the Discovery Trail and, a few yards farther, a junction with the Meadow Trail. Continue straight at both junctions, rejoining the interpretive trail near post 10. After 0.2 mile, you reach the close of the loop ▶7 and then retrace your steps 0.1 mile back to the day-use parking lot. ▶8

🚶 MILESTONES

▶1	0.0	Start at trailhead
▶2	0.1	Left at Discovery Trail junction
▶3	0.3	Straight at Upper Loop junction
▶4	0.6	Left at first Back Loop junction
▶5	0.8	Left at second Back Loop junction
▶6	1.1	Straight at Discovery Trail and Meadow Trail junctions
▶7	1.3	Right at All Access Trail junction
▶8	1.4	Return to trailhead

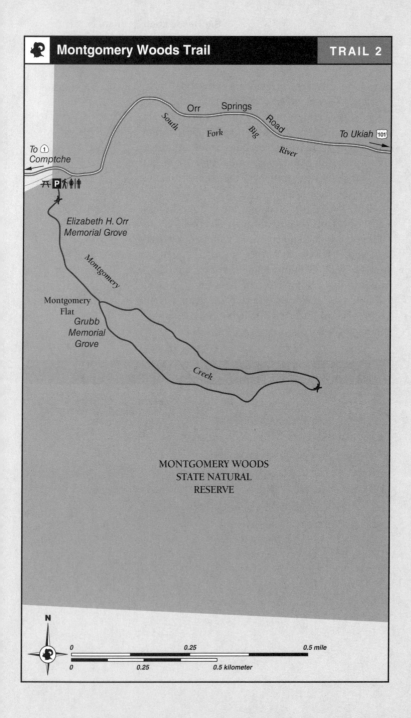

Montgomery Woods Trail

TRAIL 2

Orr Springs Road

South Fork Big River

To Ukiah 101

To 1 Comptche

Elizabeth H. Orr Memorial Grove

Montgomery

Montgomery Flat

Grubb Memorial Grove

Creek

MONTGOMERY WOODS
STATE NATURAL
RESERVE

N

0   0.25   0.5 mile

0   0.25   0.5 kilometer

Montgomery Woods Trail

Despite its seemingly out-of-the-way location, Montgomery Woods State Natural Reserve receives a fair number of visitors, due in great part to the fact that at one time it boasted the tallest known coastal redwood in existence. The unmarked 367.5-foot-tall specimen, the Mendocino Tree, was subsequently outdone by the discovery of larger trees in Humboldt Redwoods State Park and Redwood National Park. Although visitation dropped following these other discoveries, it is still high for such a remote, inland area that requires long drives on narrow, winding roads. Such popularity is no doubt a result of the magnificence of its five, unlogged groves harbored on an alluvial flat, bisected by sluggish Montgomery Creek, and sandwiched between steep canyon walls. The lush ground cover, including a patch of nearly head-high chain ferns, enhances the area's cathedral-like ambiance.

Situated in the Big River Watershed, the reserve began as a 9-acre donation from Robert Orr in 1945. Through additional purchases and donations, the Save the Redwoods League has expanded the area to 2,743 acres.

TRAIL USE
Dayhiking, Running,
Child-Friendly

LENGTH & TIME
1.5 miles, 1 hour

VERTICAL FEET
+225'/-225'

DIFFICULTY
- 1 **2** 3 4 5 +

TRAIL TYPE
Loop

START & FINISH
N39° 14.081'
W123° 23.722'

FEATURES
Redwoods
Stream

FACILITIES
Restrooms

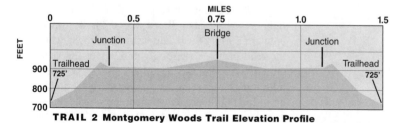

TRAIL 2 Montgomery Woods Trail Elevation Profile

Some of the *impressive redwoods in the Grubb Memorial Grove*

Best Time

The park is open year-round. Anytime it's not raining cats and dogs is a good time for a visit. However, with plenty of standing water nearby, mosquitoes can be a nuisance during early summer.

Finding the Trail

Leave US 101 in north Ukiah at Exit 551, and turn right onto North State Street. After 0.3 mile, turn left onto Orr Springs Road, and head out of town, where the road begins a twisting climb out of the valley on narrow, rough asphalt. After cresting the coastal hills, it makes an even steeper and narrower descent into the Big River Watershed, eventually entering typical redwood forest. Pass Orr Hot Springs

Resort, and reach the trailhead parking area on the left-hand side of the road, 12.6 miles from Ukiah. Renovated in 2010, the trailhead has a modern vault toilet, a deck with picnic tables, and a kiosk with interpretive signs.

If you are traveling from CA 1, take the much better Comptche-Ukiah Road from a junction just south of the town of Mendocino, and proceed eastbound to the small community of Comptche. Continue east on the only paved road heading out of town, and proceed to the trailhead parking area, approximately 30 miles from CA 1.

There are no public or private campgrounds in the immediate area.

Trail Description

Initially, the trail follows the course of an old road ▶1 through second-growth redwood forest containing laurel and tanoak, along the course of gurgling Montgomery Creek. Soon reach a stout bridge across the creek, where the first of several interpretive signs provides information about the Native Americans who once frequented this area. A primitive outhouse greets you on the opposite side, plastered with a sign stating "Closed for Repairs," but by the looks of the dilapidated structure, a person would have to be desperate to contemplate its use.

Stream

Turn left and proceed upstream, passing a plaque on a large boulder declaring this area as the Elizabeth H. Orr Memorial Grove. Just past a pair of picnic tables alongside the creek, about one-third of a mile from the parking lot, the trail begins its only significant stretch of climbing, passing additional interpretive signs on the way.

Ignore an old, unmarked road splitting away to the right near the crest of the hill, and remain on the main trail, which drops shortly to Montgomery Flat and the Grubb Memorial Grove. Here the choice

Redwoods

33

old-growth redwoods make a dramatic appearance. The flat is sandwiched between steep hillsides, sheltering the grove and creating a cathedral-like, reverential ambiance well suited to admiring this impressive collection of stately giants. The lush ground cover of ferns and redwood sorrel adds to the area's charm. Most visitors go no farther than Montgomery Flat, the scenic high point of the journey.

The flat is where the loop section begins, ►2 although the junction has become obscured over the years because visitors wandering around the grove have flattened the ground cover. Continue upstream, following a counterclockwise loop around the sometimes-marshy flat, where Montgomery Creek slows, looking more like a swamp than a free-flowing stream. Cross a short plank bridge over a tributary drainage and soon come to a more substantial wood-railed bridge spanning the sluggish creek. The bridge marks the easternmost point of the loop, ►3 despite the appearance of faint use trails continuing up the canyon into a previously logged area.

Turning downstream, the trail heads back toward the Grubb Grove just above the flat and below the steep, fern-covered north canyon wall, passing some stately redwoods along the way. A couple of short, wood-plank bridges lead across the barely running stream. ►4 From there, retrace your steps to the parking area. ►5

🚶	MILESTONES	
►1	0.0	Start at trailhead
►2	0.3	Straight at loop junction
►3	0.75	Veer left at far end of bridge
►4	1.2	Right at loop junction
►5	1.5	Return to trailhead

Fern Canyon & Pygmy Forest Loop

Van Damme State Park was named for the son of a Flemish immigrant who prospered in the logging trade, moved to San Francisco to operate a ferry, and eventually relocated back to the stunning beauty of Little River. The 1,830-acre reserve harbors a rich ecological diversity, including coastal beach and headland, second-growth redwood forest, riparian zone, and, most unique of all, a pygmy forest. This 9-mile, semiloop trip samples this diversity following Little River through aptly named Fern Canyon before climbing into redwood uplands to a pocket of pygmy forest. The return portion descends into a serene canyon bearing Little River's headwaters.

The initial 2.5-mile stretch of the Fern Canyon Trail follows a pleasantly graded old logging road, improved by the Civilian Conservation Corps (CCC) in the 1930s and now open to bicycles. (*Note that bicycles are prohibited on the upper Fern Canyon Trail.*) Beyond, along with the two-wheeled crowd, hikers make a moderate climb along the old logging road to the wheelchair-accessible Pygmy Forest Loop, where nutrient-depleted soils on an ancient marine terrace have greatly stunted the vegetation. A boardwalk with interpretive signs makes a short circuit through this unique area. The return to Little River is via a hiker-only single-track trail descending through a quiet stretch of forest.

TRAIL USE
Dayhiking, Backpacking, Running, Biking

LENGTH & TIME
9.0 miles, 4–5 hours

VERTICAL FEET
+1,450'/-1,450'

DIFFICULTY
- 1 2 **3** 4 5 +

TRAIL TYPE
Semiloop

START & FINISH
N39° 16.609'
W123° 46.832'

FEATURES
Stream
Flora
Backcountry Camping
Pygmy Forest

FACILITIES
Campground
Picnic Area
Restrooms

Best Time

The park is open year-round. Spring and early summer offer a splash of color from seasonal wildflowers.

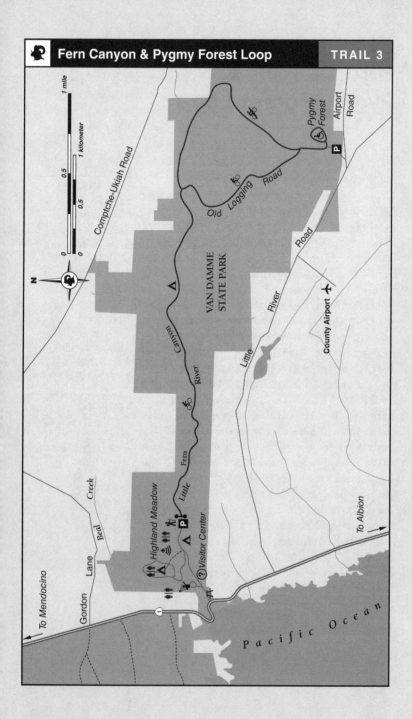

Fern Canyon & Pygmy Forest Loop   TRAIL 3

Pygmy Forest
Airport Road
Old Logging Road
VAN DAMME STATE PARK
Comptche-Ukiah Road
County Airport
Little River Road
Canyon
River
Little
Fern
Little River
Highland Meadow
Visitor Center
Bald Creek
Gordon Lane
To Mendocino
To Albion
Pacific Ocean

1 mile
1 kilometer
0.5
0.5
0
0
N

Finding the Trail

The park entrance is directly off of CA 1 at mile marker 48.03, about 2 miles south of Mendocino. The park has two developed campgrounds and an environmental campground 1.7 miles up the Fern Canyon Trail.

Trail Description

The Fern Canyon Trail begins ►1 along a closed section of an old logging skid road open to bikes, as well as pedestrians. The gently graded road heads upstream along the course of Little River, which at times harbors a recovering population of coho salmon. Interpretive signs provide interesting information about the human and natural history of the area, and numbered metal fish symbols correspond to a leaflet about the salmon (due to the state budget crisis, leaflets may be unavailable).

Stream ▶

Ferns make up much of the lush vegetation carpeting the canyon, including such varieties as bird's-foot, bracken, deer, five-finger, gold back, horsetail, lady, licorice, stamp, western sword, and wood. Blackberry, California hazel, huckleberry, elderberry, redwood sorrel, salal, salmonberry, and thimbleberry make up the rest of the vigorous understory beneath a second-growth redwood forest

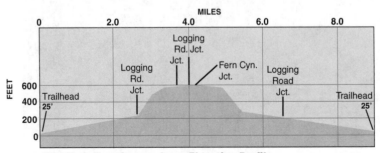

TRAIL 3 Fern Canyon Loop Elevation Profile

Little River

that also includes grand firs and western hemlocks. Occasional large stumps offer hints of the redwood's former glory in this canyon. Stone bridges built by the CCC in the 1930s, which acted like dams and degraded the salmon habitat, have been replaced by a series of gracefully arched bridges.

The walls of the canyon start to broaden, and, at 1.7 miles, you reach the environmental camp-ground. Each of the sites is equipped with a picnic table and fire pit, and old vault toilets and bearproof trash bins are nearby. The gently graded journey continues beyond the camp to an unmarked fork, where the road splits into an upper and lower sec-tion that meet up again at a turnaround. At the far end is a junction, ▶2 2.5 miles from the parking lot.

Backcountry Camping

Turn right at the junction, and immediately drop down to ford Little River, which should not present a problem unless it is running high. The old logging road then makes a moderate, 0.6-mile climb up the forested south wall of the canyon, switch-backing a couple of times on the way to the top of a ridge, where the grade once again eases. Follow the trail along the ridge, eventually entering an open, brighter section of forest on the way to the upper junction ▶3 with the Fern Canyon Trail, 1.2 miles from the lower junction.

To visit the unique pygmy forest, turn right at the junction, and walk down the road 0.2 mile to an elevated boardwalk on the left-hand side. ▶4 The short boardwalk loops through the forest, passing dwarf Bishop pine, Bolander pine, and Monterey cypress trees, as well as several varieties of stunted shrubs and plants. Interpretive signs explain the specific conditions necessary for a pygmy forest and identify some of the endemic plants. At the end of the loop, retrace your steps back to the upper Fern Canyon junction. ▶5

Pygmy Forest

Veer to the right at the junction, and stroll through an open and bright section of forest. The trail begins a moderate descent through second-growth redwood forest, which becomes darker, damper, and lusher the closer you get to Little River. Reach a short bridge across a tributary, and then soon come to a bridge over the main channel, where the trail turns and follows meandering Little River downstream. This is perhaps the best part of the route, as you walk on single-track trail (closed to bikes) through a serene stretch of lush forest alongside the tumbling headwaters of the river. Short bridges lead across a few side streams on the way to the close of the loop at the junction ▶6 with the Old Logging Road. From there, head straight ahead, and retrace your steps 2.5 miles back to the trailhead. ▶7

		MILESTONES
▶1	0.0	Start at Fern Canyon Trailhead
▶2	2.5	Right at Old Logging Road junction
▶3	3.7	Right at upper Fern Canyon junction
▶4	3.9	Left at Pygmy Forest Loop boardwalk
▶4	4.0	Right at Old Logging Road junction
▶5	4.2	Right at upper Fern Canyon junction
▶6	6.5	Straight at Old Logging Road junction
▶7	9.0	Return to Fern Canyon Trailhead

Chapman Point & Spring Ranch Headlands

Founded by William Kent in the 1860s, Spring Ranch was used as a dairy farm, sheep and cattle ranch, and vegetable garden, producing goods for the burgeoning North Coast lumber industry. The State of California acquired the property, which is blessed with stunning coastal headlands, in the 1990s. The old family residence on the east side of the highway was recently sold and renovated as a vacation home and wedding venue, and descendants of the Springs still farm the property behind the house.

Offering some of the most dramatic coastline views in the county, the 3-mile romp across mostly open prairie and along the bluffs above the ocean is a scenic delight—the gentle topography offers a huge scenic reward for minimal effort. Harbor seals are often seen bobbing in the sea, and the bluffs provide an excellent vantage for watching migrating whales. A variety of sea birds, including the occasional osprey, dart and soar across the sky. Old barns near the end of the loop add a touch of history.

Best Time

The park is open year-round. Spring and early summer offer a splash of color from seasonal wildflowers.

Finding the Trail

Drive on CA 1 to mile marker 48.94 and an unmarked dirt parking area on the west side of the road directly opposite of Gordon Lane, about 1.5 miles south of Mendocino. There are no facilities at

TRAIL USE
Dayhiking, Running,
Dogs Allowed (on leash)

LENGTH & TIME
2.9 miles, 1–2 hours

VERTICAL FEET
+200'/-200'

DIFFICULTY
- 1 **2** 3 4 5 +

TRAIL TYPE
Loop

START & FINISH
N39° 17.118'
W123° 47.617'

FEATURES
Views
Wildlife
Historic Interest
Wildflowers

FACILITIES
None

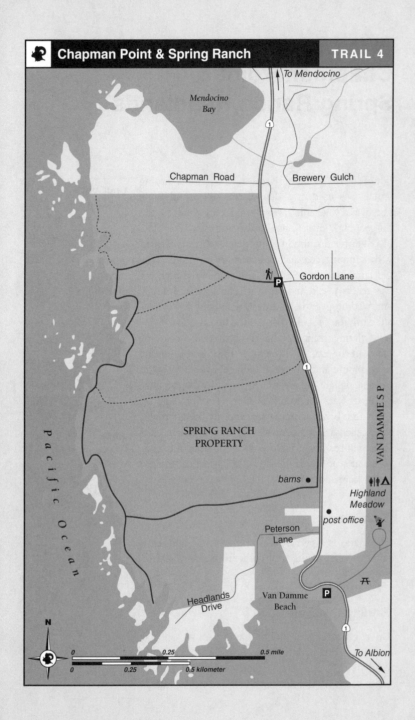

Mendocino Bay

To Mendocino

Chapman Road

Brewery Gulch

Gordon Lane

SPRING RANCH PROPERTY

VAN DAMME S P

barns

Highland Meadow

post office

Peterson Lane

Pacific Ocean

Headlands Drive

Van Damme Beach

To Albion

N

0   0.25   0.5 mile
0   0.25   0.5 kilometer

the trailhead. Nearby Van Damme State Park has two campgrounds, and there are campgrounds in Russian Gulch State Park and the Caspar Beach RV Park, both north of the town of Mendocino. The Mendocino Coast has a plethora of lodging opportunities.

Trail Description

The trail, which is closed to bikes and open to leashed dogs only, begins near a fence corner ▶1 and heads gently downhill toward the ocean along the fence line through open prairie dotted with pines. Reach a Y-junction ▶2 and veer right, heading toward the northwest corner of the reserve and a union with the path that follows the edge of the bluffs. A patch of shrubby vegetation, including Scotch broom and blackberry brambles, temporarily obscures views toward the ocean until you break out to a sweeping coastal panorama across the open prairie. Despite the presence of an architecturally stunning private residence to the north, the rugged coastline evokes a wild and dramatic landscape, with a smattering of offshore rocks absorbing the constant pounding from the tumultuous surf. The bluffs offer a fine aerie from which to observe marine mammals and seabirds.

Views

Wildlife

Upon reaching the edge of the bluff, ▶3 turn south and follow the twists and turns of the coastline path on a scenic romp above the roaring Pacific. Reach a junction with the left-hand path from the first Y-junction, and continue ahead on an incredibly scenic, winding journey southbound along the bluffs. Pass two more junctions with trails heading back toward the highway before crossing a small stream and reaching the reserve boundary at an old fence. ▶4 A log bench nearby offers an excellent spot to sit and watch the rolling waves.

From there, you could continue south into the coastal parcel of Van Damme State Park; the path

View of the *Pacific from Spring Ranch Headlands*

closest to the ocean eventually leads to a cliff above a small cove. The difficulty is navigating the various paths crisscrossing the coastal woodland back to CA 1 without trespassing. Successfully doing so would return you to a small gate on the west shoulder of the highway between Stevenson Lodge and Glendeven Inn. From there, it's a 0.5-mile walk north along the highway back to the trailhead.

Perhaps a better (and the recommended) route is to return to the junction ▶5 of the last trail heading east across the open prairie and toward a cluster of old wooden barns. After a 0.5-mile climb, you reach the barns, formerly part of the Spring Ranch operations. A short stroll leads along the access road toward the highway. ▶6 Rather than walk along the shoulder of the road, turn north along the inside of the fence, and walk along a usually mowed section of grass back toward the parking area. Pass through a gap near the fence corner to access your vehicle. ▶7

Historic
Interest

🚶	**MILESTONES**

▶1	0.0	Start at trailhead
▶2	0.3	Veer right at junction
▶3	0.6	Turn left (south) at junction
▶4	1.8	Reach boundary
▶5	1.9	Retrace steps to junction and turn right (east)
▶6	2.4	Reach CA 1 and turn left (north)
▶7	2.9	Return to trailhead

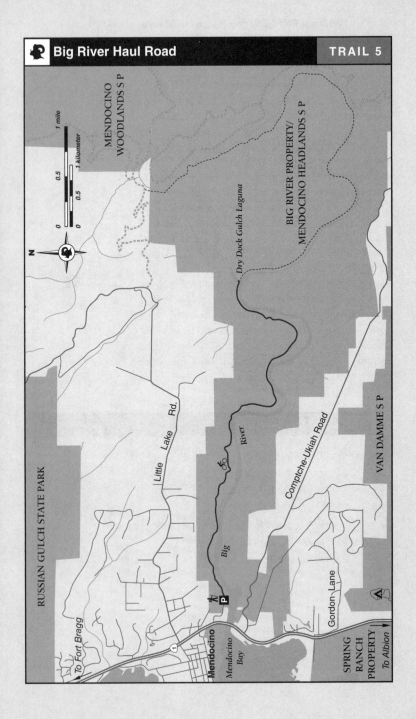

Big River Haul Road — TRAIL 5

Big River Haul Road

A cursory glance at Big River suggests that this modest waterway was misnamed. However, the appellation was granted not for the river itself but for the enormous redwoods that used to grow along its banks. The Big River Haul Road was once a flurry of activity with huge logs originally transported by rail and then truck to nearby mills. Through public and private donations and the work of countless volunteers, California State Parks acquired 7,334 acres surrounding the river in 2002.

Nowadays, hikers, mountain bikers, equestrians, dog walkers (leashed only), and runners have replaced the railroad cars and logging trucks. The nearly level grade and wide track allows recreationists to tick off miles with minimal effort. Interpretive signs add interesting tidbits of information. Patient wildlife enthusiasts may be well rewarded by the variety of animal life on the water and in the sky. Although the road is 11 miles long, most visitors travel upstream only a few miles at most, and a small but interesting laguna in Dry Dock Gulch at 4.5 miles makes an excellent turnaround point.

Best Time

The trail is open all year. Wildflowers bloom in spring and early summer.

Finding the Trail

Immediately south of Mendocino at the north end of the bridge across Big River, turn east off of CA 1 at a sign marked "Big River State Beach." Follow

TRAIL USE
Dayhiking, Running, Biking, Dogs Allowed (on leash)
LENGTH & TIME
9.0 miles, 4–5 hours
VERTICAL FEET
+100'/-100'
DIFFICULTY
- 1 **2** 3 4 5 +
TRAIL TYPE
Out & Back
START & FINISH
N39° 18.183'
W123° 47.135'

FEATURES
Stream
Historic Interest
Wildlife
Swimming
Beach

FACILITIES
Restroom
Resort Town

Dry Dock Gulch Laguna

the road downhill, and continue through a large parking area for the beach to the parking area for the Big River Haul Road near a closed gate. Vault toilets are nearby. Nearby Van Damme and Russian Gulch State Parks and Caspar Beach RV Park offer camping, and the Mendocino Coast has a plethora of lodging opportunities.

Trail Description

Pass around a closed gate, and head east away from the trailhead ►1 on the broad, gently graded old haul road past the first of several interpretive signs. The initial stretch of the road passes through mostly open vegetation, which allows you good views of Big River and the area's abundant wildlife. Within the first mile, you pass an old quarry to the left, which was used for structural fill for a railroad and then for the road. Soon after, the forest thickens and obscures the river views for most of the rest of the upstream journey, and you pass the first of several side roads that split off from the main haul road along its 11-mile course to Mendocino Woodlands State Park.

Near the 2-mile point, a break in the forest reveals the remnants of an old boom used for catching logs that were cut farther upstream and then floated downriver. Continue up the canyon as the road follows the twists and turns of Big River. At 4.5 miles from the trailhead, a use trail on the left leads shortly to a small laguna in Dry Dock Gulch, ►2 where you may spy blue herons and wood ducks. The laguna makes a good turnaround point for hikers, as the scenery remains very consistent for next 4-plus miles to the end of the tidal estuary. Return to the trailhead. ►3

Wildlife

Historic Interest

Stream

♙	**MILESTONES**	
►1	0.0	Start at trailhead
►2	4.5	Turn around at Dry Dock Gulch Laguna
►3	9.0	Return to trailhead

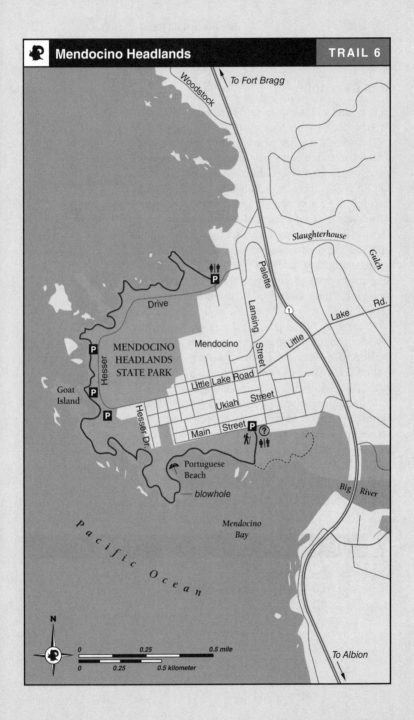

To Fort Bragg

Woodstock

Slaughterhouse

Gulch

Drive

Palette

Lansing Street

Little

Lake

Rd.

P

MENDOCINO
HEADLANDS
STATE PARK

Mendocino

Hesser

P

P

Goat
Island

P

Little Lake Road

Ukiah   Street

Hesser Dr.

Main   Street

P

?

Portuguese
Beach

blowhole

Big   River

Mendocino
Bay

P a c i f i c   O c e a n

N

0   0.25   0.5 mile

0   0.25   0.5 kilometer

To Albion

Mendocino Headlands

The quaint and picturesque hamlet of Mendocino, featured in the long-running TV series *Murder She Wrote,* starring Angela Lansbury, provides a fine backdrop to the rugged headlands bordering the town on three sides. On this 3-mile walk along the edge of the headlands and through town, hikers experience a fine contrast between the handiwork of nature and the architecture of man. Sheer bluffs offer beautiful vistas of the rocky coastline pounded by the crashing surf with excellent vantage points for observing the varied marine life, including migrating whales, dolphins, seals, and a host of sea birds. Walking through town includes the possibility of grabbing a bite to eat or quaffing a libation—a most civilized way to hike.

These headlands were threatened by a proposed development in the 1960s. Fortunately, the local citizenry banded together to successfully obtain historical status for the town and have the headlands declared as open space. The area is now protected as Mendocino Headlands State Park.

Best Time

The trail is open all year. Wildflowers bloom in spring and early summer, providing opportunities for picture-postcard views of the coastline and the quaint village of Mendocino.

Finding the Trail

At a traffic light on CA 1, turn onto Main Street, and head west into the town of Mendocino. In

TRAIL USE
Dayhiking, Running,
Dogs Allowed (on leash)

LENGTH & TIME
3.2 miles, 2–4 hours

VERTICAL FEET
+200'/-200'

DIFFICULTY
- **1** 2 3 4 5 +

TRAIL TYPE
Loop

START & FINISH
N39° 18.309'
W123° 47.826'

FEATURES
Beach
Views
Wildlife
Historic Interest
Wildflowers

FACILITIES
Restrooms
Visitor Center
Resort Town

addition to four designated parking lots farther on, the Headlands Trail can be accessed from a couple of points in town, including the historic Ford House Visitor Center (which has restrooms) at the north end of town, or at the intersection of Main and Hesser Streets at the south end. Four blocks north of Main, Hesser intersects Little Lake Road, where a left-hand turn soon leads onto northbound Hesser Drive.

Three parking areas within the next quarter mile provide short and easy connections to the Headlands Trail. Farther along, after Hesser Drive turns east, is the last parking lot, 0.1 mile prior to the intersection of Lansing Street. In addition to picnic tables, this parking lot has restrooms, although

Coastline view *from Mendocino Headlands*

they were closed in 2013 due to the budget crisis. The description below begins near the Ford House Visitor Center. Nearby Van Damme and Russian Gulch State Parks and Caspar Beach RV Park offer camping, and the Mendocino Coast has a plethora of lodging opportunities.

Trail Description

Securing a parking space on Main Street, which can be difficult on busy weekends when the weather is favorable, enables you to finish the loop in the historic part of town and then grab a post-trip brew or a bite to eat. From the Ford House, ▶1 a path leads shortly over to the top of the bluff above, from where you have a fine view of Big River entering the ocean. Turn right at the junction, ▶2 and follow the path along the bluff south of town through open prairie carpeted with seasonal wildflowers, eventually coming above Portuguese Beach.

Views

Wildflowers

Reach a junction with the lateral from the intersection of Main and Hesser Streets, and then follow the path curving south along the edge of a promontory to the site of a blowhole, encircled by a wood fence. Although you probably won't see any plumes of ocean spray erupting out of the blowhole, the churning ocean waters inside are nonetheless dramatic in their own right. Farther on, a side trail on the left ▶3 leads down a set of stairs to Portuguese Beach, known locally as Point Beach.

Beach

From the Portuguese Beach junction, the main trail continues around the point and eventually heads north. Offshore rocks and islets create a dramatic visual counterpoint to the crashing Pacific waves, as well as providing nesting grounds for a variety of seabirds in spring, including Brandt's cormorants, common murres, pigeon guillemots, and rhinoceros auklets. Other birds you might encounter in the area include egrets, loons, ospreys,

Wildlife

Historic Interest

and oystercatchers. The bluffs are also excellent vantage points for whale watchers in winter and early spring.

The largest islet, Goat Island, was once pastureland for a herd of goats. Other signs of civilization along the route include iron chains and redwood pilings, visual reminders of the logging heydays. The main path continues a wandering circuit northward along the serpentine course of the bluffs.

Eventually the shoreline and the trail curve east, arriving at the final parking area ▶4 near a grove of cypress trees. Picnic tables and restrooms invite visitors to rest and linger before heading south into the more civilized part of Mendocino. Most of the historic Victorian buildings in town were built in the mid- to late 1800s. Depending on your inclination and disposition, you can choose from a variety of routes through town. The most direct line is to follow Hesser Drive east to Lansing, ▶5 then south back to Main, ▶6, and eventually return to Ford House. ▶7

🚶	**MILESTONES**	
▶1	0.0	Start at Ford House Visitor Center
▶2	0.1	Turn right at junction
▶3	0.5	Straight at Portuguese Beach junction
▶4	2.4	Reach end of trail at parking area
▶5	2.6	Turn right at Lansing Street
▶6	3.1	Turn right at Main Street
▶7	3.2	Return to visitor center

Forest History Trail

This circuit through the Jackson Demonstration State Forest offers an informative hike amid second-growth redwood forest if you have a copy of the *Forest History Guide* in hand. Divided into five sections, the trip offers historical glimpses into our relationship with redwoods. The guide, keyed to 47 trailside posts, can be obtained free from the Cal Fire office in Fort Bragg at 802 North Main Street (it is sometimes available at Mendocino Woodlands State Park). Without the guide to pique your interest, the nearly 4-mile hike through logged redwood forest is rather mundane.

While the Forest History Trail is fully within the Jackson Demonstration Forest, laterals provide access into neighboring Mendocino Woodlands State Park. The park, located on the site of a former lumber mill, was a Recreation Demonstration Area (RDA) built in the 1930s by Civilian Conservation Corps (CCC) workers under the direction of the Works Progress Administration. The CCC erected more than 120 buildings, cabins, and other structures here, using native materials, such as redwood and rock. Of the 46 RDAs built in the United States, "Mendocino Woodlands is one of only two to maintain its historic integrity, artistic significance, and original usage," according to the park's brochure. Owned by the State of California and managed by the nonprofit Mendocino Woodlands Camp Association, the park focuses on environmental education for groups in a retreatlike setting. Together, this neighboring state park and state forest contain 25 miles of hiking trails.

TRAIL USE
Dayhiking, Running,
Biking, Dogs Allowed

LENGTH & TIME
4.1 miles, 2–3 hours

VERTICAL FEET
+1,250'/-1,250'

DIFFICULTY
- 1 2 **3** 4 5 +

TRAIL TYPE
Loop

START & FINISH
N39° 20.411'
W123° 43.147'

FEATURES
Historic Interest

FACILITIES
None

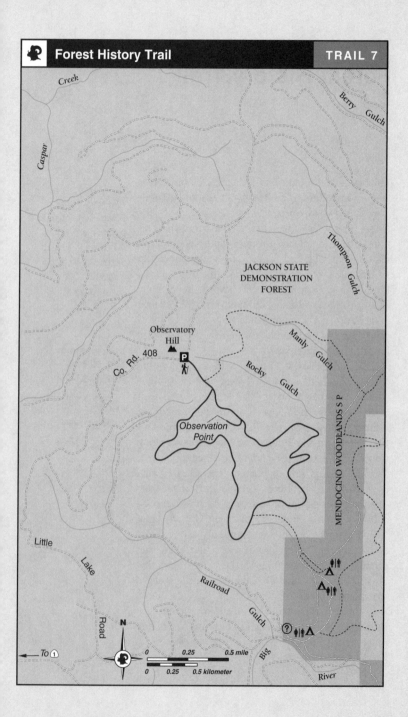

Creek

Berry Gulch

Caspar

Thompson Gulch

JACKSON STATE
DEMONSTRATION
FOREST

Observatory
Hill

Manly Gulch

Co. Rd. 408

P

Rocky Gulch

Observation
Point

MENDOCINO WOODLANDS S P

Little
Lake

Railroad

Gulch

Road

N

To ①

Big

River

0   0.25   0.5 mile

0   0.25   0.5 kilometer

Best Time

The trail is open year-round, although the access road and trail can be muddy during and after storms. Spring wildflowers add a touch of color.

Finding the Trail

Leave CA 1 at Little Lake Road, head east away from Mendocino, and drive 5.5 miles to a left-hand turn onto County Road 408, signed "Highway 20, 6 miles" (the dirt road straight ahead continues 3.3 miles to Mendocino Woodlands State Park). Follow dirt Road 408 another 1.2 miles to a small parking area on the right shoulder, unmarked except for a small hiker emblem sign above the letters "TH" (for trailhead) nailed to a redwood. The trail begins at the north end of the parking area (which does not have facilities). Nearby Van Damme and Russian Gulch State Parks and Caspar Beach RV Park offer camping, and the Mendocino Coast has a plethora of lodging opportunities.

Trail Description

Entering a mixed, second-growth redwood forest, the Redwood Forest Ecology Section of the trail ▶1 passes the first of many numbered posts to come

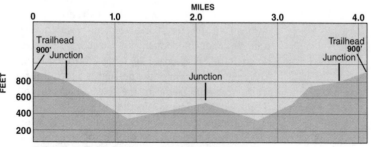

TRAIL 7 Forest History Trail Elevation Profile

Sign for the *Native American Era section of the Forest History Trail*

and descends southeast along a ridge. It reaches a junction ▶2 with a trail on the left that descends stiffly into Manly Gulch and terminates near Group Camp 3 in Mendocino Woodlands State Park. A gently rising stroll leads from there to another junction ▶3 with the beginning of the loop.

🏠 Historic Interest

To sequentially follow the numbers in the *Forest History Trail Guide,* turn right to make a counterclockwise circuit through the forest, and proceed through the Demonstration Forest Section, which chronicles some forest management research. The trail descends moderately for the next 1.3 miles down into the drainage of Little North Fork Big River. At the bottom of the descent is a junction ▶4 with a 0.6-mile lateral to the lower trailhead and Camp 1 in Mendocino Woodlands State Park.

Continue ahead on the left-hand trail to enter the Native American Era Section focusing on the Coast Pomo tribe, and begin a steady climb to regain some elevation. Along the way, the trail crosses a couple of seasonal swales via short, three-planked bridges. This section ends after 0.4 mile.

Entering the Early Logging Days section, the trail climbs even more earnestly on a sometimes steep and occasionally switchbacking ascent. Several well-placed benches will appeal to those in need of a rest. After gaining nearly 400 feet of elevation, you reach a junction ▶5 with the short lateral to Observation Point.

Back when this trail was first constructed in the 1930s, the short climb to Observation Point revealed a view of the ocean. Since then, the forest has grown up and obscured most of the view, except for a thin slice of forest to the west. A bench at the top offers a spot to sit and enjoy the forest, if not the view.

From the Observation Point junction, the trail continues northwest a short distance to the junction ▶6 at the end of the loop portion. From there, retrace your steps 0.4 mile to the trailhead. ▶7

🚶		MILESTONES
▶1	0.0	Start at upper trailhead
▶2	0.4	Straight at junction to Manly Gulch
▶3	0.5	Right at loop junction
▶4	2.1	Straight ahead (left) at Camp 1 junction
▶5	3.6	Straight ahead at Observation Point junction
▶6	3.7	Straight ahead (right) at loop junction
▶7	4.1	End at upper trailhead

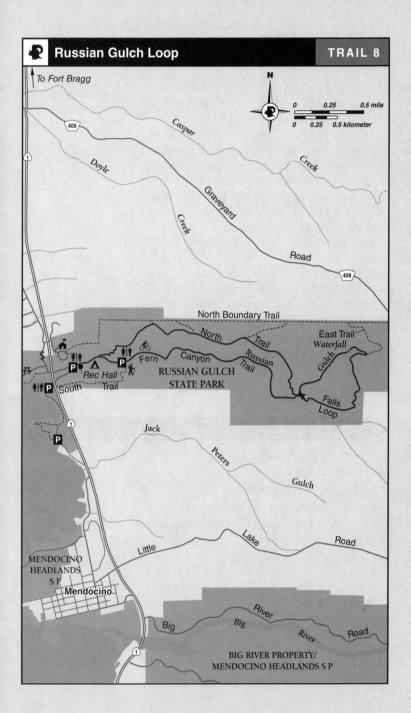

Russian Gulch Loop

TRAIL 8

To Fort Bragg

N

0   0.25   0.5 mile

0   0.25   0.5 kilometer

409

Caspar

Creek

Doyle

Graveyard

Creek

Road

409

North Boundary Trail

North   Trail

East Trail

Waterfall

Fern   Canyon

Russian

Rec Hall

RUSSIAN GULCH
STATE PARK

Gulch

South   Trail

Falls

Loop

Jack

Peters

Gulch

Lake   Road

MENDOCINO
HEADLANDS
S P

Little

Mendocino

Big   River

Big   River   Road

1

BIG RIVER PROPERTY/
MENDOCINO HEADLANDS S P

Russian Gulch Loop

Easy access from CA 1 and a straightforward hike along a wide, gently graded road combine to make the well-named Fern Canyon Trail in Russian Gulch State Park quite popular. The first 1.5 miles receive plenty of use from bicyclists, families with strollers, and wheelchair users, as well as bipeds interested in an easy stroll alongside a placid stream. The trail courses through a canyon carpeted with lush vegetation, including a second-growth redwood forest.

The traffic diminishes a bit beyond where bikes must be parked. Here the road narrows and the grade increases slightly for the next half mile to the start of the Falls Loop Trail, from where a 0.9-mile, 175-foot climb leads to a picturesque 36-foot-tall waterfall. By following the loop as described below, you will find a higher dose of peace and serenity.

Best Time

Russian Gulch State Park is open all year. Spring offers the added bonus of scattered wildflowers. During winter, when the campground is closed, you'll have to walk an additional 0.7 mile round-trip.

Finding the Trail

The well-signed entrance to Russian Gulch State Park is on the ocean side of CA 1, 2 miles north of Mendocino and 6 miles south of Fort Bragg. From the entrance station, follow the narrow park road as it curves east underneath the highway, and continue through an open gate to the day-use parking area near a locked gate just beyond the campground. The

TRAIL USE
Dayhiking, Running, Biking, Handicapped Access

LENGTH & TIME
7.1 miles, 7.8 miles (winter)
4–6 hours

VERTICAL FEET
+750'/-750'
+775'/-775' (winter)

DIFFICULTY
- 1 2 **3** 4 5 +

TRAIL TYPE
Loop

START & FINISH
N39° 19.861'
W123° 47.676'

FEATURES
Redwoods
Flora
Stream
Historic Interest
Waterfall

FACILITIES
Campground
Picnic Area
Restrooms

nearby restroom has running water. In winter, park in the lot near the first gate, which is locked when the campground is closed for the season.

Trail Description

 Stream

 Flora

Walk along the paved road 1.5 miles beyond the locked gate, ▶1 following the course of Russian Gulch Creek upstream. Officially dubbed the Fern Canyon Trail, the road passes through a narrow canyon filled with lush vegetation. Along with the namesake plants, the stream banks harbor moss-draped alders, bigleaf maples, tanoaks, and willows. Large old-growth redwood stumps scattered about the forest testify to the immense giants that once stood in this valley before logging began in the mid-1800s. The recreation hall near the trailhead is on the former site of a shingle mill. Picnic tables and a bike rack mark the end of the nearly level, 1.5-mile section of road. Bicyclists wishing to go farther will have to leave their bikes at the rack and continue on foot. ▶2

 Historic Interest

The road narrows and the grade increases a tad, although the hiking remains quite pleasant for the next 0.5 mile to where the creek forks. Reach a junction with the North Trail angling sharply behind and to your left (the return route for the full loop). Ten yards farther ahead, you reach a second junc-

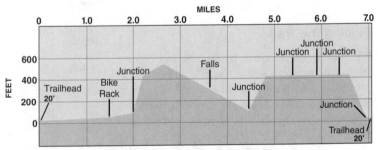

TRAIL 8 Russian Gulch Loop Elevation Profile

tion ▶3 with the Falls Loop Trail. For the shortest route to the falls and back, take the left-hand fork, reaching the falls in 0.9 mile. Otherwise, veer onto the right-hand fork of the Falls Loop.

The right-hand trail crosses the main branch of Russian Gulch Creek on a wood bridge and then starts climbing stiffly up the hillside above the south fork, switchbacking once on the way to the top of a ridge, where the grade eases. After 0.2 mile the trail turns north and continues the pleasant stroll through mixed forest for another 0.4 mile back toward Russian Gulch. At the brink, you hear the creek again, as the trail descends toward the bottom of the canyon amid Oregon grape, rhododendron, and tanoak, reaching a junction ▶4 with the East Trail at 3.5 miles. Continue heading downstream above the creek for a short distance to the top of the falls.

Steep, often slippery stone steps lead to the base of the 36-foot-high falls, ▶5 where a stout wood bridge spans the creek. Little sun reaches the area, creating a cool and moist environment for the lush vegetation bordering the silvery falls. You will no doubt be sharing this delightful scene with fellow admirers, especially on weekends.

Waterfall ▌▌

Away from the falls, the trail closely follows the creek southwest down Russian Gulch. Wood-berm steps and a trio of bridges aid the 0.9-mile descent to the close of the loop at the Fern Canyon Trail junction ▶6 and the North Trail junction shortly beyond. The fastest and easiest route back to the trailhead would be to retrace your steps along the gently graded Fern Canyon Trail. However, with a little extra effort, you can vary your return by veering uphill to the right and following the North Trail back to the campground.

From the junction, the North Trail makes a stiff but short, switchbacking, 250-foot climb up the wall of the canyon and then follows a gently

Waterfall in *Russian Gulch State Park*

graded route through mixed forest along the north rim of Russian Gulch. Soon after crossing the last of four bridges over seasonal swales, you reach a junction ►7 with the first of three laterals to the North Boundary Trail, 0.7 mile from the Fern Canyon Trail junction. The easy, forested stroll continues a half mile to the next lateral junction ►8 and another half mile to the third lateral junction. ►9

After another quarter mile along the rim, the trail starts a switchbacking descent toward the floor of the canyon and a junction ►10 with the Fern Canyon Trail in the middle of the campground. Unless you're here in winter, turn left and follow the paved road 0.2 mile to the trailhead parking area ►11 (winter visitors should turn right and walk along the road for 0.2 mile to the trailhead near the first gate).

MILESTONES

►1	0.0	Start at Fern Canyon Trailhead
►2	1.5	End of road open to bikes
►3	2.0	Turn right at Falls Loop junction
►4	3.5	Straight at East Trail junction
►5	3.6	Waterfall
►6	4.5	Turn right at Falls Loop junction and right at North Trail junction
►7	5.4	Straight at first lateral to North Boundary Trail junction
►8	5.9	Straight at second lateral to North Boundary Trail junction
►9	6.4	Straight at third lateral to North Boundary Trail junction
►10	6.9	Turn left at Fern Canyon junction
►11	7.1	Return to Fern Canyon Trailhead

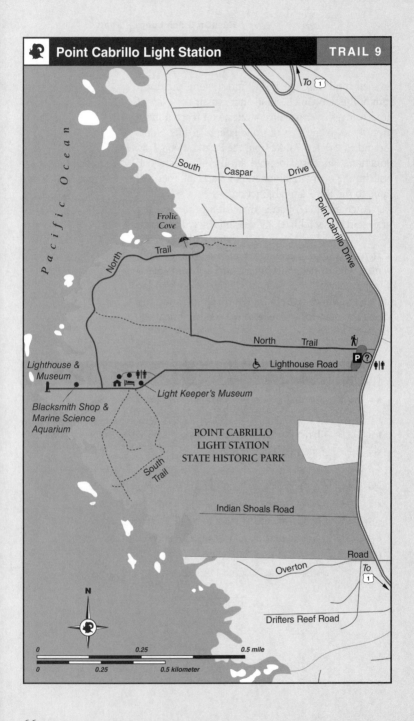

Point Cabrillo Light Station

TRAIL 9

Pacific Ocean

South Caspar Drive

Point Cabrillo Drive

Frolic Cove

North Trail

North Trail

Lighthouse & Museum

Lighthouse Road

Blacksmith Shop & Marine Science Aquarium

Light Keeper's Museum

South Trail

POINT CABRILLO LIGHT STATION STATE HISTORIC PARK

Indian Shoals Road

Overton

Road

To 1

Drifters Reef Road

To 1

N

0   0.25   0.5 mile

0   0.25   0.5 kilometer

Point Cabrillo Light Station

The Point Cabrillo Light Station was originally constructed after the great San Francisco earthquake of 1906, which created a huge demand for lumber to rebuild the city. The lighthouse guided ships along the rugged North Coast to and from tiny doghole ports, where the lumber was loaded onto schooners. A century later, the property had been transferred to California State Parks, and 11 of the original 15 buildings were eventually restored. Today, visitors may tour the lighthouse and some of the other buildings, as well as the picturesque grounds, all of which are part of the state historic park.

Along with its historical interest, Point Cabrillo sits on some prime coastal property, offering stunning views of the Pacific and the rugged coastline from the top of the bluffs. This 2-mile-plus hike travels across coastal prairie, visits a sandy strip of beach with a short waterfall at Frolic Cove, and tours the lighthouse and other structures. Along the way, you may see numerous shorebirds and marine mammals.

Best Time

The park is open year-round. Avoid the exposed area during fierce winter storms.

Finding the Trail

Between the tiny community of Caspar and the town of Mendocino, turn west from CA 1 onto Point Cabrillo Drive at milepost 54.66. Drive 1.7 miles to the park entrance on the west side of the road, and park in the visitor center parking lot (which has

TRAIL USE
Dayhiking, Running,
Dogs Allowed (on leash),
Handicapped Access,
Child-friendly

LENGTH & TIME
2.3 miles, 2–3 hours

VERTICAL FEET
+150'/-150'

DIFFICULTY
- **1** 2 3 4 5 +

TRAIL TYPE
Loop

START & FINISH
N39° 20.976'
W123° 48.778'

FEATURES
Views
Beach
Wildlife
Historic Interest
Lighthouse

FACILITIES
Museum
Restrooms
Lodging

The Wreck of the *Frolic*

This picturesque cove was not too kind to San Francisco–bound clipper *Frolic,* which hit a reef to the north in 1850. The captain and crew were able to get the crippled ship into the cove, with its Chinese cargo still intact. By the time a salvage team made their way north, however, members of the Pomo tribe had pilfered most of the cargo. When the team returned to San Francisco, not only did they inform their boss, lumberman Harry Meiggs, of the loss but also of the giant redwoods and lesser Douglas firs covering the slopes beyond the coast. A year later, the town of Mendocino was founded, and a sawmill was built at Big River.

restrooms). The nearest camping is at Caspar Beach RV Park. Van Damme and Russian Gulch State Parks offer camping near Mendocino, and the Mendocino Coast has a plethora of lodging opportunities.

Trail Description

The most direct path to the historic light station is to leave the parking lot at its south end and follow the paved Lighthouse Road for 0.75 mile. However, doing so misses some of the park's best natural scenery. Instead, follow an old gravel road dubbed the North Trail that exits the parking area on the north side ▶1 and parallels the road before angling slightly northwest. Reach a junction ▶2 after 0.4 mile and veer right, remaining on the North Trail, which now heads north across grasslands with fine views of the Pacific toward Frolic Cove. Soon the cove comes into view on the way to a T-junction. ▶3

 Views

Turn right at the junction, and arc around to where the path descends into the cove via some steps and then onto the beach below a small but scenic waterfall. ▶4 After fully enjoying Frolic Cove, retrace your steps back to the T-junction. ▶5

 Beach

 Waterfall

From the T-junction, head west on the North Trail along the top of the bluff overlooking the ocean, with gorgeous views of the coastline and offshore rocks. Along with the possibility of seeing more than 50 species of birds, keen eyes may spot harbor seals, sea lions, dolphins, gray whales, orcas, humpback whales, and occasionally a blue whale. Continue along the bluff to a junction ►6 with a connector back to the parking lot, and proceed another 0.3 mile to Lighthouse Road and the Point Cabrillo Light Station complex. ►7

Wildlife

Turn right and follow a sidewalk along the old gravel road toward the ocean, soon passing the blacksmith shop, which houses the Marine Science Aquarium, and continue to the lighthouse, which has a small museum on the bottom floor. The lighthouse was operational by 1909, with various technological improvements made in the 1930s and early 1970s. The original Fresnel lens was relit in

Lighthouse

Historic
Interest

Point Cabrillo Lighthouse

1999, and the property was transferred to California State Parks in 2002.

After thoroughly examining the lighthouse and surrounding buildings, head east on Lighthouse Road, soon encountering the residences that housed the families of the light keeper and his assistants. The fully restored head light keeper's home and two cottages to the north are available as overnight rentals (see **pointcabrillo.org** for more information). The Light Keepers Museum is housed in the farthest north building. For further wanderings, the short South Trail leaves the parking lot opposite the head light keeper's residence. Picnic tables provide fine spots for a relaxing lunch.

From the residences, a straightforward 0.6-mile walk along the paved road leads back to the parking area. Periodically placed signs about whales may keep youngsters engaged during the ascent. Reach the close of the loop at the parking lot. ▶8

🚶	**MILESTONES**	
▶1	0.0	Start at parking area
▶2	0.5	Right at junction
▶3	0.6	Right at T-junction
▶4	0.65	Frolic Cove
▶5	0.7	Right at junction
▶6	1.2	Straight at junction
▶7	1.5	Light station
▶8	2.3	Return to trailhead

Ecological Staircase Trail

At first glance, the landscape of Jug Handle State Natural Reserve appears fairly ordinary. However, the area is one of the best examples of defined plant communities and corresponding soil types in the Northern Hemisphere, with an "ecological staircase" that comprises five distinct, uplifted terraces. The 2.5-mile Ecological Staircase Trail visits some of the five communities, the highlight of which is the pygmy forest. Occupying a flat terrace, plants of the pygmy forest are stunted by highly acidic soils overlaying a layer of hardpan. A free brochure keyed to 40 numbered posts provides insight into the area's geology and flora. The trail also allows access to the broad beach of Jug Handle Cove via a short side trail.

Best Time

The area is open year-round. Portions of the trail can be muddy following rainy periods. Springtime offers the added bonus of wildflowers.

Finding the Trail

About 4 miles south of Fort Bragg, turn into the signed parking area for Jug Handle State Natural Reserve, which is on the west side of CA 1 and immediately south of the Jug Handle Creek Bridge. The parking area has a portable toilet, and there are picnic tables nearby. The nearest camping is at Caspar Beach RV Park. Van Damme and Russian Gulch State Parks offer camping near the town of Mendocino, and the Mendocino Coast has a plethora of lodging opportunities.

TRAIL USE
Dayhiking, Running

LENGTH & TIME
4.7 miles, 2–4 hours

VERTICAL FEET
+400'/-400'

DIFFICULTY
- 1 2 **3** 4 5 +

TRAIL TYPE
Out & Back

START & FINISH
N39° 22.477'
W123° 48.982'

FEATURES
Pygmy Forest
Beach
Views
Stream
Flora
Wildflowers

FACILITIES
Picnic Area
Restroom

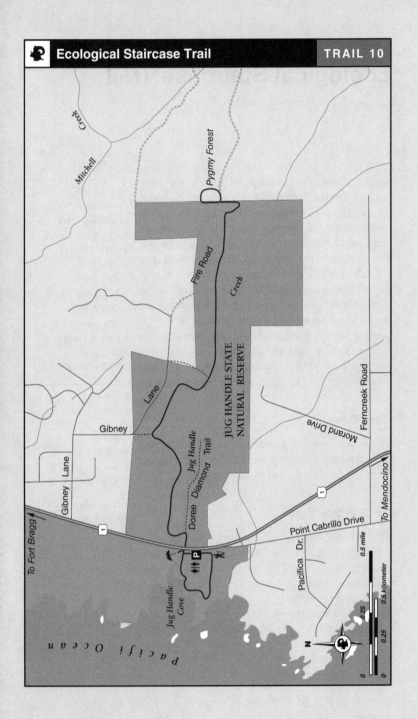

Trail Description

From the well-signed trailhead, ▶1 head toward the ocean through a forest of mostly Monterey pines, and immediately reach the first of 40 numbered posts corresponding to entries in a pamphlet available at the trailhead about the natural history of the plant communities along the 2.6-mile route. Break out of the trees onto coastal prairie made up mainly of introduced grasses, the first of the five uplifted terraces that make up the Ecological Staircase. Springtime wildflowers include daisy, angelica, goldfields, lupine, poppy, and sea thrift. Follow the trail on a clockwise arc around the headlands above rugged sea-stacks and the sandy beach of Jug Handle Cove, ignoring a couple of steep use trails down to the cove.

Proceed into a forest of Sitka spruce, grand fir, and wax myrtle intermixed with Monterey, Bishop, and shore pines. The trail passes to the north of the parking area, where a junction ▶2 with a short lateral (your return route) provides access back to your vehicle. Soon, between posts 8 and 9, you reach a junction ▶3 with a spur on the left heading downslope and providing the best access to the large beach at the mouth of Jug Handle Cove (dogs are prohibited). The sandy beach backdropped by the gracefully arched CA 1 bridge is an often photographed scene.

Flora

Wildflowers

Views

Beach

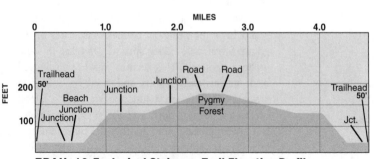

TRAIL 10 Ecological Staircase Trail Elevation Profile

Pygmy Forest foliage

 Stream

Continue ahead from the junction, soon passing below the bridge. A short way from the bridge, the trail descends via a series of steps into the lush riparian vegetation along the creek and then heads across a stout bridge and adjoining boardwalk. Just before the bridge, the obscure Doree Diamond Trail heads upstream on a boardwalk above a picturesque swamp before climbing into Sitka spruce forest. Beyond the boardwalk, the trail climbs stiffly west. Watch for poison oak intermixed with ceanothus, gooseberry, and Scotch broom. At the top of the climb, the trail turns east and gently ascends through Sitka spruce forest and across small pockets of grasslands.

Eventually you reach the second terrace, where grand fir is the principal conifer. Associates of the grand fir include Sitka spruce, Douglas fir, and western hemlock. This section was heavily logged back in the early 1960s and now has a varied ground cover. Reach a junction ►4 with a lateral on the left heading north to Gibney Lane, 1.2 miles from the trailhead. After another 0.3 mile, you pass beneath a set of power lines running through the old right-of-way for the Caspar Railroad, which transported timber between Jug Handle Creek and a mill near the mouth of Caspar Creek in the late 1800s.

Continue east, eventually entering second-growth redwood forest with an increasing ground cover of redwood sorrel. At 1.9 miles, you reach a second junction ►5 with a trail heading north toward Gibney Lane. As the ground transitions from well-drained sandy soils to hardpan, the redwood associates switch from conifers to tanoaks and myrtles. Near post 30, a dramatic change occurs as you reach the start of the pygmy forest.

Proceed north on gravel tread to an intersection with the east-west-running dirt Fire Road, ►6 and following arrowed directions on a post, continue north to the start of the loop through the unique pygmy forest. A sharp right turn leads onto the boardwalk and past the dwarf vegetation, including Bolander pine, a miniature relative of the typically straight and tall lodgepole pine. Farther on, a raised deck provides an elevated view of this unique environment. At the end of the boardwalk, continue to the intersection with the Fire Road, ►7 turn left at the next junction, ►8 and retrace your steps back to the trailhead. ►9

Pygmy Forest

🚶	**MILESTONES**	
►1	0.0	Start at trailhead
►2	0.4	Straight at junction to parking lot
►3	0.5	Straight at beach junction
►4	1.2	Right at junction to Gibney Lane
►5	1.9	Straight at junction to Gibney Lane
►6	2.3	Cross Fire Road and turn right onto pygmy forest boardwalk
►7	2.6	Return to Fire Road
►8	4.6	Left at junction to parking lot
►9	4.7	Return to trailhead

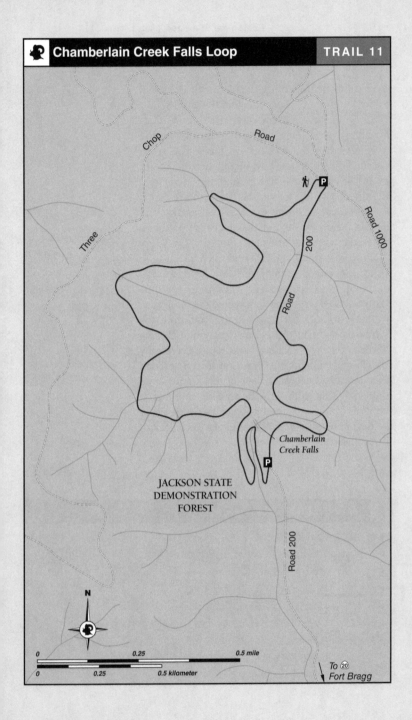

Chamberlain Creek Falls Loop

TRAIL 11

Chop Road

Three

Road 1000

Road 200

Chamberlain Creek Falls

Road 200

JACKSON STATE
DEMONSTRATION
FOREST

N

0   0.25   0.5 mile

0   0.25   0.5 kilometer

To 20
Fort Bragg

Chamberlain Creek Falls Loop

Directly east of the scenic coastline that most people associate with Mendocino County lies the nearly forgotten forests of the coastal hills. Hidden away amid the trees are redwood groves, tumbling streams, and waterfalls. This trip visits one such wonder, a 50-foot-tall waterfall near an untouched stand of virgin redwoods in a deep, narrow canyon within the 50,000-acre, multiple-use Jackson State Demonstration Forest.

Best Time

Although the area is typically open year-round, the only time the dirt access road to the trailhead is suitable for driving is when it's dry. Portions of the road can be extremely muddy following rainy periods and impassable to the average sedan. The falls are showiest at peak flows, usually from late winter to early spring. Spring offers the added bonus of wildflowers.

TRAIL USE
Dayhiking, Running, Dogs Allowed

LENGTH & TIME
2.9 miles, 1½–2 hours

VERTICAL FEET
+600'/-600'

DIFFICULTY
- 1 2 **3** 4 5 +

TRAIL TYPE
Loop

START & FINISH
N39° 24.391'
W123° 34.484'

FEATURES
Waterfall
Redwoods
Wildflowers

FACILITIES
None

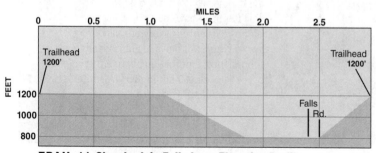

TRAIL 11 Chamberlain Falls Loop Elevation Profile

Chamberlain Creek Falls

Finding the Trail

Leave CA 1 near the south end of Fort Bragg, and head east on CA 20 for 17 miles to mile marker 17.4, just beyond Dunlap Conservation Camp and the Chamberlain Creek Bridge. Turn left onto Road 200, and drive 1.2 miles to a fork, where you turn sharply left to remain on Road 200. Follow the dirt road on a stiff climb, continuing past a small parking area by a wood fence on the left for the unmarked Chamberlain Falls Trail, 4.7 miles from CA 20. Continue another 0.4 mile to an intersection with Road 1000 (Three Chop Road), and park your vehicle where space allows.

Marked by a small sign, the Camellia Trail begins at the southwest corner of the intersection. There are no facilities near the trailhead. The nearest campground, Dunlap, is administered by the Jackson State Demonstration Forest and is located on CA 20 at mile marker 16.9 (reservations not accepted).

Trail Description

From the intersection, ▶1 follow the Camellia Trail into shady forest on a general traverse around the nose of a minor ridge and into a side canyon of a tributary of Chamberlain Creek. Periodic redwood stumps testify to the area's logging days. Cross the usually trickling creek, and repeat the process for the next drainage. At the third side canyon, the trail descends a hillside with the aid of several switchbacks down to a flat and an untouched grove of impressive redwoods, spared from the lumberman's axe because it is hidden in a narrow, steep canyon.

Redwoods 🌲

A short distance farther up the trail is Chamberlain Falls, ▶2 a 50-foot silver shower dropping down a cliff of black rock. The trail passes immediately below the base of the waterfall, allowing you an intimate view. Fallen logs offer good

Waterfall

spots on which to linger. A plaque nearby designates the area as the Eric Swanson Grove.

When the time has come to tear yourself away from this serene locale, continue ahead on the counterclockwise loop to a set of steep switchbacks up the canyon wall, a set of stairs, and up to Road 200 and the unmarked Chamberlain Falls Trailhead. ▶3

Turn left onto the road, and climb 0.4 mile to the intersection at the start of the trip. ▶4

🚶	**MILESTONES**	
▶1	0.0	Start at intersection of Roads 200 and 1000
▶2	2.4	Chamberlain Falls
▶3	2.5	Left at Road 200 and Chamberlain Falls Trailhead
▶4	2.9	Return to intersection

Ten Mile Beach

Duncan MacKerricher and his wife, Jessie, came to the north coast from Canada in 1864, subsequently purchasing 1,000 acres for a spread he named Rancho de la Laguna. His descendants sold the ranch to the State of California in 1949. Replacing a rail line, the Haul Road was built in 1949 to transport logs from the Ten Mile River Watershed to the Union Lumber Company mill in Fort Bragg. Modern recreationists used the old road until sections were destroyed by recurring Pacific storms.

Today MacKerricher State Park is a fine place to camp, picnic, beachcomb, and watch wildlife. Nine miles of shoreline, acres of sand dunes, a freshwater lake, and the last coastal fen remaining in California create a seaside paradise without equal. While the section of the Haul Road north of Laguna Point is no longer a viable route, hiking along the beach as far as Ten Mile River remains a scenic delight. (If you're looking for a shorter hike, you can turn around wherever you prefer.)

Best Time

Although the park is open all year and the coastline scenery is always exceptional, walking along sections of the beach during high tide may be dangerous, especially during winter storms.

Finding the Trail

Turn west from CA 1, about 3 miles north of Fort Bragg, at the entrance to MacKerricher State Park. Continue along the park access road past the

TRAIL USE
Dayhiking, Running,
Dogs Allowed (on leash)

LENGTH & TIME
11.0 miles, 5–7 hours

VERTICAL FEET
Nominal

DIFFICULTY
- 1 2 **3** 4 5 +

TRAIL TYPE
Out & Back

START & FINISH
N39° 29.341'
W123° 47.972'

FEATURES
Beach
Views
Wildlife

FACILITIES
Campgrounds
Picnic Areas
Restrooms
Visitor Center

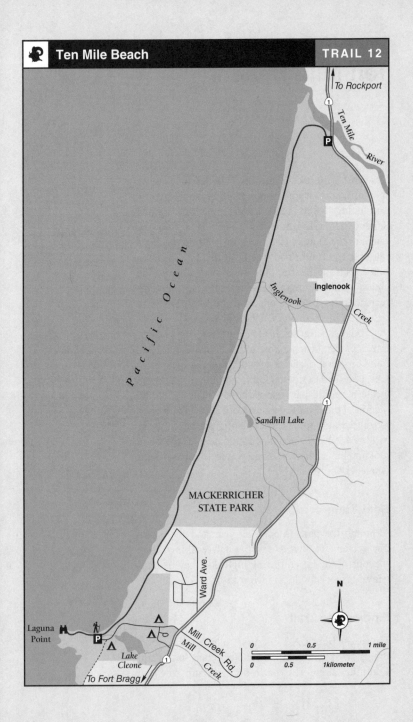

To Rockport

Ten Mile River

P

Pacific Ocean

Inglenook

Inglenook

Creek

Sandhill Lake

1

MACKERRICHER
STATE PARK

Ward Ave.

N

Laguna
Point

P

Lake
Cleone

Mill Creek Rd.

Mill Creek

1

To Fort Bragg

| 0 | | 0.5 | | 1 mile |
| 0 | | 0.5 | | 1kilometer |

entrance station to an intersection with Mill Creek Road. Turn left and continue past the campground and Lake Cleone to the Laguna Point day-use parking area. The park has four campgrounds: East Pine, West Pine, Cleone, and Surfwood.

Trail Description

The boardwalk extending from the parking lot to the seal-watching station at Laguna Point provides an excellent spot from which to watch harbor seals, migrating gray whales, or a variety of seabirds. Steps lead down to a rocky area (accessible during low tide) for tidepooling. Recreationists also heavily use the intact portion of the old Haul Road heading south from Laguna Point and over the restored Pudding Creek Trestle to Glass Beach. Contrary to published reports, hiking the Haul Road from Laguna Point north to Ten Mile River is no longer possible. Although a section accessible from Ward Avenue remains suitable for walking, most of the remaining road has been washed out, undercut, or buried with sand. California State Parks has proposed a plan to remove most of what remains.

Wildlife

All is not lost, however, as you can still hike the beach all the way to Ten Mile River. The coastline scenery is superb, including views to the north of the distant Lost Coast. The farther north you travel, the fewer people you'll see—you may even have the beach to yourself. As is usual for beach hikes, walking on wet sand is much easier than plodding through dry sand. Between the parking area ▶1 and the river are two stream crossings, the creek ▶2 draining Sandhill Lake at 3.5 miles and Inglenook Creek ▶3 at 4 miles, neither of which should present major difficulties.

Beach

Views

The complete trip to the south bank of Ten Mile River ▶4 is 5.5 miles, but you can turn around at any point, fully satisfied with the stunning scenery.

▶5 Dogs are *not* allowed in the Inglenook Fen-Ten Mile Dunes Preserve portion of the park (north of Ward Avenue and east of the Haul Road).

If you would like to plan a one-way shuttle trip, you could leave a second car in a parking area 4.6 miles north of the park entrance on the shoulder of CA 1. To reach the parking area from the northern end of the beach, follow an intact section of the Haul Road, which bends east and parallels the south bank of Ten Mile River to a use trail. Follow this trail steeply up the hillside and through a tunnel of vegetation to the parking area.

🚶	MILESTONES	
▶1	0.0	Start at Laguna Point Trailhead
▶2	3.5	Cross creek draining Sandhill Lake
▶3	4.0	Cross Inglenook Creek
▶4	5.5	Reach Ten Mile River
▶5	11.0	Return to trailhead

Opposite *Mendocino Headlands State Park*

King Range & Sinkyone Wilderness

King Range & Sinkyone Wilderness

Rising 4,000 feet above the Pacific Ocean to the apex of the King Range in a little more than 4 miles, the rugged and steep topography of the Lost Coast has few equals. The terrain is so steep that highway engineers abandoned the coastline route of the Shoreline Highway (CA Highway 1) and relocated the road farther inland. Nowadays the wild-looking landscape is contained within the King Range National Conservation Area and Sinkyone Wilderness State Park. However, during the logging heyday, mills, railroads, ports, and settlements littered the area. Fortunately, nature has done a fabulous job of returning the land to a pristine state. Today hikers, backpackers, and equestrians travel through an untamed and highly picturesque wilderness, usually with little or no company, which creates perhaps the premier coastal hiking area in the nation.

The Lost Coast offers not only incomparable scenery, but also the opportunity to see a diverse and prolific assortment of wildlife. Stretches of pristine beach are complemented by sightings of a wide variety of marine mammals, including harbor seals, sea lions, and migrating whales. Low tide provides plenty of opportunities for tidepooling. And the skies are commonly filled with an assortment of birds, with the occasional osprey or eagle making an appearance. Inland trails offer the occasional stunning coastline vista, as well as potential sightings of Roosevelt elk or black bear.

Unlike the majority of the North Coast's hiking trails, the Lost Coast is a backpacker's paradise, with the namesake trail the main highlight. Remote, rugged, and lonely, the path is arguably the quintessential coast backpacking trip.

Rugged topography *of the Lost Coast*

Permits

Permits are required for overnight trips into the King Range National Conservation Area (north section) and Sinkyone Wilderness State Park (south section). Overnight permits for the King Range NCA are free and can be obtained by self-registration at trailheads. Overnight permits for stays within Sinkyone Wilderness cost $5 per night and can be bought at the Needle Rock Visitor Center midway through the south section of the Lost Coast Trail.

Bear canisters are required for backpacking trips within the King Range NCA and are a good idea in Sinkyone Wilderness as well. Canisters can be rented from the BLM office in Arcata, the King Range NCA ranger station on Shelter Cove Road, or the Petrolia Store. Campfires are often banned in these areas—check with the appropriate agencies for current conditions.

Maps

USGS 7.5-minute maps covering the Lost Coast from north to south are: *Petrolia, Cooskie Creek, Shubrick Peak, Honeydew, Shelter Cove, Bear Harbor, Mistake Point,* and *Hales Grove.* In addition, the BLM publishes a handy map, *King Range National Conservation Area: The Lost Coast,* which covers the north section. *California's Lost Coast,* published by Wilderness Press, is a fair complement to the USGS maps for the south section through Sinkyone Wilderness State Park.

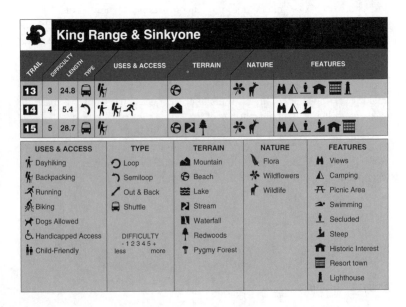

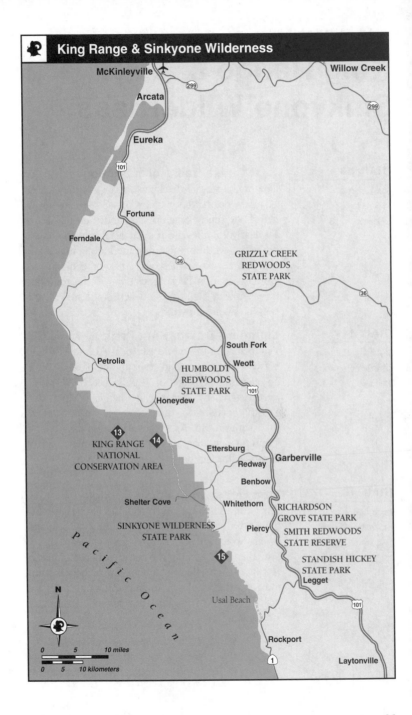

King Range & Sinkyone Wilderness

McKinleyville

Willow Creek

299

Arcata

299

Eureka

101

Fortuna

Ferndale

36

GRIZZLY CREEK
REDWOODS
STATE PARK

36

South Fork

Petrolia

Weott

HUMBOLDT
REDWOODS
STATE PARK

101

Honeydew

13 14

KING RANGE
NATIONAL
CONSERVATION AREA

Ettersburg

Garberville

Redway

Benbow

Shelter Cove

Whitethorn

RICHARDSON
GROVE STATE PARK

SINKYONE WILDERNESS
STATE PARK

Piercy

SMITH REDWOODS
STATE RESERVE

15

STANDISH HICKEY
STATE PARK

Legget

Pacific Ocean

N

Usal Beach

101

0   5   10 miles

0   5   10 kilometers

Rockport

1

Laytonville

King Range & Sinkyone Wilderness

Lost Coast Trail: North Section 93

The premier beach backpacking trip in the Golden State, the north section of the Lost Coast Trail travels across the sandy beach or just above on the dunes for nearly 25 miles. Beautiful coastal scenery and the abundant wildlife, including marine mammals and numerous bird species, are constant companions. Exercise caution because sections of the route are impassable at high tide, and ticks, rattlesnakes, and poison oak are present.

Lightning Trail to King Peak 103

Few places in the world can boast the relief found between the ocean and the summit of King Peak, an elevation change of 4,088 feet in 3 miles. Fortunately, by starting at the 2,180-foot-high Lightning Trailhead, hikers can get a head start on their summit bid. As expected, fogless days offer a stunning view from the top of the mountain, site of a former fire lookout.

Lost Coast Trail: South Section 108

The antithesis to the north section's flat beach hike, the Lost Coast Trail's south section moves inland on an up-and-down course with significant elevation changes, reaching the ocean only occasionally. Similar to its northern neighbor, the scenery is stunning and the wildlife abundant. Although tides are not a concern, ticks, rattlesnakes, and poison oak are present.

Lost Coast Trail: North Section

The Lost Coast is a strip of rugged Northern California coastline between where CA 1 bends inland in the south and the Mattole River enters the ocean near Petrolia in the north. The steep topography forced highway engineers to retreat inland to find more hospitable terrain suitable for a north-to-south byway. Combined with some outstanding scenery, the lack of a road and the inevitable, corresponding development has created a veritable hikers' paradise. The area's premier long-distance path, the Lost Coast Trail is also perhaps the finest trail along the entire Pacific Coast. The seaside community of Shelter Cove near the midpoint divides the trail; the following description covers the north segment.

Ocean beach is the dominant landform of this north section, as the route is either directly over the black sand or immediately above on grassy benches. The trail's proximity to the ocean permits glorious views of the Pacific Ocean, the undeveloped coastline, and the towering King Range. Along with magnificent scenery, the area is teeming with an abundance of wildlife. Offshore animals commonly seen include harbor seals, sea lions, migrating gray whales during winter and spring, and tidepool creatures during low tide. If you don't see any black-tailed deer or black bear, you will almost certainly see their prints in the sand where streams spill into the ocean. Birds, including gulls, pelicans, cormorants, terns, herons, sandpipers, ravens, and the occasional bald eagle, are everywhere. Spring visitors will be treated to a fine wildflower display. The decommissioned Punta Gorda Lighthouse provides a touch of historical interest.

TRAIL USE
Backpacking

LENGTH & TIME
24.8 miles, 3–4 days

VERTICAL FEET
+200'/-100'

DIFFICULTY
- 1 2 **3** 4 5 +

TRAIL TYPE
Shuttle

START & FINISH
N40° 17.347'
W124° 21.352'

FEATURES
Beach
Wildflowers
Wildlife
Views
Secluded
Historic Interest
Lighthouse
Backcountry Camping

FACILITIES
Campground
Resort Town

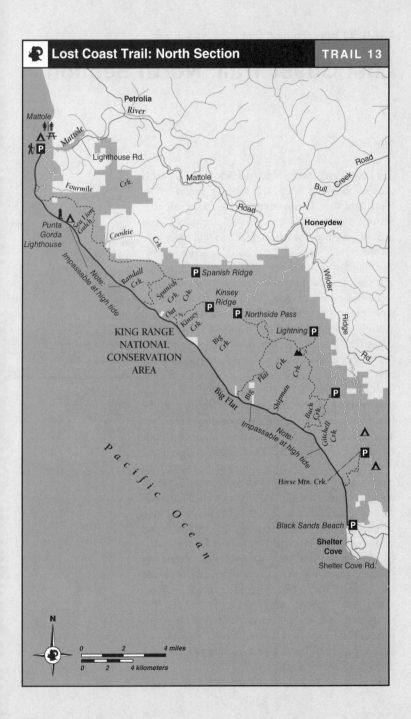

Petrolia

River

Mattole

Mattole

Lighthouse Rd.

Mattole

Fourmile

Crk.

Road

Bull

Creek

Road

Honeydew

Punta Gorda Lighthouse

Sea Lion Gulch

Note: Impassable at high tide

Cooskie

Crk.

Randall Crk.

Spanish Crk.

P *Spanish Ridge*

Oat

Crk.

Kinsey Ridge

P

Kinsey Crk.

P *Northside Pass*

Big Crk.

Lightning P

Wilder

Ridge

Rd.

KING RANGE NATIONAL CONSERVATION AREA

Big Flat

Big Flat

Shipman

Crk.

Crk.

Buck Crk.

P

Note: Impassable at high tide

Gitchell Crk.

P

Pacific Ocean

Horse Mtn. Crk.

P

Black Sands Beach P

Shelter Cove

Shelter Cove Rd.

N

| 0 | 2 | 4 miles |

| 0 | 2 | 4 kilometers |

While hikers need not worry about significant elevation gains and losses, walking on some of the beach sections can be tiring. In additions, hikers must look up the tide schedule ahead of time, as three sections of the trail are impassable during high tide. Be aware that rattlesnakes, although uncommon, are present in this community, as are poison oak and ticks (particularly in spring). Traveling from north to south keeps the prevailing wind at your back.

Best Time

Even though the Lost Coast Trail can be hiked any time the weather is accommodating, spring and fall are usually the two best seasons. While temperatures are generally moderate during summer, fog often-times drapes the Northern California coastline with an omnipresent veil. Along with clearer skies, spring offers the added bonus of a vibrantly colorful array of wildflowers on the bluffs above the beach from late April to early May, enhanced by the annual migration of California gray whales. Fall also offers generally clear weather, with the characteristic dried grasses of the Golden State replacing the spring flowers.

Finding the Trail

Leave US 101 in Garberville at Exit 639B, and follow Redwood Drive for 2.5 miles to the town of Redway. Turn left (west) onto Briceland Thorn Road, and proceed for 12.2 miles to Thorn Junction, where the road straight ahead is Shelter Cove Road. Continue another 8 miles to the beach resort town of Shelter Cove and an intersection with Beach Road on your right. Proceed on Beach Road for 0.75 mile to the signed parking lot for Black Sands Beach Trailhead, where you can leave your shuttle vehicle. Your hike begins from the Mattole River Trailhead, so backtrack to the Shelter Cove Road, and drive 10.8 miles to a left-hand turn onto Ettersburg Honeydew Road. Follow this road 6 miles to an intersection with Etter Ranch Road. Continue ahead, now on Wilder Ridge Road, for another 13.5 miles to a junction with Mattole Road in the tiny burg of Honeydew. Head straight onto Mattole Road, and proceed westbound for 13.7 miles to a left-hand turn onto Lighthouse Road. Follow this narrow paved and then gravel road for 0.4 mile to the Mattole Trailhead parking area.

Logistics

Shuttling to both trailheads without two vehicles or a kind friend willing to commit to a multihour drive is possible by using one of the two Bureau of Land Management–permitted commercial shuttle companies servicing the Lost Coast (the shuttle between Shelter Cove and Mattole cost $200 in 2012). Contact Lost Coast Shuttle (707-986-7437, 707-223-1547, sherriluallin@gmail.com, **lostcoast shuttle.com**) or Lost Coast Trail Transport Service (707-986-9909, roxanne@saber.net, **lostcoasttrail .com**) for more information.

With a small handful of lodging and dining options, the seaside town of Shelter Cove can be a fine base camp, especially for hikers attempting to complete both the north and south sections of the Lost Coast Trail.

Trail Description

After filling out an overnight use form at the trail-head signboard, ►1 avoid the tendency to follow the path toward the beach, and veer left near a closed gate, following an inland trail with more solid footing. At low tide, however, the stretch of beach to the south offers some fantastic tidepools that will compensate for the more difficult hiking on the sand. Following the inland trail, you soon pass by an archaeological site and then continue across sand dunes for quite a while. At 1.3 miles, the trail crosses a seasonal stream coursing through Smith Gulch and then continues until it drops onto the sandy beach, 1.6 miles from the trailhead.

 Historic Interest

A relatively short walk along the beach leads around the promontory known as Windy Point. After another 0.7 mile, you skirt Punta Gorda (Spanish for "fat point"), which is impassable at high tide, and then forsake the sand to return to the bluffs directly above the beach. Reach a ford of

Beach

Caution ⚠

Punta Gorda Lighthouse

OPTIONS

Although a lighthouse was requested as early as 1888 to warn mariners of Windy Point, a rock spur jutting dangerously into the ocean, construction was delayed until 1910. A foghorn was operational a year before the lighthouse was finally completed in 1912.

In the interim, nine vessels were lost at sea near here. The most famous disaster was the sinking of the *Columbia,* a cargo and passenger steamship that set sail in 1907 from San Francisco bound for Portland, Oregon, with 251 passengers and crew.

Despite being enveloped by dense evening fog and within earshot of the whistle from the *San Pedro,* a lumber schooner in the immediate vicinity, Captain Peter Doran refused to slow the *Columbia.* Unfortunately, the pilot of the *San Pedro,* First Officer Hendricksen, also failed to reduce his ship's speed, and it slammed into the *Columbia*'s starboard side, ultimately resulting in the loss of 88 passengers and crewmembers.

The Punta Gorda Lighthouse was operational until 1951, when it was replaced by a navigational buoy. In 1970, the Bureau of Land Management burned down the neighboring outbuildings used to house the lighthouse keepers and their families to discourage squatters; they left only the lighthouse and oil house standing. Placed on the National Register of Historic Places in 1976, the lighthouse was restored in 1989 and is preserved today by the Honeydew Volunteer Fire Department.

Fourmile Creek at 2.5 miles, just beyond two old cabins located on a strip of private land. At 0.4 mile from Fourmile Creek is a junction with the Cookie Creek Trail, ►2 which climbs 2,000 feet above the coast and provides a more than 12-mile, strenuous alternative to an upcoming section of the Lost Coast Trail that is impassable at high tide.

Historic Interest

Wildflowers

Another 0.3 mile of easy hiking from the junction leads to the Punta Gorda Lighthouse, where a short side trail leads up to two structures with interpretive signs. In spring a colorful display of wildflowers graces the slopes around the lighthouse.

As you head away from Punta Gorda Lighthouse, the trail rolls along the steep, grass-covered hillside above the beach on the way to a stiff descent into Sea Lion Gulch, 3.8 miles from the trailhead. Just before the creek crossing is a small campsite, the last place to pitch a tent before a stretch of beach that is impassable at high tide. You may hear a chorus of barking sea lions from a group of rock outcroppings aptly named Sea Lion Rocks. The trail heads briefly downstream along the creek onto the sand and the beginning of a nearly 4-mile section of beach that should be traveled only at low tide.

Backcountry Camping

Wildlife

Caution

Caution

Sandwiched between the steep bluffs to the left and the pounding surf on the right, the Lost Coast Trail follows a sandy strip of beach for about a quarter mile toward Hat Rock, where a rock promontory blocks forward progress. Lacking an officially designated trail, you must scramble up and over this obstacle via one of a number of possible routes to reach the beach again on the far side. Once you are across, be assured that this brief scramble is the hardest part of your hike. Just south of Hat Rock is a junction with the Cookie Spur Trail, ►3 a 1.2-mile connector to the Cookie Creek Trail mentioned earlier. From the junction, you could bypass the remainder of the beach route by following the spur up to the Cookie Creek Trail, heading 5.2 miles east to the Spanish Ridge Trail junction and then descending 2.9 miles back to the beach.

Beyond the Cooskie Spur junction, the Lost Coast Trail continues along the narrow beach for 1.1 miles to a crossing of Cooskie Creek. Campsites may be available upstream above the high tide line.

Backcountry Camping

Another 2 miles of beach hiking leads to Randall Creek and the end of the section that is impassable at high tide. After fording the creek, the trail briefly climbs onto a grassy bench, a popular camping area with several scenic campsites adorned by California poppies in spring.

Backcountry Camping

Beyond Randall Creek, the trail stays above the beach on an extended journey across Spanish Flat, a bench covered by tall grasses. After 1.2 miles, you reach a junction with the Spanish Ridge Trail, ▶4 which climbs 2,000 feet in 2.9 miles to connect with the Cooskie Creek Trail.

Another 0.7 mile of hiking through similar terrain leads to a log crossing of Spanish Creek and some nearby campsites. Beyond the creek the trail passes below a private home on the way to a usually easy ford of Oat Creek. Farther on, 1.4 miles from Spanish Creek, you reach a junction with the Kinsey Ridge Trail, ▶5 a 4-mile, 2,000-foot climb leading to the Kinsey Ridge Trailhead.

Backcountry Camping

Shortly past the Kinsey Ridge junction, the trail drops back onto the beach near another private residence. Along the way, dead snags on the hills above give testament to the forest fire that visited here. Approaching the next canyon, the trail enters the wide mouth of Big Creek, 1.7 miles from Kinsey Creek, where a few possible campsites will tempt overnighters. A couple of logs provide a usually straightforward crossing of the stream.

Backcountry Camping

South of Big Creek, the Lost Coast Trail returns to the beach for a lengthy romp above the surf. Although bear prints and scat are common sights on the sand near Big Creek, your chances of seeing

Approaching *Punta Gorda Lighthouse*

a bear remain slim and typically decrease the farther you travel from the creek.

Eventually, the trail forsakes the sandy beach for a route across the high, fairly wide, grass-covered bench of Big Flat. Near one of the seasonal streams draining the slopes of Shubrick Peak above, erosion forces the trail back onto the beach, which at this point is covered with ankle-twisting cobbles; fortunately this stretch is short. After a bit a sandy trail angles steeply away from beach and up onto the bluffs. The extended journey along Big Flat continues along the course of an old road and then an abandoned landing strip. Near the far end of the strip, you pass what must have been a fairly impressive home in its heyday on the way to a marked junction with the Rattlesnake Ridge Trail. ►6 This infrequently used trail climbs 4.9 miles to Bear Hollow Camp and then another 0.8 mile to a junction with the King Crest Trail.

At the junction, the Lost Creek Trail turns sharply toward the beach and then makes either a

log crossing or a ford, depending on the season, of
Big Flat Creek, 2.8 miles from Big Creek. There are
numerous campsites on Big Flat before the crossing
and on Miller Flat above the south side of the creek
channel.

**Backcountry
Camping**

Away from Big Flat Creek, the route traverses
Miller Flat for 0.6 mile, passing below a newer landing strip mowed out of the thick grass. From the edge
of the flat, the trail plunges steeply down to a 4.5-
mile stretch of beach that is impassable at high tide.

Caution

The going may be slow because much of the
stretch is covered with small rocks. Cliffs even
steeper than those south of Sea Lion Rocks provide
no hope for escape for anyone unfortunate enough
to disregard the tide tables. The first possible exit
occurs 1.9 miles from Big Flat Creek, where the
narrow canyon of Shipman Creek offers some fine
campsites on both banks. Another 1.4 miles of
beach hiking leads to Buck Creek, with one decent
campsite located on a bench above the south bank.
Shortly beyond the creek is a junction with the
Buck Creek Trail, ►**7** a 3.6-mile, 3,000-foot ascent
to a connection with the King Crest Trail near
Saddle Mountain. Another 1.5 miles on the beach
is necessary to travel out of the impassable-at-high-
tide zone. If you happen to be here for a very low
tide, look for excellent tidepools on the way to the
narrow canyon of Gitchell Creek. There may be
campsites on the beach above the high tide line on
the south side of the creek, tucked below a bluff.

**Backcountry
Camping**

Wildlife

**Backcountry
Camping**

Now less than 4 miles of beach hiking separates
Gitchell Creek from the Black Sands Beach Trailhead.
Although the route to the south is generally passable
at any tide, lower tides are preferable, as some of the
initial stretches are quite narrow and hemmed in by
cliffs. While the route is straightforward, it can also be
somewhat tiring, depending on the condition of the
sand and the fact that much of the beach is covered
with pebbles. At 1.9 miles from Gitchell Creek is a

⚠ Backcountry Camping

junction with the Horse Mountain Creek Trail, ▶8 a 4.2-mile climb to a trailhead on King Peak Road. Just beyond the junction is the canyon of Horse Mountain Creek, a fine spot for a last night's camp.

Another 1.8 miles across Black Sands Beach brings you to the north edge of the town of Shelter Cove. Hop across Telegraph Creek, ignoring a very steep gash of sand climbing up the bluff above, continue down the beach a short distance, and then turn up the canyon of Humboldt Creek to where a path switchbacks up to the Black Sands Beach Trailhead ▶9 and the handicapped parking lot. If your car is parked in the overnight lot, walk steeply up the road to the signed parking area.

𝘅 MILESTONES

▶1	0.0	Start at Mattole Trailhead
▶2	2.9	Straight at Cooskie Creek Trail
▶3	5.2	Straight at Cooskie Spur Trail
▶4	9.5	Straight at Spanish Ridge Trail
▶5	11.6	Straight at Kinsey Ridge Trail
▶6	16.0	Right at Rattlesnake Ridge Trail
▶7	19.5	Straight at Buck Creek Trail
▶8	22.9	Straight at Horse Mountain Creek Trail
▶9	24.8	End at Black Sands Beach Trailhead

Lightning Trail to King Peak

Few places in the world can boast a relief similar to that of the King Range, where the land rises from sea level to an elevation of 4,088 feet at the summit of King Peak in a mere 3 miles. Fortunately, hikers don't have to conquer that entire amount, as the Lightning Trail starts at 2,180 feet and reaches the summit in only 2.7 miles. The summit offers a superb coast view, with forested slopes plunging precipitously toward the ocean. The view of the interior is also quite striking, with distant Lassen Peak visible on very clear days. Although this hike works best as a dayhike, backpackers can stay overnight at shady Maple Camp, where water is available year-round.

Best Time

Provided the access roads are in good condition and there is no snow on King Peak, this hike can be done at any time of year. However, in winter, the weather can be miserable and the roads may be impassable; summer offers a high probability of coastal fog, which makes clear days in spring or fall the best time to scale King Peak.

Finding the Trail

Leave US 101 in Garberville at Exit 639B, and follow Redwood Drive for 2.5 miles to the town of Redway. Turn left (west) onto Briceland Thorn Road, and proceed for 12.2 miles to Thorn Junction, where the road straight ahead is Shelter Cove Road.

TRAIL USE
Dayhiking, Backpacking, Running

LENGTH & TIME
5.4 miles, 3–5 hours

VERTICAL FEET
+2,000'/-2,000'

DIFFICULTY
- 1 2 3 **4** 5 +

TRAIL TYPE
Semiloop

START & FINISH
N40° 10.379'
W124° 06.721'

FEATURES
Mountain
Backcountry Camping
Views
Steep

FACILITIES
None

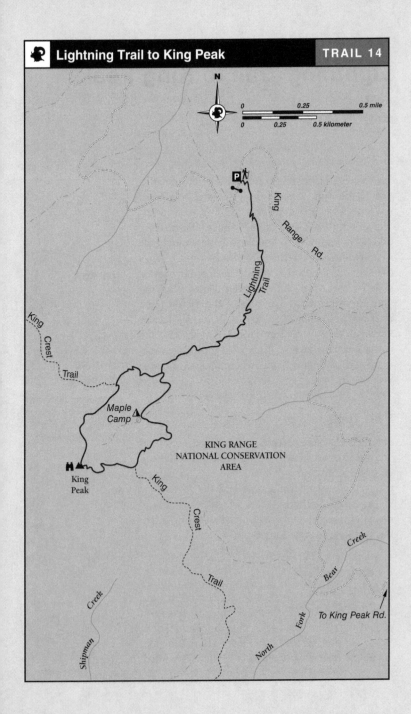

Lightning Trail to King Peak

TRAIL 14

N

0   0.25   0.5 mile

0   0.25   0.5 kilometer

King Range Rd.

Lightning Trail

King Crest Trail

Maple Camp

King Peak

KING RANGE
NATIONAL CONSERVATION
AREA

King Crest Trail

Creek

Bear Creek

Shipman Creek

North Fork

To King Peak Rd.

Continue on Shelter Cove Road another 4 miles to a right-hand turn onto dirt King Peak Road.

Follow narrow King Peak Road north, passing by the Paradise Royale Mountain Bike Trailhead at 2.4 miles (not shown on the *King Range NCA Lost Coast* map), Tolkan Campground at 3.6 miles, and Horse Mountain Creek Trailhead at 4.7 miles on the way to the south junction of Saddle Mountain Road at 6.5 miles. Continue ahead on King Peak Road for another 2 miles to a junction, veer left onto King Range Road, and proceed another 8.6 miles to the Lightning Trailhead, passing through the north junction of Saddle Mountain Road after 2.3 miles. Along the way you will cross a few streams, which should not be a problem for the average sedan except during and after significant rainstorms (check with the Bureau of Land Management King Range Office 1 mile west of Thorn Junction for current conditions).

Tolkan and Horse Mountain Campgrounds are located along King Peak Road.

Trail Description

The well-signed Lightning Trail steadily climbs away from the parking area ▶1 via occasional switchbacks through a mixed forest of madrones, oaks, and Douglas firs. Higher up the slope, a series

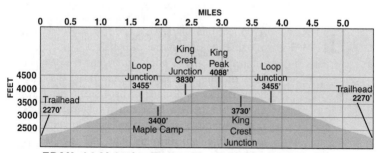

TRAIL 14 Lightning Trail to King Peak Elevation Profile

View from *the summit of King Peak*

of moderate to moderately steep switchbacks lead up a ridge with filtered views to the east on the way to the King Peak loop junction, ►2 1.7 miles from the trailhead.

Turn left (south) at the junction, losing some of that hard-gained elevation on the way through open and then shady forest to Maple Camp, where a year-round spring feeds a tributary of the East Fork Honeydew Creek. Above the creek, the camp features one good, tree-shaded campsite and a few marginal ones. Past the camp, the trail climbs stiffly up the sometimes-dry streambed before veering away to the southeast to gain the east ridge of the peak. The trail zigzags up the ridge through forest cover until it breaks out onto open, manzanita-covered slopes, which allow a taste of the views to come from the summit. At 0.7 mile from the previous junction, you reach the south junction ►3 of the King Crest Trail.

Backcountry Camping

Steep

Turn right at the junction, and make a 0.3-mile, 200-foot climb across open slopes to the summit. ►4 Here the expanse of the Northern California coast stretches to the northwest and southeast. The view from the highest piece of terra firma in the vicinity punctuates the immediate topography's steep nature; it drops more than 4,000 feet in 3 miles to the coast. The view of the interior is nearly as impressive. The deck of an old lookout remains near the summit, a reminder of past days before fire lookouts were replaced by aerial and satellite technology.

Mountain

Views

Once you can pull yourself away from the magnificent vista, follow switchbacks down from the summit, then continue along an open ridge. Farther on, the trail reenters mixed forest and comes to the north junction ►5 of the King Crest Trail, a half mile from the top of King Peak.

Veer to the right (northeast), switchbacking down a steep shady slope. Head briefly back into the open, then reach the close of the loop ►6 just where the trail reenters dense forest cover. From there, retrace your steps to the trailhead. ►7

		MILESTONES
►1	0.0	Start at Lightning Trailhead
►2	1.7	Left at loop junction
►3	2.4	Right at south junction with King Crest Trail
►4	2.7	Summit of King Peak
►5	3.3	Right at north junction with King Crest Trail
►6	3.7	Left at loop junction
►7	5.4	End at Lightning Trailhead

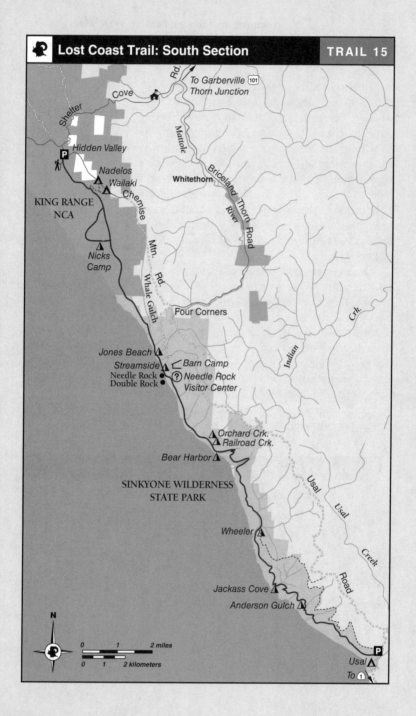

To Garberville 101
Thorn Junction

Shelter

Cove

Rd.

Mattole

Brideland Thorn Road

Whitethorn

River

Hidden Valley

P

Nadelos

Wailaki

Chemise

KING RANGE
NCA

Nicks
Camp

Mtn. Rd.

Whale Gulch

Four Corners

Indian

Crk.

Jones Beach

Streamside

Barn Camp

Needle Rock

Double Rock

? Needle Rock
Visitor Center

Orchard Crk.

Railroad Crk.

Bear Harbor

SINKYONE WILDERNESS
STATE PARK

Usal

Usal

Wheeler

Creek

Jackass Cove

Road

Anderson Gulch

N

0   1   2 miles

0   1   2 kilometers

Usal

P

To 1

Lost Coast Trail: South Section

Unlike the beach route of the northern half of the Lost Coast Trail, the southern half moves inland and at times climbs steeply over mostly forested ridges between brief forays to the ocean. Although this section's ocean views are less frequent, they're arguably more impressive, as the higher vantage points provide for longer-range vistas. Where the trail does reach the beach, the scenery is quite striking. This hike passes through some old-growth redwood groves. The abundant marine wildlife includes harbor seals, sea lions, migrating gray whales, and tidepool creatures. On land, you may see black-tailed deer, black bear, or Roosevelt elk (reintroduced to the area in 1982). The area has a profusion of birds, including brown pelicans, black oystercatchers, cormorants, sandpipers, terns, gulls, ravens, and an occasional osprey or bald eagle.

The area's remote location and resulting potential for solitude belies the human population it boasted in the late 1800s and early 1900s, when there was a dairy in the Needle Rock area, a wharf and narrow gauge railroad operated out of Bear Harbor, and Usal Beach had a lumber mill. While most evidence of human activity around Bear Harbor and Usal Beach is gone, the Needle Rock Visitor Center occupies the old ranch house. A road provides vehicle access to the visitor center, which is about a third of the way into the hike, increasing your chances of encountering other people. Otherwise, you'll likely see few other souls out on the trail.

Due to its inland route, tides are not a concern on this section of the Lost Coast. Hikers should be aware that rattlesnakes, although uncommon, are

TRAIL USE
Backpacking

LENGTH & TIME
28.7 miles, 3–5 days

VERTICAL FEET
+8,850'/-8,850'

DIFFICULTY
- 1 2 3 4 **5** +

TRAIL TYPE
Shuttle

START & FINISH
N40° 01.854'
W124° 01.552'

FEATURES
Beach
Stream
Redwoods
Wildflowers
Wildlife
Secluded
Steep
Historic Interest
Backcountry Camping
Views

FACILITIES
Campground
Resort Town

present in this community, as are poison oak and ticks (particularly in spring). Traveling from north to south keeps the prevailing wind at your back.

Best Time

Even though the Lost Coast Trail can be hiked any time the weather is accommodating, spring and fall are usually the two best seasons. While temperatures are generally moderate during summer, fog oftentimes drapes the Northern California coastline with an omnipresent veil. Along with clearer skies, spring offers the added bonus of a vibrantly colorful array of wildflowers on the bluffs above the beach, enhanced by the annual migration of California gray whales. Fall also offers generally clear weather and the characteristic dried grasses of the Golden State.

Finding the Trail

From the junction of US 101 and CA 1 near Legget, head westbound on CA 1, and continue for 14.9 miles to an unsigned junction with Usal Road (County Road 431) at milepost 90.88 (3 miles north of Rockport). Turn right and follow this narrow, dirt road for 6.2 miles to the Usal Trailhead, passing through Usal Campground on the way. Usal Road should be passable to the typical sedan during dry

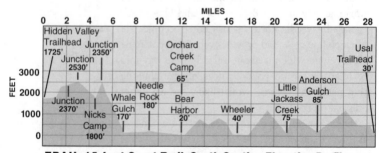

TRAIL 15 Lost Coast Trail: South Section Elevation Profile

weather, but prolonged rain may make the road impassable to all but four-wheel-drive vehicles. For a car campground, at $25 per night the Usal Campground is a dump, with very primitive outhouses, no running water, and no trash pickup.

Your hike begins from the Hidden Valley Trailhead, so backtrack to US 101, and head north for 23 miles to the town of Garberville. Leave US 101 at Exit 639B, and follow Redwood Drive for 2.5 miles to the town of Redway. Turn left (west) onto Briceland Thorn Road, and proceed for 12.2 miles to Thorn Junction, where the road straight ahead is Shelter Cove Road. Continue another 5.25 miles on Shelter Cove Road to an intersection with Chemise Mountain Road. Turn left and proceed on Chemise Mountain Road for 0.2 mile to the signed parking lot for Hidden Valley Trailhead on the right.

Nearby Nadelos and Wailaki Campgrounds are farther along Chemise Mountain Road.

Logistics

Shuttling to both trailheads without two vehicles or a kind friend willing to commit to a multihour drive is possible by using one of the two Bureau of Land Management–permitted commercial shuttle companies servicing the Lost Coast (the shuttle between the Hidden Valley Trailhead and the Usal Trailhead cost $350 in 2012). Contact Lost Coast Shuttle (707-986-7437, 707-223-1547, sherri luallin@gmail.com, **lostcoastshuttle.com**) or Lost Coast Trail Transport Service (707-986-9909, roxanne@saber.net, **lostcoasttrail.com**) for more information.

With a small handful of lodging and dining options, the seaside town of Shelter Cove can be a fine base camp, especially for hikers attempting to complete both the north and south sections of the Lost Coast Trail.

Trail Description

A gently graded trail heads away from the Hidden Valley Trailhead ►1 through a typical coast forest composed of Douglas firs (the most common coastal evergreen), Jeffrey pines, Pacific madrones, and tanoaks. Soon, the path skirts the tall grasses of lush Hidden Valley along the forest edge on the way to a stiff, switchbacking climb up the north slope of Chemise Mountain, the first of many steep climbs you'll encounter. From the top, you follow the undulating ridge to a junction with the Chemise Mountain Trail ►2 on the left coming 1.5 miles up from the Nadelos and Wailaki Campgrounds along the Chemise Mountain Road.

 Steep

Continue ahead at the junction ►3 on a gradual ascent of the ridgeline for 0.8 mile to a junction on the left with a short lateral to a viewpoint. Although this vantage offers a fine view of numerous ridges and peaks of Northern California to the east and south, trees block any ocean vistas.

 Views

Away from the junction, continue along the ridge, soon reaching a junction with the Chinquapin Loop Trail ►4 on the right, a 2.1-mile detour offering much better scenery than the 1.4-mile, featureless stretch ahead.

If you're in a hurry, then proceed ahead on an up-and-down, but mostly downhill journey to the south junction of the Chinquapin Loop. Otherwise, turn right and moderately descend for a mile or so, enjoying some fine views of the ocean. After a short ascent to the crossing of a rivulet, you come to the spur to Nicks Camp, where you can pitch your tent and enjoy an excellent view of the coast. From the camp junction, the Chinquapin Loop Trail climbs

Views

 Backcountry Camping

View of *Wheeler Cove and the Lost Coast*

0.7 mile back up to the south junction ▶5 of the Lost Coast Trail, passing more fine vistas.

From the south junction of the Chinquapin Loop Trail, the Lost Coast Trail makes an initially mild ascent along the spine of Chemise Mountain, followed by an oftentimes steep, 2,000-foot descent via some long-legged switchbacks toward Whale Gulch. Reaching a small meadow, a post marks the crossing from the King Range National Conservation Area into the Sinkyone Wilderness. Nearby are the crumbling remnants of an old structure, perhaps a residence that must have had an incredible coast view before the neighboring trees matured. Fortunately, a short distance farther down the trail, you're treated to your own fine ocean vista. Just beyond, the approach to an occupied private home may be heralded by the sound of barking dogs.

 Views

A series of switchbacks drop away from the house and the canine commotion on a steep descent to the bottom of Whale Gulch, ▶6 which is 7.1 (6.4) miles from the Hidden Valley Trailhead, where either a boulder-hop or a ford awaits (this crossing may be impassable in winter).

Across the stream in Whale Gulch, the grade eases considerably as you head downstream toward the ocean. Soon the trail passes above the small, rocky beach, offering fine coastal views of the high cliffs to the north. Beyond a faint use trail leading to the driftwood-choked lagoon, the Lost Coast Trail passes a slim marsh and then traverses grassy meadows above the beach for nearly 2 miles to the Needle

 Views

Rock Visitor Center. Excellent ocean views accompany you on this pleasant stroll. This lovely setting is also the location of two trail camps, complete with picnic tables, fire rings, and primitive outhouses. The first is Jones Beach Camp, with four sites near a stream shaded by eucalyptus trees, occupying the site of an abandoned ranch house. From the camp, lovely Jones Beach Cove is accessible via a quarter-mile lateral.

Backcountry Camping

Beach

A quarter mile beyond Jones Beach Camp, the trail crosses Low Gap Creek and then continues another half mile to a short spur to Streamside Camp near an unnamed creek. This camp has three sites, two in the trees and one on a grassy bench with an incredible 180-degree view of the coastline. In addition to the spectacular scenery, Roosevelt elk are often seen in this area, especially in the morning and early evening hours. Another quarter mile of easy hiking leads past a view of the area's namesake feature, Needle Rock, a rock arch that used to be topped by a spire, and Barn Camp, where for $30 per night (rates in 2012) you could spend the night under a large shelter. Soon after you pass Barn Camp, you arrive at the Needle Rock Visitor Center. ▶7

Views

Wildlife

Camping

From the visitor center, you follow the course of Briceland Road, a narrow, dirt road providing vehicle access to Orchard Creek Camp. The road is only open to vehicles with a valid camping permit, so automobile traffic is usually light. A section of the road was washed out during heavy rains in the winter of 2012 and was not repaired by the following autumn due to California's budget crisis. Without adequate funding, the road may end up being decommissioned, which would limit use to foot and horseback travel.

For the next 2.7 miles, the road rolls up and down toward Orchard Creek Camp, crossing Flat Rock Creek and passing the promontory of High

Views

Backcountry Camping

Backcountry Camping

Views

Beach

Steep

Redwoods

Views

Redwoods

Tip. Beautiful ocean views are frequent accompaniments to the journey. The road ends at a large grassy parking area, with Orchard Creek Camp ►8 a short walk upstream along the trickling brook.

From the parking area, the Lost Coast Trail makes a bridged crossing of Orchard Creek and heads downstream for 0.2 mile to reach Railroad Creek Camp, where three sites are tucked beneath some eucalyptus trees. Cross Railroad Creek on a bridge, and continue another 0.2 mile downstream on a pleasant grade to Bear Harbor. ►9 Of the three camps in the vicinity, Bear Harbor is by far the most attractive, with four sites with beach views of the ocean.

Leave Bear Harbor, the beach, and the easy hiking behind, climbing stiffly up a lush side canyon, crossing a stream, and then scaling a steep, forested ridge. After gaining about 700 feet, the trail loses about half that elevation on a descent into Duffys Gulch. On the way, you pass beneath the first coast redwoods of the trip, a part of the J. Smeaton Chase (1864–1923) Grove, named for an early California author whose most famous work was *California Coastal Trails*. A short climb leads to a fine coastal view, the first of a handful of such vistas ahead on an up-and-down romp, where the trees part just enough or the trail crosses small open patches of grass. Eventually, the trail begins a steady descent toward North Fork Jackass Creek and the old townsite of Wheeler, plunging downhill through more redwoods from the School Marm Grove.

At the bottom of the descent is a green valley where an old logging town sprung up in the 1950s. Although all of the buildings are gone, you may spy an old artifact or two still lying around. ►10 There are several campsites spread around the immediate area near the crossing of North Fork Jackass Creek, 4.3 miles from Bear Harbor, but more attractive sites wait farther down the trail, which continues

Bear Cove Harbor

As remote and wild as the Lost Coast seems today, this area was once the western terminus of the Bear Harbor & Eel River Railroad, as still evidenced by rusting rails dangling over the rocks on the north side of the Bear Cove. A small wharf was completed in 1885 to ship tanbark and railroad ties. Construction of a 10-mile railroad connecting Bear Harbor to a site near Indian Creek began in 1893. The terminus was named for Lew Moody, who built a hotel and saloon nearby. The Southern Humboldt Lumber Company took over the railroad in 1902 for the purposes of transporting lumber, finishing the extension of the line 7.5 miles in 1905 to a mill and millpond at Andersonia (across the river from present-day Piercy). A new, larger wharf at Bear Harbor was also built.

Although logs were eventually delivered to the millpond via the railroad, a series of tragedies prevented the mill from producing lumber. Harvey Anderson, president of the lumber company, died as a result of being struck in the head by a timber brace pulled by a steam engine in November 1905. Tax problems, right-of-way issues, and finally damage from the Great Earthquake of 1906 halted milling operations before they could begin. Subsequent litigation and a flood during the winter of 1925–1926, which broke the millpond's dam and sent logs into the Eel River, prevented new buyers from restarting the operation. Ultimately, the Southern Humboldt Lumber Company's legacy became "the million-dollar mill that never milled." The locomotives were later restored and placed at Fort Humboldt State Park. Andersonia became a ghost town, but it was temporarily used as a construction camp during the building of US 101.

another 0.3 mile to a somewhat obscure junction. Go straight at the junction, and then boulder-hop the main branch of Jackass Creek to the camp area. The trail continues ahead a short distance to a grass-covered bench above a small stretch of beach near Wheeler Cove.

The Lost Coast Trail departs Wheeler Cove on another stiff ascent up a gulch, zigzagging 650 feet to the crest of a ridge above Anderson Cliff. Fine coast

Backcountry Camping

Beach

Steep

Views

Wildflowers

views and spring wildflowers will raise your spirits on the way. Don't neglect the unmarked use trail to a grassy knoll and an expansive view of the coastline in both directions.

Steep

From the ridge, the trail bounces up and down but mostly downhill for the next 0.3 mile to the crossing of a small creek. A stiff ascent follows, as the trail winds up to the crest of an 1,100-foot ridge. Just as steeply, the trail then plunges through alternating sections of meadow and forest almost all the way to the ocean, reaching a junction ▶11 above Little Jackass Creek near a dilapidated outhouse.

Beach

At the junction, the right-hand path drops shortly down to the beach at Little Jackass Cove, one of the trip's more picturesque spots. The steep cliffs above Mistake Point frame the coastline view to the north, while a rock arch provides a fine focal point for watching the crashing surf. A cluster of offshore rocks harboring a sea lion colony highlights the southern view. If the weather is accommodating, a campsite just off the beach offers a near-idyllic setting. More protected sites under the trees can be had by walking upstream along the main trail for 0.2 mile.

Wildlife

Backcountry Camping

From the junction with the trail to the beach, the Lost Coast Trail heads upstream into the forest past some campsites and then attacks the south side of the canyon on a steep, switchbacking climb. At the top of the ridge, the trail traverses the head of Northport Gulch, crosses a ridge, and then descends via switchbacks to a crossing of the stream in Anderson Gulch. ▶12 Just before the creek is Anderson Gulch Camp, perhaps the least scenic camp area in Sinkyone Wilderness. Additionally, beach access is nonexistent.

Steep

Backcountry Camping

A relatively short, 250-foot climb leads out of Anderson Gulch, followed by a gentle downhill jaunt that switchbacks across open, grassy slopes with excellent views of the coast. However, this picturesque segment is short-lived, as the trail dives into Dark Gulch to eventually cross its little stream.

Views

The last major ascent now lies before you, a mile-long, 1,000-foot, switchbacking climb to near the top of Timber Point across grass-covered slopes and redwood-dotted forest. Beyond, a mostly enjoyable ramble makes an undulating descent over open, grassy slopes blessed with long-ranging coast vistas. The less-enjoyable part of this nearly 2-mile section is frequently sloping, oftentimes overgrown, sometimes steep, and occasionally washed-out trail surface. Eventually, it enters the woods for good, where the grade eases before a steeper half-mile descent leads to the Usal Trailhead. ▶13

Steep

Views

⚲ MILESTONES

▶1	0.0	Start from Hidden Valley Trailhead
▶2	2.2	Straight at Chemise Mountain Trail
▶3	3.0	Straight at viewpoint junction
▶4	3.1	Right at north junction of Chinquapin Loop Trail
▶5	5.2	Right at south junction of Chinquapin Loop Trail
▶6	7.1 (6.4)	Whale Gulch
▶7	9.3 (8.6)	Needle Rock Visitor Center
▶8	12.0 (11.3)	Orchard Creek Camp
▶9	12.4 (11.7)	Bear Harbor
▶10	16.7 (16.0)	Wheeler
▶11	21.2 (20.5)	Little Jackass Creek
▶12	23.7 (23.0)	Anderson Gulch
▶13	28.7 (28.0)	Out to Usal Trailhead

CHAPTER 3

Humboldt

Humboldt

Humboldt Redwoods State Park harbors the most impressive redwood groves on the planet. If not for the nearby presence of US 101 and the Avenue of the Giants, which runs right through the middle of the park, this redwood haven would be an idyllic spot for admiring the tall trees in a reverential atmosphere. As is, the park is still perhaps the premier place to witness some of the last remaining stands of old-growth redwoods in a cathedral-like setting. Straddling the course of the main and south forks of the Eel River, the adjacent alluvial flats provide the prime growing conditions for creating towering *Sequoia sempervirens,* some approaching 400 feet tall.

Although the park is well inland compared to most redwood parks and, therefore, has warmer temperatures and drier conditions, summer fog creeps up the river and nourishes the coast redwoods. Because of this pattern, the trees in the north end of the park are more impressive, and they diminish in stature as you head farther south.

Backpackers and long-distance hikers will be disappointed with the lack of opportunities in Humboldt Redwoods. Although some longer trails exist, they forsake the tall trees to travel through unimpressive second-growth forest, better suited for mountain bikers looking for a fun ride than hikers wishing to experience the majesty of the forest. Day-trippers will find an abundant collection of short trails, most of which require little elevation gain. The combination of impressive redwood groves, easy paths, and a closer proximity to major population centers than other redwood parks makes Humboldt Redwoods an attractive destination for tourists. Hikers looking to enjoy the redwoods in peace and tranquility should gravitate toward lesser-used trails or visit the park during the off-season.

Permits

Permits are not required for dayhikes. Humboldt Redwoods State Park does not charge an entrance fee. Although visitors must pay a fee to enter the

Redwoods along *the High Rock River Trail*

main section of Grizzly Creek Redwoods State Park, there is no charge for entry to the Cheatham Grove (Trail 28).

Maps

By far, the best map covering Humboldt Redwoods State Park is the 1:25,000-scale map published by Redwood Hikes Press. This full-color, accurate, and detailed topographic map shows both trails with mileages and the location of footbridges and memorial redwood grove signs and benches.

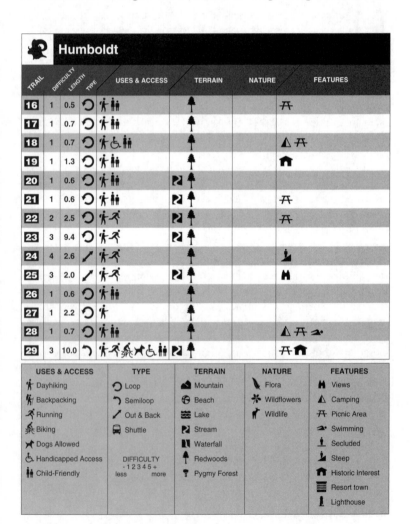

Humboldt

TRAIL	DIFFICULTY	LENGTH	TYPE	USES & ACCESS	TERRAIN	NATURE	FEATURES
16	1	0.5	Loop	Dayhiking, Child-Friendly	Redwoods		Picnic Area
17	1	0.7	Loop	Dayhiking, Child-Friendly	Redwoods		
18	1	0.7	Loop	Dayhiking, Handicapped Access, Child-Friendly	Redwoods		Camping, Picnic Area
19	1	1.3	Loop	Dayhiking, Child-Friendly	Redwoods		Historic Interest
20	1	0.6	Loop	Dayhiking, Child-Friendly	Stream, Redwoods		
21	1	0.6	Loop	Dayhiking, Child-Friendly	Stream, Redwoods		Picnic Area
22	2	2.5	Loop	Dayhiking, Running	Stream, Redwoods		Picnic Area
23	3	9.4	Loop	Dayhiking, Running	Stream, Redwoods		
24	4	2.6	Out & Back	Dayhiking, Running	Redwoods		Secluded
25	3	2.0	Out & Back	Dayhiking, Running	Stream, Redwoods		Views
26	1	0.6	Loop	Dayhiking, Child-Friendly	Redwoods		
27	1	2.2	Loop	Dayhiking	Redwoods		
28	1	0.7	Loop	Dayhiking, Child-Friendly	Redwoods		Camping, Picnic Area, Swimming
29	3	10.0	Semiloop	Dayhiking, Running, Biking, Dogs Allowed, Handicapped Access, Child-Friendly	Stream, Redwoods		Picnic Area, Historic Interest

USES & ACCESS	TYPE	TERRAIN	NATURE	FEATURES
Dayhiking	Loop	Mountain	Flora	Views
Backpacking	Semiloop	Beach	Wildflowers	Camping
Running	Out & Back	Lake	Wildlife	Picnic Area
Biking	Shuttle	Stream		Swimming
Dogs Allowed		Waterfall		Secluded
Handicapped Access	DIFFICULTY	Redwoods		Steep
Child-Friendly	- 1 2 3 4 5 +	Pygmy Forest		Historic Interest
	less more			Resort town
				Lighthouse

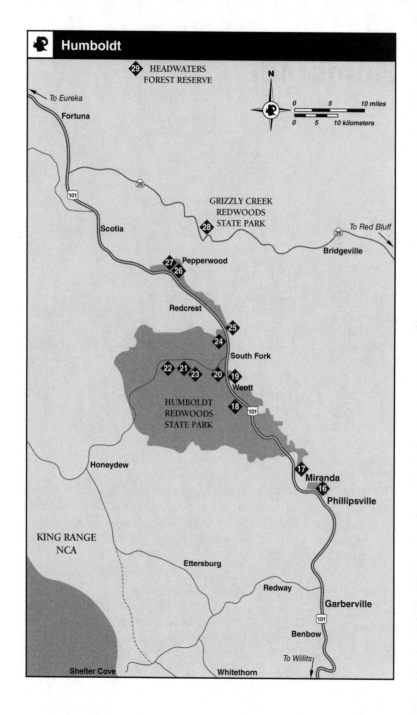

Humboldt

Franklin K. Lane Loop

This short, virtually flat loop trail is many people's introduction to the wonders of the coast redwoods. This is the first significant grove in Humboldt Redwoods State Park that visitors encounter coming from the major population centers to the south.

Best Time

The trail is open all year. As the first path encountered by northbound motorists on the Avenue of the Giants, the Frances K. Lane day-use area receives considerable interest, despite the lack of restrooms. As with redwood groves in general, spring offers an added sprinkling of color from scattered wildflowers.

Finding the Trail

A sign marks the turnout for the Frances K. Lane parking area on the east side of Avenue of the Giants at milepost 28.6, just north of the community of Phillipsville. Northbound drivers should leave US 101 at Exit 645 and drive 2.8 miles; southbound motorists should leave US 101 at Exit 650 and drive 1.9 miles. The trailhead is equipped with picnic tables and bearproof trash bins. The park has three campgrounds: Hidden Springs, Burlington, and Albee Creek. In the community of Myers Flat is the privately owned Giant Redwoods RV and Camp.

TRAIL USE
Dayhiking,
Child-Friendly

LENGTH & TIME
0.5 mile, ½ hour

VERTICAL FEET
Negligible

DIFFICULTY
- **1** 2 3 4 5 +

TRAIL TYPE
Loop

START & FINISH
N40° 12.892'
W123° 47.169'

FEATURES
Redwoods

FACILITIES
Picnic Area

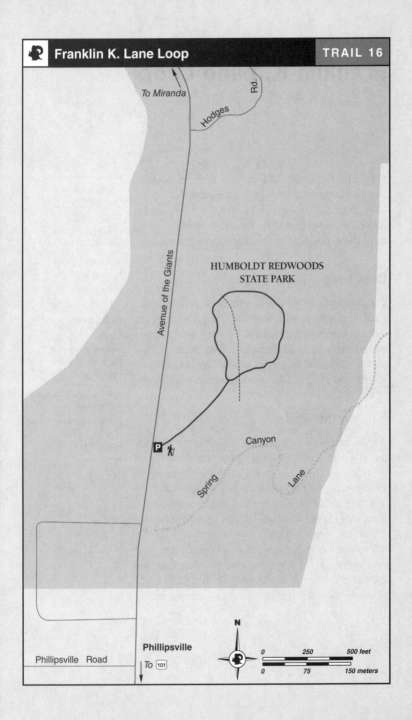

Franklin K. Lane Loop — TRAIL 16

To Miranda

Hodges Rd.

Avenue of the Giants

HUMBOLDT REDWOODS
STATE PARK

Canyon

Lane

Spring

Phillipsville

Phillipsville   Road

To 101

N

| 0 | 250 | 500 feet |
| 0 | 75 | 150 meters |

Franklin K. Lane plaque

Trail Description

From the parking area ▶1 the trail heads north into a shady forest with initially very little ground cover, soon reaching a junction ▶2 at the bottom of a low berm. Go straight ahead and climb quickly to the top of the berm, where redwood sorrel and ferns suddenly carpet the forest floor. This part of the grove is blessed with some fairly impressive redwood trees, as you pass through a sawed gap in a large downed specimen and continue toward a hill. Keen eyes will spot the roadbed of the former alignment of the highway, which was relocated to its present position in the early 1900s. Proceed to the base of the hill, and then curve along the base following a counterclockwise loop through the forest.

Redwoods 🌲

Eventually, the trail reaches a downed redwood near a four-by-four post with directional arrows.

On the back side of this log is a large stone with a plaque, a memorial to the grove's namesake, Franklin K. Lane, a California politician and the first president of the Save the Redwoods League. Lane also served under President Woodrow Wilson as Secretary of the Interior, helping to establish the National Park Service during his tenure. Generally, the redwoods seem to be less impressive on the west side of the grove, but you do pass a massive downed sequoia on the way to the close of the loop. ▶3 From there, retrace your steps shortly to the parking area. ▶4 Watch for poison oak, especially on the second half of the loop.

🚶 MILESTONES

▶1	0.0	Start at Franklin K. Lane Trailhead
▶2	0.1	Proceed ahead at loop junction
▶3	0.3	Proceed ahead at loop junction
▶4	0.4	Return to trailhead

Stephens Grove Loop

This unmarked trail passes through a grove of old-growth redwoods near the southern end of Humboldt Redwoods State Park. The short distance and minimal elevation gain provides an easy introduction to the park's namesake features for northbound motorists on the Avenue of the Giants, which unfortunately is adjacent to the grove.

Best Time

As with many of the trails in Humboldt Redwoods State Park, the Stephens Grove Loop is open all year. However, given its location immediately off the Avenue of the Giants, a visit in the off-season or at least early in the day will help to minimize the accompanying road noise.

Finding the Trail

The unsigned parking area is on the west side of the Avenue of the Giants, just north of the community of Miranda. On Avenue of the Giants, drive 2.1 miles north of the intersection of the access road from Exit 650 from US 101, or 3.4 miles south of Elk Creek Road. The park has three campgrounds: Hidden Springs, Burlington, and Albee Creek. In the community of Myers Flat is the privately owned Giant Redwoods RV and Camp.

Trail Description

The unmarked trail dives down the hillside away from the parking area, ▶1 immediately reaching the

TRAIL USE
Dayhiking,
Child-Friendly

LENGTH & TIME
0.7 mile, ½ hour

VERTICAL FEET
Negligible

DIFFICULTY
- **1** 2 3 4 5 +

TRAIL TYPE
Loop

START & FINISH
N40° 14.658'
W123° 49.311'

FEATURES
Redwoods

FACILITIES
None

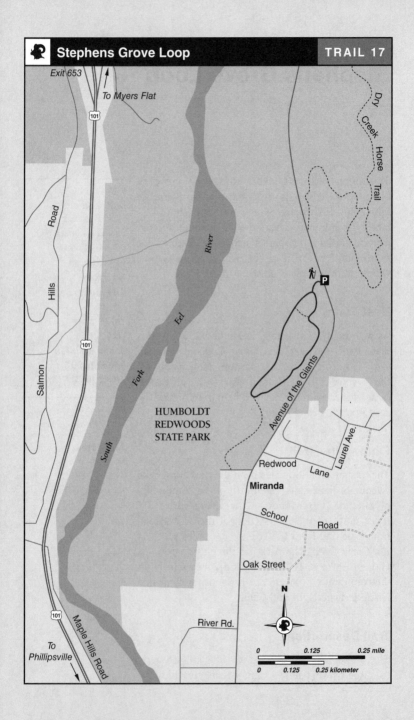

Stephens Grove Loop

TRAIL 17

Exit 653

To Myers Flat

101

Dry Creek Horse Trail

Road

Hills

River

Salmon

101

Eel

Fork

South

HUMBOLDT
REDWOODS
STATE PARK

Avenue of the Giants

Laurel Ave.

Redwood Lane

Miranda

School Road

Oak Street

N

River Rd.

| 0 | 0.125 | 0.25 mile |

| 0 | 0.125 | 0.25 kilometer |

To
Phillipsville

Maple Hills Road

loop junction. ►2 Taking the left-hand path, pass through a cut in a downed redwood, and follow a clockwise loop through an old-growth redwood forest with a smattering of redwood sorrel and ferns on the forest floor. Intermittent road noise from cars on the Avenue of the Giants distracts from the otherwise cathedral-like nature of the grove. Heading generally southwest, you wind through the forest, crossing a couple of short wood bridges over gurgling streams on the way to an unmarked junction ►3 at the south end of the loop (the left-hand heads south to the town of Miranda).

Redwoods

Veer right at the junction to continue on the loop, which travels along the edge of the forest adjacent to the broad gravel bed of the South Fork Eel River. The brightness of the river corridor contrasts starkly with the dark and shady forest. Old stumps from former logging days litter the otherwise stately grove. Eventually the trail crosses a pair of bridges over usually dry streambeds and reaches the close of the loop ►4 just below the parking area. From there, retrace your steps shortly uphill to the trailhead. ►5

🚶	**MILESTONES**		
►1	0.0	Start at Stephens Loop trailhead
►2	0.01	Turn left at loop junction
►3	0.3	Veer right at junction with trail to Miranda
►4	0.69	Turn left at loop junction
►5	0.7	Return to trailhead

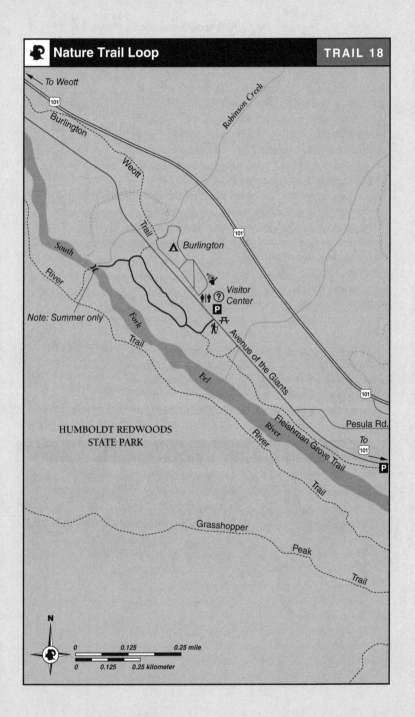

To Weott

101

Burlington

Robinson Creek

Weott

Trail

Burlington

South

River

Visitor
Center

P

Fork

Note: Summer only

Avenue of the Giants

Trail

Eel

River

Fleishman Grove Trail

Pesula Rd.

101

To
101

P

HUMBOLDT REDWOODS
STATE PARK

River

Trail

Grasshopper

Peak

Trail

N

0   0.125   0.25 mile

0   0.125   0.25 kilometer

Nature Trail Loop

The Nature Trail across from the visitor center and the Burlington Campground in Humboldt Redwoods State Park offers a short and easy ramble through a fine grove of old-growth redwoods. Interpretive signs provide a good introduction to the ecology of the tall trees, and the trail is wheelchair accessible.

Best Time

The trail is open all year.

Finding the Trail

Follow the Avenue of the Giants to the visitor center, which is between Exit 656 at Meyers Flat and Exit 661 at Weott from US 101. The trail begins on the opposite side of the road near a crosswalk immediately south of the visitor center. The park has three campgrounds: Hidden Springs, Burlington (adjacent to the visitor center), and Albee Creek. In the community of Myers Flat is the privately owned Giant Redwoods RV and Camp.

Trail Description

From the visitor center parking lot, ▶1 follow the crosswalk across the Avenue of the Giants, and pick up the wide track of a gravel path on the far side, soon reaching a junction ▶2 with the Nature Trail on the right and the first interpretive sign nearby. The upturned base of a stump lying on the forest floor offers some perspective on the immense size

TRAIL USE
Dayhiking,
Child-Friendly,
Handicapped Access

LENGTH & TIME
0.7 mile, ½ hour

VERTICAL FEET
Negligible

DIFFICULTY
- **1** 2 3 4 5 +

TRAIL TYPE
Loop

START & FINISH
N40° 18.432'
W123° 54.433'

FEATURES
Redwoods

FACILITIES
Campground
Picnic Area
Restrooms
Visitor Center

Redwoods

of the coast redwoods. A short distance down the trail is a second junction ▶3 with the beginning of the loop section.

Turning left at the junction, the trail heads northwest across a flat not far from South Fork Eel River past several fine examples of tall redwoods shading a forest floor carpeted with ferns. Reach a junction ▶4 with a connector down to the river and, from June through September, across a footbridge to the River Trail on the opposite bank.

From the River Trail junction, continue the clockwise circuit through the forest past more interpretive signs and large redwoods to the end of the loop. ▶5 Retracing your steps, continue straight ahead a short distance to the next junction. ▶6 Turn left and return to the parking lot. ▶7

		MILESTONES
▶1	0.0	Start at trailhead
▶2	0.05	Right at junction
▶3	0.1	Left at loop junction
▶4	0.3	Right at River Trail junction
▶5	0.6	Straight at loop junction
▶6	0.65	Left at junction
▶7	0.7	Return to trailhead

Fallen redwood stump *along the Nature Trail*

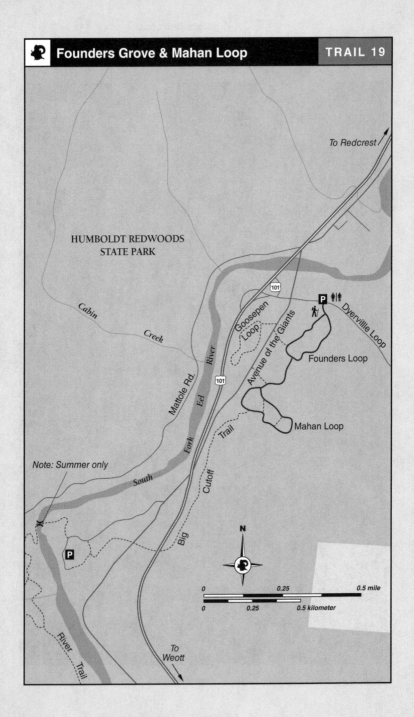

To Redcrest

HUMBOLDT REDWOODS
STATE PARK

Cabin

Creek

101

Goosepen
Loop

Avenue of the Giants

Dyerville Loop

Founders Loop

Mattole Rd.

Eel

River

101

Mahan Loop

Fork

Cutoff

Trail

Note: Summer only

South

Big

N

P

River

Trail

To
Weott

0   0.25   0.5 mile

0   0.25   0.5 kilometer

Founders Grove & Mahan Loop

The premier area for coastal redwoods in Humboldt Redwoods State Park (some would say in all of California) occurs on the alluvial flats near the union of the Eel River and its South Fork. Dyerville Flat near this confluence harbors the Founders Grove, the park's most popular, which contains two of the tallest specimens, the Founders Tree and the Dyerville Giant. Three short loop trails provide access to Dyerville Flat and the Founders and Canfield Groves of redwoods. By using a short connecting trail, you can connect the Founders and Mahan Loops to create a 1.3-mile stroll through some of the park's most impressive scenery. West of this trip is the Goosepen Loop, a half-mile-long, little-used trail through dark forest sandwiched between the Avenue of the Giants and US 101.

TRAIL USE
Dayhiking,
Child-Friendly

LENGTH & TIME
1.3 miles, 1–1½ hours

VERTICAL FEET
Negligible

DIFFICULTY
- **1** 2 3 4 5 +

TRAIL TYPE
Loop

START & FINISH
N40° 21.180'
W123° 55.415'

FEATURES
Redwoods
Historic Interest

FACILITIES
Restrooms

Best Time

The trail is open all year. However, the tourist season reaches its zenith during the summer months when the temperatures are also at their highest; both conditions contribute to a congested and uncomfortable feel. Other than during periods of heavy rain, the Founders Grove may be best enjoyed during the off-season. If you do visit the grove during the summer, come early in the morning to avoid the largest crowds and to minimize the traffic noise from US 101 and, to a lesser extent, the Avenue of the Giants.

Finding the Trail

The Avenue of the Giants provides straightforward access to the grove. Drive to the intersection with

The Dyerville Giant

Dyerville Loop Road, which is 0.25 mile south of Exit 663 from US 101 and directly south of a highway bridge over the Eel River. Turn east and proceed about 100 yards to a parking area on the left-hand side of the road. The trail begins on the south side of the road, opposite the parking lot. The park has three campgrounds: Hidden Springs, Burlington (adjacent to the visitor center), and Albee Creek. In the community of Myers Flat is the privately owned Giant Redwoods RV and Camp.

Trail Description

From the parking lot, ▶1 follow a crosswalk over
Dyerville Loop Road and continue south, ignoring a path that angles in from the bus parking
area. Proceed shortly to a boardwalk encircling the
immense Founders Tree. A high percentage of tourists go no farther than this soaring giant, so take heart
if you happen to be here at the same time as a large
crowd. Turn left at a junction ▶2 immediately in
front of the Founders Tree, and very shortly bear left
again, following the broad path dubbed derisively as
the "Founders Freeway" into the heart of the grove.
Redwood sorrel and ferns carpet the forest floor, as
you pass several fine examples of coast redwoods,
a goosepen tree, and a number of fallen monarchs.
Reach a junction ▶3 with a connector to the Mahan
Loop at the south end of the Founders Loop.

Redwoods 🌲

Turn left onto the connector and head southwest.
Shortly after passing a path on the right to the highway, you reach a junction ▶4 with the Mahan Loop,
0.2 mile from the junction with the Founders Loop.

Turn right at the junction to begin a counterclockwise circuit, passing through a cutout in a large
fallen redwood on the way to yet another junction, ▶5
this one with a connector heading west to a pullout
on the Avenue of the Giants. Turn left and head past
some tanoak trees to the base of a hill and a junction
▶6 with the Big Cutoff Trail heading southwest below
Duckett Bluff. Continue ahead along the base of the
hill, passing a use trail on the left and soon encountering the Mahan plaque attached to a large boulder
positioned between two enormous redwood stumps.

From the plaque, the Mahan Loop turns sharply
north and then northwest, winding through a forest
with several large redwoods back to the junction ▶7
with the connector trail back toward the Founders
Loop.

After retracing your steps on the connector back
to the junction ▶8 of the Founders Loop, turn left

near the enormous root base of the Dyerville Giant and the equally sizable hole it left behind. With a length of 362 feet and a diameter of 17 feet, the tree is estimated to have been approaching 2,000 years old when it fell thunderously to the forest floor in March 1991. Some of the residents in the nearby communities thought a train wreck had generated the deafening sound. Arcing back toward the northeast, you wander among more redwoods on the way back to the close of the loop at the Founders Tree. ►9 From there, retrace your steps the short distance back to the parking area. ►10

🚶	MILESTONES	
►1	0.0	Start at Founders Grove parking area
►2	0.05	Left at Founders Loop junction
►3	0.2	Left at junction with connector
►4	0.4	Left at Mahan Loop junction
►5	0.5	Left at connector junction
►6	0.55	Straight at Big Cutoff junction
►7	0.9	Right at Mahan Loop and connector junction
►8	1.1	Left at connector and Founders Loop junction
►9	1.25	Left at Founders Loop junction
►10	1.3	Return to Founders Grove parking area

Rockefeller Grove Loop

The redwoods in the Rockefeller Grove may be slightly less impressive than their counterparts in the Founders Grove, but this grove has one major advantage over its more popular neighbor—less highway noise. Located across South Fork Eel River from the Avenue of the Giants and US 101 and on a flat next to Bull Creek, the Rockefeller Grove emits a more serene ambiance, a much better atmosphere in which to pay homage to the tall trees. You may hear the occasional vehicle on nearby Mattole Road, but the volume of traffic is much less than the well-traveled highways to the east.

The short, nearly flat loop through the grove is suitable for anyone who is ambulatory and, although the circuit could be walked fairly easily in just 15 minutes, the majesty of the grove dictates a much longer stay in order to appreciate the tall trees. Most of the classic redwood features, including extremely tall and massive sequoias, burls, redwood sprouts, fallen monarchs, and a ground cover of redwood sorrel, are all well represented.

TRAIL USE
Dayhiking,
Child-Friendly

LENGTH & TIME
0.6 mile, 1 hour

VERTICAL FEET
Negligible

DIFFICULTY
- **1** 2 3 4 5 +

TRAIL TYPE
Loop

START & FINISH
N40° 20.520'
W123° 56.469'

FEATURES
Redwoods
Stream

FACILITIES
None

Best Time

The trail is open all year. Fewer tourists travel the extra mile from the Avenue of the Giants than those who visit the Founders Grove adjacent to the highway, but the area still receives a lot of use during summer. A visit early in the morning or in spring or fall should feel less crowded. During periods of fair weather in the winter, you may have the entire grove to yourself.

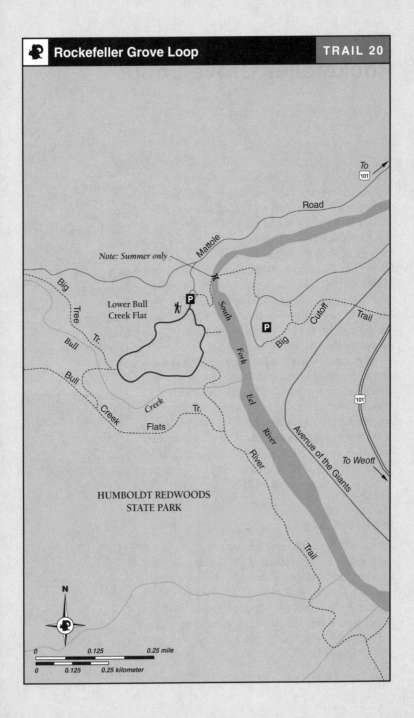

Rockefeller Grove Loop

TRAIL 20

To 101

Road

Mattole

Note: Summer only

P

South

Big

Tree

Tr.

Lower Bull
Creek Flat

Bull

P

Big

Cutoff

Trail

Bull

Fork

Creek

Creek

Flats

Tr.

Eel

101

River

River

Avenue of the Giants

To Weott

HUMBOLDT REDWOODS
STATE PARK

Trail

N

0   0.125   0.25 mile

0   0.125   0.25 kilometer

Finding the Trail

The Mattole Road branches west away from the Avenue of the Giants immediately south of Exit 663 from US 101 and immediately north of the highway bridge over South Fork Eel River. Drive on Mattole Road for 1.3 miles to the obscure-looking turnoff to the Rockefeller Grove parking lot. Pay close attention to your odometer, as the dirt access road plunging steeply down an embankment on the left-hand side of Mattole Road is extremely easy to miss, as is the nearby sign. Follow the road a short distance to the parking area. The park has three campgrounds: Hidden Springs, Burlington (adjacent to the visitor center), and Albee Creek. In the community of Myers Flat is the privately owned Giant Redwoods RV and Camp.

Trail Description

The trail begins at the southwest edge of the parking area ►1 and travels a short distance to the start of the loop. ►2 Turn right and begin a counterclockwise circuit through a forest of tall redwoods shading a pretty carpet of redwood sorrel. Pass through a sawed gap in a massive downed redwood, and continue past a use trail on the right that leads to another massive fallen monarch.

Redwoods

After 0.25 mile, you reach a junction ►3 with the Big Tree Loop and a lateral to the Bull Creek Trail. The Big Tree Loop heads northwest for 3.7 miles to a trailhead farther up Mattole Road (see Trail 23). The connector leads shortly to Bull Creek, where, in summer, a footbridge provides dry access across the creek to the far bank and a junction with the Bull Creek Flats Trail (see Trail 23). Veer left at the junction to continue the loop, walking amid more impressive redwoods, some with numerous redwood sprouts around the base and others with gnarly burls, soon reaching the Rockefeller plaque on the left.

Stream

Just beyond the Rockefeller plaque, you reach a junction ►4 with a side trail leading down to the banks of Bull Creek, the waters of which can provide a refreshing diversion on a hot summer day. Veer left at the junction, pass beneath a fallen giant, and continue a slightly winding course back to the close of the loop. ►5 From there, turn right and retrace your steps the short distance back to the parking area. ►6

MILESTONES

►1	0.0	Start at trailhead
►2	0.05	Right at loop junction
►3	0.25	Left at Big Tree Loop junction
►4	0.4	Left at junction to Bull Creek
►5	0.55	Right at loop junction
►6	0.6	Return to trailhead

Big Tree Loop

The short Big Tree Loop is one of the main high-lights for summer visitors to Humboldt Redwoods State Park, when a seasonal footbridge allows easy access across Bull Creek to a stand of impressive old-growth redwoods. The most notable tree, the Giant holds the distinction of being the National Champion Redwood, awarded based upon a num-ber of factors, including diameter, height, and crown spread. Additionally, visitors can gain a better perspective on just how massive a mature redwood can be while viewing the Flatiron Tree, a huge downed redwood sprawling across the forest floor. Away from these popular tourist attractions, the loop travels through a cathedral-like forest con-taining many fine redwood specimens. The picnic area at the trailhead offers the opportunity for lunch following the short and easy hike.

TRAIL USE
Dayhiking,
Child-Friendly

LENGTH & TIME
0.6 mile, 1 hour

VERTICAL FEET
Nominal

DIFFICULTY
- **1** 2 3 4 5 +

TRAIL TYPE
Loop

START & FINISH
N40° 21.045'
W123° 59.506'

FEATURES
Redwoods
Stream

FACILITIES
Restroom
Picnic Area

Best Time

The seasonal bridge allowing straightforward access to the Big Tree Loop is only in place during summer, usually from late May to the end of September. In the fall, when the water level is low, you can easily ford Bull Creek and have the area mostly to yourself.

Finding the Trail

Narrow Mattole Road branches west away from the Avenue of the Giants immediately south of Exit 663 from US 101 and immediately north of the highway bridge over South Fork Eel River. Drive your vehicle on Mattole Road for 4.4 miles to a left-hand turn onto the access road for the Big Tree Day Use Area.

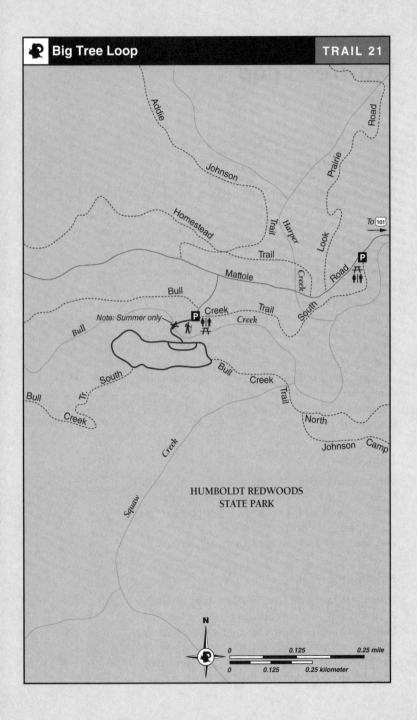

HUMBOLDT REDWOODS
STATE PARK

Note: Summer only

To 101

N

0   0.125   0.25 mile

0   0.125   0.25 kilometer

The Tall Tree

Follow this road a short distance to the parking area on the north side of Bull Creek. The park has three campgrounds: Hidden Springs, Burlington (adjacent to the visitor center), and Albee Creek. In the community of Myers Flat is the privately owned Giant Redwoods RV and Camp.

Trail Description

Stream

From the parking area, ▶1 you head briefly down to alder- and willow-lined Bull Creek to cross the seasonal footbridge ▶2 to the far bank. Turn left and begin a clockwise loop, ▶3 initially following the creek briefly downstream, with excellent views across the creek of the tall redwoods on the opposite bank.

Redwoods

Soon the trail bends into the forest near the Giant Tree, an incredibly large redwood granted the distinction in 1991 of being the National Champion Redwood. Not surprisingly, many tourists go no farther than the Giant Tree. Continue the loop, soon reaching a junction ▶4 with the Bull Creek Trail.

Turn right at the junction, and follow a section of the Bull Creek Flats Trail heading west through magnificent redwood forest. After another 0.2 mile, you reach a junction ▶5 where your trail bends northwest before arcing around to the end of the loop. ▶6 From there, turn left and retrace your steps back to the Big Tree Day Use Area. ▶7

🚶	MILESTONES	
▶1	0.0	Start at trailhead
▶2	0.025	Cross Bull Creek
▶3	0.05	Turn left at loop junction
▶4	0.1	Right at Bull Creek junction
▶5	0.3	Right at loop junction
▶6	0.55	Left at day-use area junction
▶7	0.6	Return to trailhead

Big Tree & Homestead Loop

Bull Creek is home to the largest remaining contiguous redwood stand in existence, and this short loop allows access to a picturesque portion known as the Rockefeller Forest. The route follows a section of the Tall Tree Trail and the Homestead Trail on a circuit through Upper Bull Creek Flat immediately north of the creek. The redwoods are most impressive along the Tall Tree Trail, which travels alongside the creek, but the slightly elevated Homestead Trail offers an enjoyable perspective as well. While the loop parallels Mattole Road, traffic is generally light enough, particularly in the off-season, to only occasionally interrupt the tranquility of the grove.

Best Time

The trail is open all year. Summer is the busiest season, which makes spring or fall a more attractive time for a visit.

Finding the Trail

Narrow Mattole Road branches west away from the Avenue of the Giants immediately south of Exit 663 from US 101 and immediately north of the highway bridge over South Fork Eel River. Drive your vehicle on Mattole Road for 4.4 miles to a left-hand turn onto the access road for the Big Tree Day Use Area. Follow this road a short distance to the parking area on the north side of Bull Creek. The park has three campgrounds: Hidden Springs, Burlington (adjacent to the visitor center), and Albee Creek. In the community of Myers Flat is the privately owned Giant Redwoods RV and Camp.

TRAIL USE
Dayhiking, Running

LENGTH & TIME
2.5 miles, 1–2 hours

VERTICAL FEET
+150'/-150'

DIFFICULTY
- 1 **2** 3 4 5 +

TRAIL TYPE
Loop

START & FINISH
N40° 21.045'
W123° 59.506'

FEATURES
Stream
Redwoods

FACILITIES
Restroom
Picnic Area

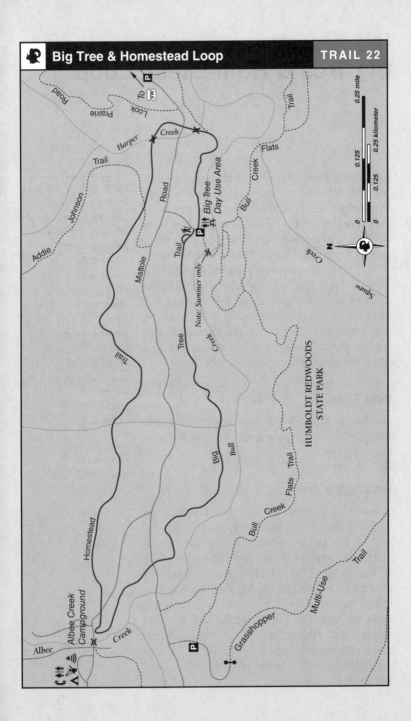

Big Tree & Homestead Loop

TRAIL 22

Trail Description

Trails head away from the day-use area in just about every direction, and the signs can be confusing. The most popular route in the summer heads down to a seasonal bridge across Bull Creek and onto the Big Tree Loop (see Trail 23). However, from the parking area, you should walk back toward Mattole Road a short distance to find the Big Tree Loop ►1 heading west, marked by a pair of four-by-four posts. Following signs to Albee Creek Campground, head down the trail, and soon encounter a junction with a short lateral to the 350-foot-plus Tall Tree, a worthy diversion. Continue ahead from this giant on a short loop back to the main trail.

Redwoods

With the sound of the gurgling creek to the left, stroll easily along a nearly level path through old-growth forest, one of the most impressive stands of redwoods on the planet. Redwood sorrel and ferns dot the shaded forest floor. Along the way, you cross short wood bridges over seasonal drainages. Just after crossing a wood plank bridge, 0.9 mile from the trailhead, the trail crosses Mattole Road ►2 and merges with an old dirt road on the far side. Immediately past a stream-gauging station, single-track resumes, drawing near Albee Creek and passing through riparian vegetation. A short climb leads to the edge of the paved access road to Albee Creek Campground directly east of a bridge across the creek and 0.2 mile from Mattole Road.

Stream

Angle sharply to the right at a nearby post, ►3 follow the Homestead Trail shortly to a crossing of the campground road, and proceed into lighter forest. Approaching a wood bridge over a seasonal drainage, the forest returns to a more redwood-dominant grove, with a healthy ground cover, principally ferns and redwood sorrel. The trail contours across the hillside just above the flat, offering a fine view of the redwood forest. Cross a couple more short bridges, and make a short descent to a

Redwood forest *along the Big Tree & Homestead Loop*

junction ►4 with the Addie Johnson Trail on the left, 1.0 mile from the campground.

Continue ahead from the junction and, just after a railed bridge over usually flowing Harper Creek, the trail intersects gated, multiuse Look Prairie Road near the shoulder of Mattole Road, ►5 0.2 mile from the Addie Johnson junction.

Cross Mattole Road and pick up single-track trail heading southwest. Immediately cross back over Harper Creek on a bridge, and proceed upstream along Bull Creek through redwood forest 0.2 mile to the close of the loop. ►6

🚶	MILESTONES	
►1	0.0	Start at trailhead
►2	0.9	Cross Mattole Road
►3	1.1	Right at Homestead Trail junction
►4	2.1	Straight at Addie Johnson junction
►5	2.3	Cross Mattole Road
►6	2.5	Return to trailhead

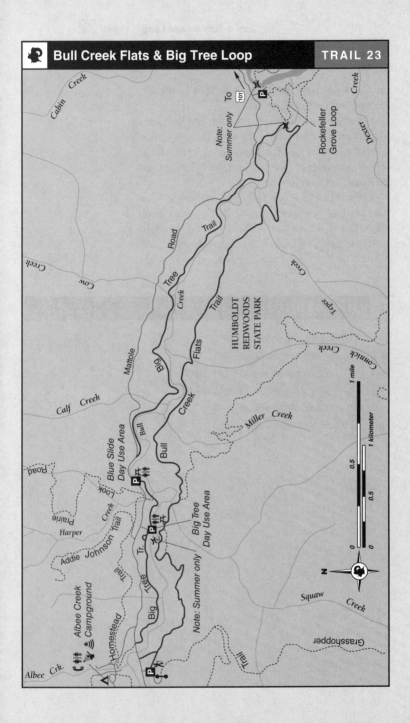

Bull Creek Flats & Big Tree Loop

For those looking for a longer hike among impressive redwoods, there's a lot to like on the Bull Creek Flats and Big Tree Loop. The trip begins by heading downstream along Bull Creek and passing through an old-growth redwood forest, reaching a crescendo in the Big Tree area on Upper Bull Creek Flat. Farther on is a second climax at Lower Bull Creek Flat, where a side trip on the 0.6-mile Rockefeller Grove Loop (see Trail 21) leads beneath some impressive redwood monarchs. Crossing a seasonal bridge over the creek, the loop then turns upstream, closely following the north bank. The redwood forest on this side of Bull Creek is less impressive, and the route merges with Mattole Road for a couple of short stretches.

There are restrooms and picnic areas at the nearby Blue Slide and Big Tree Day Use Areas.

Best Time

While the area is open year-round, the seasonal bridge across Bull Creek is in place only during

TRAIL USE
Dayhiking, Running
LENGTH & TIME
9.4 miles, 4–6 hours
VERTICAL FEET
+300'/-300'
DIFFICULTY
- 1 2 **3** 4 5 +
TRAIL TYPE
Loop
START & FINISH
N40° 21.012'
W124° 00.441'

FEATURES
Redwoods
Stream

FACILITIES
None

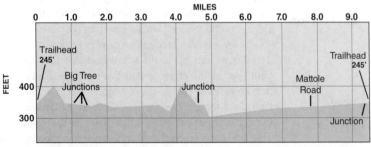

TRAIL 23 Bull Creek Flats & Big Tree Loop Elevation Profile

the summer, usually from late May to the end of September. Perhaps an ideal time for this hike is in spring or fall, when the water is low enough for you to easily ford the creek; without the bridge, visitation is light.

Finding the Trail

Narrow Mattole Road branches west away from the Avenue of the Giants immediately south of Exit 663 from US 101 and immediately north of the highway bridge over South Fork Eel River. Drive your vehicle on Mattole Road for 5.4 miles to a left-hand turn onto Grasshopper Road, and proceed a short distance to the Bull Creek Flats Trailhead on the left. Park along the side of the road as space allows. The park has three campgrounds: Hidden Springs, Burlington, and Albee Creek. In the community of Myers Flat is the privately owned Giant Redwoods RV and Camp.

Trail Description

Away from the trailhead, ▶1 follow slightly rising tread through rather ordinary forest, soon coming to a wood plank bridge over a trickling side stream. The trail dips briefly into a couple of usually dry side canyons, traveling above the flats adjacent to Bull Creek for the first mile or so. Eventually, the trail drops onto Upper Bull Creek Flat on the way to a junction ▶2 with the Big Tree Loop, 1.1 miles from the trailhead. Here you find yourself among towering redwoods.

🌲 **Redwoods**

Unless you've already done or plan to do the Big Tree Loop, turn left at the junction, and follow the path toward the creek, eventually reaching a junction ▶3 with the path to the seasonal bridge over Bull Creek and the Big Tree Day Use Area on the far side. Continue ahead on gravel to the base of the Giant Tree, and then proceed a short distance to a junction ▶4 with the reunion of the Bull Creek Flats Trail.

Back on the main trail, continue east across a stout bridge over Squaw Creek and to a T-junction ►5 with the Johnson Camp Trail on the right, 0.2 mile from the previous junction.

Go straight at the junction for 0.7 mile to a bridged crossing of Miller Creek. The trail draws closer to the south bank of picturesque Bull Creek for a stretch and crosses a small grassy clearing. Back under the trees, cross Connick Creek on a wood bridge, 0.4 mile from Miller Creek. Beyond the creek, the trail climbs above the flats for a while, which offers a slightly more detached view of the redwood forest below. After crossing a short bridge over Tepee Creek, the trail switchbacks higher into upland redwood forest and then drops down to Lower Bull Creek Flat and a junction ►6 with the trail heading across Bull Creek, 4.7 miles from the trailhead.

Leaving the Bull Creek Flats Trail, turn left and head steeply down to Lower Bull Creek Flat and the seasonal bridge across Bull Creek, reaching the Rockefeller Grove Loop ►7 on the far side. Unless you're going to walk the 0.6-mile loop through this magnificent stand of tall redwoods, turn left and follow the Big Tree Loop upstream close to the north bank of Bull Creek. Soon the trail draws near Mattole Road, curves away to follow a bend in the river, and then comes close to the road again near a pair of short bridges over seasonal swales. After 0.25 mile, you move away from the road for an extended romp through redwood forest, following the creek across Upper Bull Creek Flat.

After the bridged crossings of Cow and Calf Creeks, about 3 miles from the Rockefeller Grove Loop junction, Mattole Road comes right alongside Bull Creek, forcing the trail onto the edge of the asphalt ►8 around a sweeping curve. Fortunately, the distance is short, as you move off the road at the east end of the meadow ►9 at the Blue Slide Day Use Area.

Redwood on the *Bull Creek Flats Trail*

Stroll across the meadow to the picnic area, and find the single-track trail heading west back under forest cover, soon reaching a lateral ▶10 to the Look Prairie Multiuse Trail on the far side of Mattole Road. Continue ahead, crossing a bridge over Harper Creek and proceeding to the Big Tree Day Use Area. ▶11

Find the trail on the far side of the access road, marked by a pair of four-by-four posts. Following directions to Albee Creek Campground, head down the trail, soon encountering a junction with a short lateral to the 350-foot-plus Tall Tree, a worthy diversion. Continue ahead from this giant on a short loop back to the main trail.

With the sound of the gurgling creek to the left, stroll easily along a nearly level path through old-growth forest, one of the most impressive stand of redwoods on the planet. Redwood sorrel and ferns dot the shaded forest floor. Along the way, you cross short wood bridges over seasonal drainages. Just after crossing a wood plank bridge, 0.9 mile from the trail-head, the trail reaches Mattole Road. ▶12

Turn left onto Mattole Road, walk across the highway bridge, and find single-track trail ▶13 heading south just beyond. Soon you cross a short wood bridge, and proceed to a T-junction with the Bull Creek Flats Trail. From there, turn right ▶14 and retrace your steps the short distance back to the trailhead.

Redwoods

| ![walking icon] | **MILESTONES** |

▶1	0.0	Start at Big Tree Trailhead
▶2	1.1	Turn left at Big Tree Loop junction
▶3	1.3	Straight at junction to Big Tree Day Use Area
▶4	1.4	Left at Bull Creek Flats junction
▶5	1.6	Straight at Johnson Camp junction
▶6	4.7	Left at junction with trail across Bull Creek
▶7	4.8	Left at Rockefeller Grove Loop junction
▶8	7.8	Merge onto Mattole Road
▶9	8.0	Leave Mattole Road at Blue Slide Day Use Area
▶10	8.1	Straight at lateral to Look Prairie Multiuse Trail
▶11	8.3	Big Tree Day Use Area
▶12	9.2	Left onto Mattole Road
▶13	9.3	Left at junction of single-track trail
▶14	9.4	Right at junction and return to trailhead

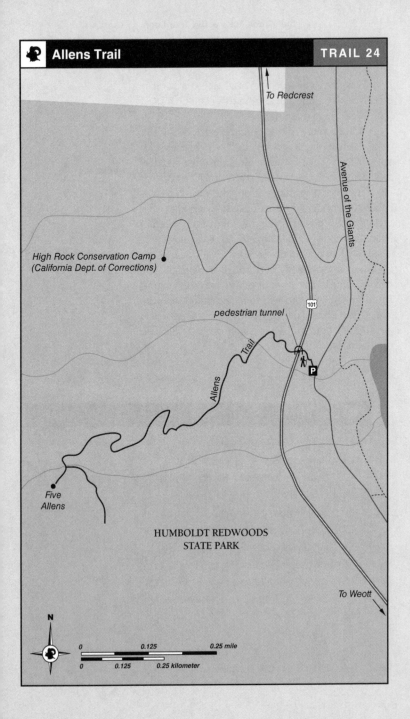

Allens Trail

TRAIL 24

To Redcrest

Avenue of the Giants

High Rock Conservation Camp
(California Dept. of Corrections)

pedestrian tunnel

101

Allens Trail

P

Five
Allens

HUMBOLDT REDWOODS
STATE PARK

To Weott

N

| 0 | | 0.125 | | 0.25 mile |

| 0 | | 0.125 | 0.25 kilometer |

Allens Trail

Most of the trails into the old-growth redwoods of Humboldt Redwoods State Park are relatively flat, visiting the impressive giants on alluvial flats. The Allens Trail is the polar opposite, gaining more than 1,000 feet in a little more than a mile of switchbacks on the way to a redwood-filled grove high above the Eel River. Because of the steep grade, you probably won't have a lot of company. The ever-present traffic noise from US 101 mars the first part of the climb, but it fades away by the time you reach serene Allens Grove.

Best Time

Although the trail is open all year, this steep climb is best done when the air is cool. If you happen to be here during summer, get an early start to beat the heat.

Finding the Trail

The trailhead is difficult to find at first, despite being right off of the Avenue of the Giants. Park

TRAIL USE
Dayhiking, Running
LENGTH & TIME
2.6 miles, 2–3 hours
VERTICAL FEET
+1,100'/-1,100'
DIFFICULTY
- 1 2 3 **4** 5 +
TRAIL TYPE
Out & Back
START & FINISH
N40° 22.355'
W123° 55.541'

FEATURES
Redwoods
Steep

FACILITIES
None

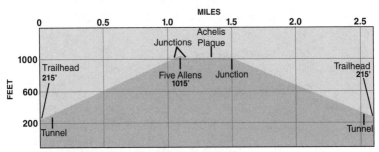

TRAIL 24 Allens Trail Elevation Profile

Trillium

your vehicle on the highway shoulder near mile-post 22.1 (0.3 mile south of the road to High Rock Conservation Camp). A sign nearby reads "Maria McKead Allen Grove." The trail begins at a sign attached to a four-by-four post. The park has three campgrounds: Hidden Springs, Burlington, and Albee Creek. In the community of Myers Flat is the privately owned Giant Redwoods RV and Camp.

Trail Description

 Steep

From the Avenue of the Giants ▶1 climb steeply up a hillside covered with a mixed forest of Douglas firs and tanoaks. After six short-legged switchbacks, the trail passes through a pedestrian tunnel ▶2 beneath US 101. Beyond the underpass, the switchbacking climb resumes through mixed redwood forest with the sound of gurgling Matthews Creek to the left, which fails to drown out the persistent noise of passing cars.

After 0.3 mile, cross the lushly lined creek on a wood-railed bridge and keep climbing. Eventually, you enter a small vale covered with an almost pure stand of redwood forest, with a typical understory of redwood sorrel and ferns. The highway noise is finally left behind, as you reach the crossing of a thin, fern-lined rivulet and an unmarked junction ▶3 just beyond, 1.1 miles from the trailhead. Continuing straight ahead, climb shortly to the end of the trail near a sign for the Five Allens, ▶4 named for a quintet of conservationists.

Redwoods

After enjoying the sanctuary surrounding the Five Allens, retrace your steps to the junction and turn right. ▶5 This lateral cuts across the hillside and ends at a dead tree with a plaque for Elisabeth Achelis ▶6 amid an open redwood forest. Retrace your steps to the junction ▶7 and then down to the trailhead. ▶8

🚶 MILESTONES

▶1	0.0	Start at trailhead
▶2	0.1	Pedestrian tunnel
▶3	1.1	Straight at junction
▶4	1.15	Five Allens
▶5	1.2	Right at junction
▶6	1.35	Achelis plaque
▶7	1.5	Right at junction
▶8	2.6	Return to trailhead

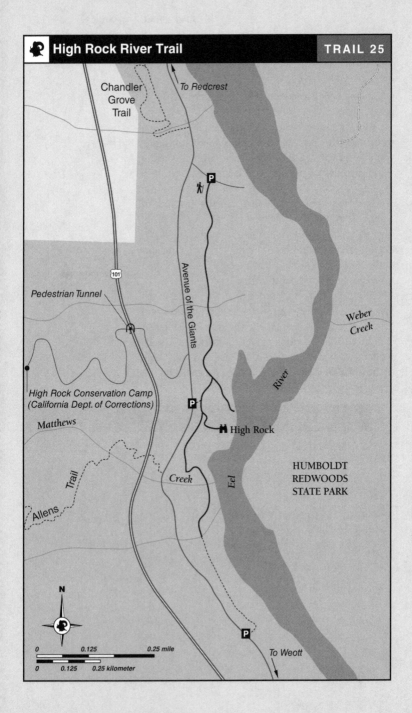

High Rock River Trail

TRAIL 25

Chandler Grove Trail

To Redcrest

101

Avenue of the Giants

Pedestrian Tunnel

High Rock Conservation Camp
(California Dept. of Corrections)

Matthews

Trail

Allens

Creek

High Rock

Weber Creek

River

Eel

HUMBOLDT
REDWOODS
STATE PARK

To Weott

N

| 0 | 0.125 | 0.25 mile |
| 0 | 0.125 | 0.25 kilometer |

High Rock River Trail

If the High Rock River Trail were farther away from the Avenue of the Giants, this trip would offer an opportunity to enjoy some impressive redwoods and a view of the Eel River in peace and serenity. Most likely you won't have to rub elbows with any fellow humans. Traffic noise, however, might disturb the otherwise reverential ambiance. The trail passes through several memorial groves of old-growth redwoods, climbs into upland forest on the way to a lovely vista of the Eel River from the top of High Rock, and then descends back into lowland forest, offering a wealth of variety for such a short hike.

TRAIL USE
Dayhiking, Running

LENGTH & TIME
2.0 miles, 1 hour

VERTICAL FEET
+200'/-200'

DIFFICULTY
- 1 2 **3** 4 5 +

TRAIL TYPE
Out & Back

START & FINISH
N40° 22.866'
W123° 55.449'

FEATURES
Stream
Redwoods
Views

FACILITIES
None

Best Time

The trail is open all year. Traffic noise from the Avenue of the Giants will be less noticeable during the off-season. To avoid as much road noise as possible, summer visitors should arrive early.

Finding the Trail

The trailhead, located just off the Avenue of the Giants between Exit 663 at Dyerville and Exit 667A from US 101 at Redcrest, is not marked. Drive to milepost 22.8 on Avenue of the Giants, where a dirt road heads east toward Eel River (this junction is 0.3 mile north of the road to High Rock Conservation Camp). Turn down this road a short distance to the vicinity of a steel gate, and park your vehicle as space allows. The trail begins on the south side of the road. The park has three campgrounds: Hidden

View of *South Fork Eel River from High Rock*

Springs, Burlington, and Albee Creek. In the community of Myers Flat is the privately owned Giant Redwoods RV and Camp.

Trail Description

Redwoods

The unmarked trail heads ►1 south beneath the impressive redwoods of the Bowman, Lewis, and Starr Groves occupying an alluvial flat adjacent to the Eel River. The understory comprises redwood sorrel, false Solomon's seal, and poison oak. The flat soon begins to narrow between the river and a steep hillside. After crossing a stout wood bridge over a small creek, you encounter a plaque and a bench for the Wentworth Grove. Soon after, the trail begins a mild-to-moderate climb, passing beneath some utility lines and proceeding shortly to an unmarked junction, ▶2 where the left-hand trail drops down to the sandy riverbank.

River

Taking the right-hand path, you soon climb to a second unmarked junction, ▶3 where the trail on the right leads shortly to the edge of the highway. Continuing straight ahead, the main trail switchbacks up the hillside through upland forest to the top of a ridge. A brief walk east along the ridge leads to a fenced viewpoint ▶4 at the edge of High Rock, offering a fine view of the Eel River below.

Views

Beyond High Rock, the main trail becomes indistinct, descending into a fine stand of redwoods in the Olson Gove, ▶5 crossing bridges over Matthews Creek and an unnamed seasonal stream along the way. Beyond, the forest is choked with small trees and, unless you have a ride waiting at the southern trailhead, this would be a good place to turn around and head back to your starting point. ▶6

Redwoods 🌲

🚶	**MILESTONES**	
▶1	0.0	Find the trailhead
▶2	0.3	Veer right at junction to river
▶3	0.35	Straight at second junction
▶4	0.6	High Rock viewpoint
▶5	1.0	Olson Grove
▶6	2.0	Return to trailhead

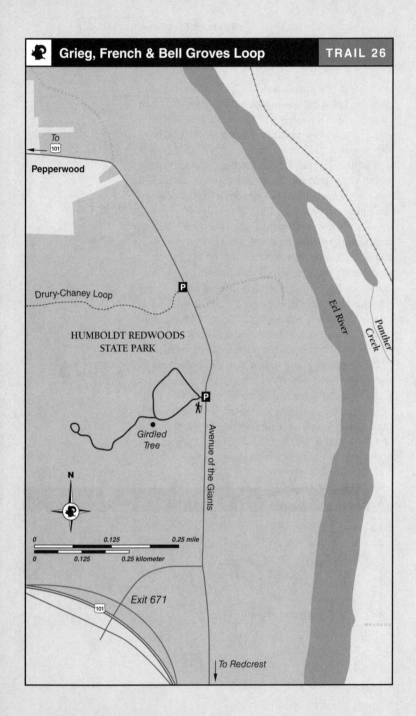

To
101

Pepperwood

Drury-Chaney Loop

HUMBOLDT REDWOODS
STATE PARK

*Girdled
Tree*

Avenue of the Giants

Eel River

Panther Creek

N

0   0.125   0.25 mile
0   0.125   0.25 kilometer

Exit 671

101

To Redcrest

Grieg, French & Bell Groves Loop

This short loop is a fine way to spend a half hour or so in the midst of some impressive redwoods towering over a thick carpet of redwood sorrel.

Best Time

The trail is open all year. Located near the north end of Humboldt Redwoods State Park, this grove receives less foot traffic than those farther south, but it still sees a fair share of tourists during the summer season. Fall and spring may be the optimum time for a visit.

Finding the Trail

The trail on the west side of the Avenue of the Giants is 0.2 mile south of the more clearly marked Drury-Chaney Loop (Trail 29), south of Pepperwood and 0.3 mile north of the off-ramp road from Exit 671 from US 101. The park has three campgrounds: Hidden Springs, Burlington, and Albee Creek. In the community of Myers Flat is the privately owned Giant Redwoods RV and Camp.

Trail Description

A number of paths head away from the Avenue of the Giants ▶1 and into redwood forest, making it difficult to select the right one. The correct path is on the left and heads directly southwest into tall trees of the Grieg Grove. Beyond the foot-trampled bare ground next to the road, redwood sorrel and a few ferns carpet the forest floor on the way through

TRAIL USE
Dayhiking,
Child-Friendly

LENGTH & TIME
0.6 mile, ½ hour

VERTICAL FEET
Nominal

DIFFICULTY
- **1** 2 3 4 5 +

TRAIL TYPE
Loop

START & FINISH
N40° 26.476'
W123° 59.143'

FEATURES
Redwoods

FACILITIES
None

Redwoods

173

Redwood sorrel, *ferns, and old-growth redwoods in the French Grove*

the French Grove to the Girdled Tree. Many years ago a ring of bark was removed from this massive redwood's trunk and transported to San Francisco for an exposition. Despite the affront, the tree has continued to live. A bench near it offers the opportunity to sit and contemplate the tree's scar and the more pleasant surroundings.

Continue ahead on a winding course through the redwoods to a small clearing with a couple of picnic tables. Beyond the picnic area a short loop circles through Bell Grove ▶2 at the conclusion of the journey. From there, retrace your steps, or follow any one of the social trails back to the trailhead. ▶3

🚶	**MILESTONES**

▶1	0.0	Start at trailhead
▶2	0.3	Bell Grove
▶3	0.6	Return to trailhead

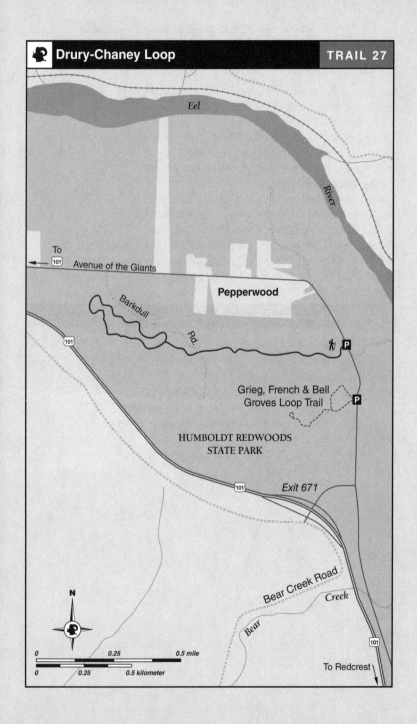

Drury-Chaney Loop

The Drury-Chaney Loop is a short, easy romp through an impressive redwood forest. A carpet of redwood sorrel at the beginning is so uniform that it almost appears to be unnatural. As the northern-most maintained trail in Humboldt Redwoods State Park, this path is not as well used as some others.

TRAIL USE
Dayhiking

LENGTH & TIME
2.2 miles, 1½ hours

VERTICAL FEET
Nominal

DIFFICULTY
- **1** 2 3 4 5 +

TRAIL TYPE
Loop

START & FINISH
N40° 26.593'
W123° 59.215'

Best Time

The trail is open all year. Summer is the most popular time to visit the park, making a trip in spring or fall a more attractive proposition for solitude seekers.

FEATURES
Redwoods

FACILITIES
None

Finding the Trail

The well-marked trailhead is just south of Pepperwood and north of Exit 671 from US 101, on the west side of the Avenue of the Giants near mile-post 28.8. Park your vehicle on the west shoulder as space allows. The park has three campgrounds: Hidden Springs, Burlington, and Albee Creek. In the community of Myers Flat is the privately owned Giant Redwoods RV and Camp.

Trail Description

An area map, interpretive signs providing informa-tion about logging practices in the redwood forest, and a boulder with a memorial plaque mark the beginning of a gravel path, ▶1 which begins in a clearing next to the road but soon heads into dense redwood forest. The forest floor is carpeted with a mat of nearly unbroken redwood sorrel that has an

Redwoods

177

Beautiful forest *of the Drury-Chaney Loop*

almost manicured appearance. After 0.6 mile, you pass below a set of utility lines and cross Barkdull Road, and then come to the loop junction ►2 0.1 mile farther. A detour down the road to the right leads to some impressively large redwoods.

Turn left at the junction, immediately cross a wood railed bridge over a trickling stream, and proceed on a clockwise loop through redwood forest on an alluvial flat. Cross a second bridge over a seasonal swale, where you may notice the increasing sound of traffic from US 101 to the west. Where the trail bends back to the east, a very short side trail on the left accesses a memorial bench. Shortly afterward, you pass another path on the left heading toward Barkdull Road and the Cantfield-Andrews Memorial Grove. Continue through old-growth forest, passing through some cutouts in downed redwoods on the way to the end of the loop, ►3 and then retrace your steps back to the trailhead. ►4

MILESTONES

►1	0.0	Start at trailhead
►2	0.7	Left at loop junction
►3	1.5	Left at loop junction
►4	2.2	Return to trailhead

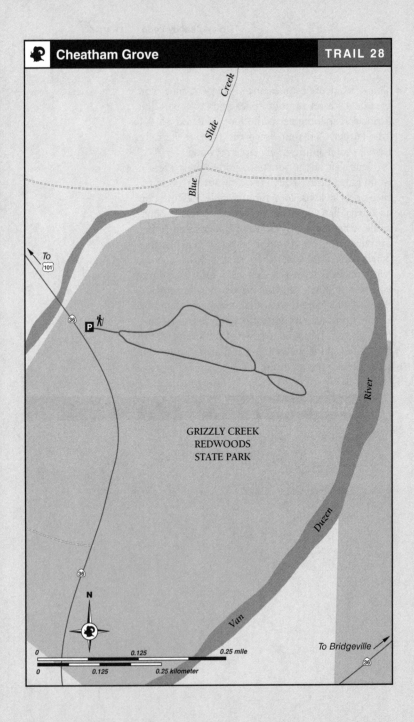

Slide Creek

Blue

To 101

36

P

GRIZZLY CREEK
REDWOODS
STATE PARK

River

Duzen

N

Van

To Bridgeville

36

36

0   0.125   0.25 mile
0   0.125   0.25 kilometer

Cheatham Grove

Well away from the more popular parks close to US 101, far-flung Grizzly Creek Redwoods State Park harbors the farthest inland coast redwood forest. Three separate parcels are strung out along the banks of the meandering Van Duzen River. The most impressive stand of redwoods is on an alluvial flat in the Cheatham Grove, the westernmost parcel adjacent to Van Duzen County Park.

The grove was named for Owen R. Cheatham, president of Georgia Hardwood Lumber Company (later renamed Georgia Pacific Plywood and Lumber Company), who was so taken by the area's beauty that he spared the area from logging. Others have been equally impressed by the straight, soaring redwoods and the well-ordered ground cover of redwood sorrel and ferns, including the filmmakers of *Return of the Jedi,* who used the grove for the set of the speeder bike chase. Because of its remote location and the light traffic on nearby CA 36, visitors to the grove should have a reasonable expectation of peace and quiet.

TRAIL USE
Dayhiking,
Child-Friendly

LENGTH & TIME
0.7 mile, ½–1 hour

VERTICAL FEET
Nominal

DIFFICULTY
- **1** 2 3 4 5 +

TRAIL TYPE
Loop

START & FINISH
N40° 28.986'
W123° 57.767'

FEATURES
Redwoods
Swimming

FACILITIES
Campground
Visitor Center
Picnic Area

Best Time

Although the trail is open all year, the area can be a muddy mess during and after rainstorms.

Finding the Trail

From US 101 south of Fortuna, take the Fowler Lane exit, and proceed eastbound on CA 36, passing through the tiny communities of Hydesville and Carlotta and then continuing past Van Duzen County

Cheatam Grove *in Grizzly Creek Redwoods State Park*

Park. About 14 miles from US 101, and just past the far end of the J. Dwight Odell Memorial Bridge over the Van Duzen River, turn left onto a short road at a sign for the Owen R. Cheatham Grove. Drop down from the highway to a small, dirt parking area. The road is 3 miles west of the main entrance into Grizzly Creek Redwoods State Park. The park's campground has 30 regular campsites, a group site, and a hiker and biker site. The Cheatham Grove has first-come, first-served environmental sites.

Trail Description

Redwoods

Head east away from the parking area ▶1 into an open, old-growth redwood forest on an alluvial flat sandwiched in a bend of the Van Duzen River. The tall, straight sequoias tower over a dense, lush understory of redwood sorrel and ferns arranged in such a manner that you may think Grizzly Creek Redwoods State Park employs a gardener. Very soon you reach the big loop junction ▶2 near a bench.

Continue straight ahead, traveling deeper into this serene redwood forest. Farther on, you bypass the big loop trail ▶3 branching away to the left and soon reach the small loop junction ▶4 near the root system of a large upturned redwood, 0.2 mile from the trailhead. A counterclockwise loop circles through the east end of the grove and returns you in short order back to this junction. ▶5

At the end of the small loop, retrace your steps 0.05 mile to the junction ▶6 with the big loop and turn right. Wind through the forest and come to a short path leading to a clearing with a bench near a large maple tree. Farther on, near another bench, ignore a path on the right that heads to the edge of the grove and continues toward the river. Veering ahead on the left-hand trail, you soon close the big loop at the first junction ▶7 and then retrace your steps back to the parking area. ▶8

Swimming ⌐⏀•

🚶	**MILESTONES**	
▶1	0.0	Start at trailhead
▶2	0.05	Straight at Big Loop junction
▶3	0.2	Straight at Big Loop junction
▶4	0.25	Right at Small Loop junction
▶5	0.35	Right at junction
▶6	0.4	Right at Big Loop junction
▶7	0.65	Right at junction
▶8	0.7	Return to trailhead

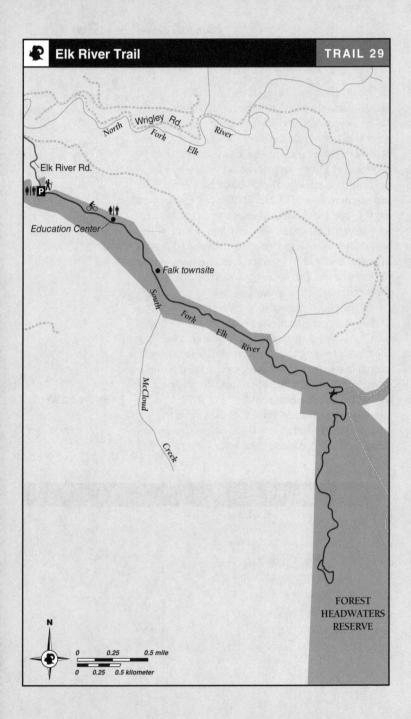

Elk River Trail

After years of heated controversy, the Headwaters Forest Reserve was acquired and protected in 1999, creating the sixth largest redwood park in California. The vast majority of the area is off-limits to the public to prevent environmental degradation. The sole portal into this redwood sanctuary, the Elk River Trail barely penetrates the old-growth section. The initial stretch follows the pleasant grade of an old logging road along the banks of the South Fork Elk River through serene second-growth forest, offering some history along the way. Beyond, single-track trail climbs up to a short loop through a small stand of old-growth redwoods.

Note: Dogs and bikes are allowed on only the first 3 miles. Only the first mile is accessible to wheelchair users.

Best Time

Except during and after rainstorms, when the path can be quite muddy, the Elk River Trail can be hiked year-round. Spring is perhaps the best time, when a smattering of wildflowers lines the trail.

Finding the Trail

Just south of Eureka, leave US 101 at the Herrick Avenue and Elk River Road exit, and turn south onto Elk River Road. Continue for about 1.7 miles to a junction, and veer right to remain on Elk River Road. Proceed for another 3.4 miles, cross a bridge over North Fork Elk River, and then continue another 0.9 mile to the well-marked trailhead. There

TRAIL USE
Dayhiking, Running, Biking, Dogs Allowed, Handicapped Access, Child-Friendly

LENGTH & TIME
10.0 miles, 4½–6 hours

VERTICAL FEET
+1,460'/-1,460'

DIFFICULTY
- 1 2 **3** 4 5 +

TRAIL TYPE
Semiloop

START & FINISH
N40° 41.523'
W124° 08.440'

FEATURES
Redwoods
Stream
Historic Interest

FACILITIES
Restrooms
Picnic Area

are no campgrounds in the vicinity. Eureka has numerous motels and a couple of RV parks.

Trail Description

 Stream

From the trailhead ▶1 the route follows a gently graded, slightly undulated, paved road up the second-growth forested canyon of South Fork Elk River. You quickly come to the first of several interpretive signs placed alongside the first mile of trail, where a pair of ornamental yew trees marks the beginning of a path leading to the abandoned site of a caretaker's residence. Continue up the wheelchair-accessible road, soon reaching the Headwaters Education Center on the left. The center occupies the building that once housed the mill's locomotive, which was carefully disassembled, transported, and rebuilt on this site. Additional interpretive signs nearby provide interesting historical information and a plea for continued protection of the area's sensitive resources. Toward the rear of the building is a modern vault toilet.

Historic Interest

After 0.1 mile, the old road leads to the former townsite of Falk, ▶2 where up to 400 people once resided and a mill processed lumber from the surrounding forest. Without the accompanying photograph of the town on the interpretive sign, imagining such a community here would be next

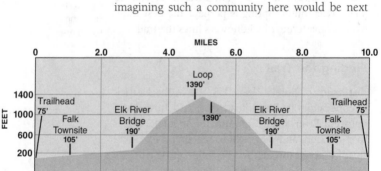

TRAIL 29 Elk River Trail Elevation Profile

Headwaters Education Center Building

to impossible; the forest has recovered remarkably since the mill closed in 1937. In the late 1970s, the landowners tore down and burned the last of the town's decaying structures. Shortly beyond Falk, the asphalt surface changes to well-packed gravel.

While the gravel section remains relatively easy to travel, you must negotiate some steeper hills. Farther on, a short single-track section of trail was built to bypass a washed-out section of the old road. Past this detour, you continue up the gravel road-bed enjoying the pleasant sound of the river below. At the 3-mile marker near a picnic table, the road bends sharply downhill to a steel-plate bridge ▶3 over the river. At the far end of the river, a sign and wood rail gate mark the end of the section open to mountain bikes and dogs.

The gravel road continues uphill for a while on the way to a sign for Little South Fork Elk River

Trail, where single-track trail doubles back uphill on the right. Steeper switchbacks lead up the slope and away from the river, as the forest canopy closes in and the sound of the rushing river soon fades. This combination of the lack of sound from moving water and the darkness of the forest creates an extremely serene ambiance, especially if you're alone. Periodic wood-beam-and-dirt steps attempt to mitigate erosion along this stretch of trail, which can be muddy in spots during wet conditions.

At the end of the switchbacks, you reach the top of a ridge, which the trail follows for a bit. You drop off the ridge and then make a generally ascending traverse across the upper slopes of Little South Fork Elk River canyon. Ferns carpet the forest floor and a stand of red alders graces the forest on the way to the loop junction near a burned-out redwood stump. ►4

An arrow directs you to the right onto a counterclockwise route through the forest. A switchback leads up the slope and past several more stumps before you reach a section of old-growth forest. Wind past fallen logs and tall redwoods to the high point at a small gully. A winding descent eventually leads back into second-growth forest near the close of the loop. ►5 From there, retrace your steps 5 miles to the trailhead. ►6

 Redwoods

🚶	**MILESTONES**	
►1	0.0	Start at trailhead
►2	1.1	Falk townsite
►3	3.0	Elk River Bridge
►4	4.5	Right at loop junction
►5	5.0	Left at Little South Fork Elk River junction
►6	10.0	Return to trailhead

Opposite *High Rock River Trail*

Redwood National Park & Vicinity

Redwood National Park & Vicinity

Redwood is the only national park along the far north coast of California. Set aside in the 1960s, the park protects a section of the Redwood Creek drainage, along with a strip of coastline. Although the national park lacks some of the majesty of the old-growth stands found in the state parks due to its late arrival to the party, Redwood National Park offers more of a wilderness feel. US 101 runs right through the area, but since many of the trails are located well away from the road, they offer a higher dose of tranquility than many of the state park trails. Along with three neighboring state parks, Redwood offers a variety of hikes with stunning coastline vistas, sandy beaches, serene forests, and enchanting streams.

Permits

Permits are not required for dayhiking. Overnight trips require a free backcountry camping permit, available from the Thomas H. Kuchel Visitor Center. Backcountry camping is limited to designated campsites and areas. Patrick's Point State Park charges an entrance fee.

Maps

By far, the best map covering Redwood National Park and vicinity is the 1:25,000-scale map *Redwood National and State Parks South*, published by Redwood Hikes Press. The accurate, detailed, full-color, topographic map shows both trails with mileages and the location of footbridges and memorial redwood grove signs and benches.

Overleaf and opposite: *Wedding Rock, Patrick's Point State Park*

TRAIL	DIFFICULTY	LENGTH	TYPE	USES & ACCESS	TERRAIN	NATURE	FEATURES
30	3	1.4	Loop	Dayhiking, Running, Dogs Allowed			Views, Historic Interest, Resort town, Lighthouse
31	3	0.6 or 4.2	Out & Back	Dayhiking, Running	Beach	Wildlife	Views, Camping, Picnic Area, Historic Interest, Resort town
32	2	8.0	Out & Back	Dayhiking, Running	Beach, Lake	Wildflowers	Views, Picnic Area
33	3	16.4	Out & Back	Dayhiking, Backpacking, Running	Stream, Redwoods		Camping
34	1	1.4	Semiloop	Dayhiking, Handicapped Access, Child-Friendly	Redwoods		Historic Interest
35	3	3.2	Semiloop	Dayhiking, Running	Stream, Redwoods		
36	4	5.2	Loop	Dayhiking, Running	Stream, Redwoods	Wildflowers	Swimming
37	3	10.4	Out & Back	Dayhiking, Running	Stream	Wildflowers	Views, Picnic Area, Historic Interest
38	3	4.5	Semiloop	Dayhiking, Running	Stream	Wildflowers	Views, Historic Interest, Picnic Area
39	4	8.0	Out & Back	Dayhiking, Running	Beach, Stream	Flora, Wildflowers	Views, Secluded, Steep
40	2	2.6	Loop	Dayhiking, Running, Child-Friendly	Stream, Waterfall, Redwoods	Wildflowers, Wildlife	Picnic Area

USES & ACCESS	TYPE	TERRAIN	NATURE	FEATURES
Dayhiking	Loop	Mountain	Flora	Views
Backpacking	Semiloop	Beach	Wildflowers	Camping
Running	Out & Back	Lake	Wildlife	Picnic Area
Biking	Shuttle	Stream		Swimming
Dogs Allowed		Waterfall		Secluded
Handicapped Access	DIFFICULTY	Redwoods		Steep
Child-Friendly	- 1 2 3 4 5 +	Pygmy Forest		Historic Interest
	less more			Resort town
				Lighthouse

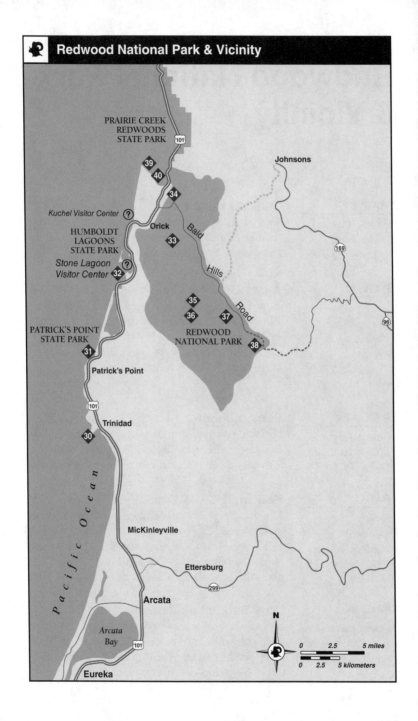

Redwood National Park & Vicinity

PRAIRIE CREEK
REDWOODS
STATE PARK

101

Johnsons

39

40

34

169

Kuchel Visitor Center (?)

Orick

HUMBOLDT
LAGOONS
STATE PARK

Bald

33

*Stone Lagoon
Visitor Center* (?) 32

Hills

35

36

37

Road

REDWOOD
NATIONAL PARK

38

96

PATRICK'S POINT
STATE PARK

31

Patrick's Point

101

Trinidad

30

P a c i f i c   O c e a n

MicKinleyville

Ettersburg

299

Arcata

*Arcata
Bay*

101

Eureka

N

0   2.5   5 miles

0   2.5   5 kilometers

Redwood National Park & Vicinity

Tall Trees Grove 225

Housing a former record holder for the tallest red-wood, the Tall Trees Grove provides the serene, cathedral-like mood that should accompany any pilgrimage to these old-growth trees. Access to this peaceful grove, nestled in a pocket of forest far from any major road, is limited each day by the Park Service. Visit the Thomas H. Kuchel Visitor Center for a permit.

Emerald Ridge Loop 230

A longer loop option, the Emerald Ridge Loop incorporates a visit to the Tall Trees Grove with a journey to a much less visited part of the forest and a sometimes-wet journey downstream along Redwood Creek.

Dolason Prairie Trail 236

Beginning near an elevation of 2,400 feet in the open prairie of Bald Hills Ridge, the Dolason Prairie Trail descends all the way to the forest along Redwood Creek, providing a fine cross section of the topography of Redwood National Park.

Lyons Ranch Loop 241

This journey across an upland prairie leads to the historic site of an old ranch, offering grand views of the Redwood Creek drainage along the way.

Coastal Trail: Skunk Cabbage Section 246

A little-used trail travels through a section of lush coastal forest before climbing stiffly to the top of a bluff and then descending just as stiffly to a strip of isolated sandy beach. Springtime visitors may see acres of skunk cabbage in bloom.

Trillium Falls Loop 251

Roosevelt elk, a short waterfall, and old-growth red-woods are highlights of this short loop from the Elk Meadows Day Use Area.

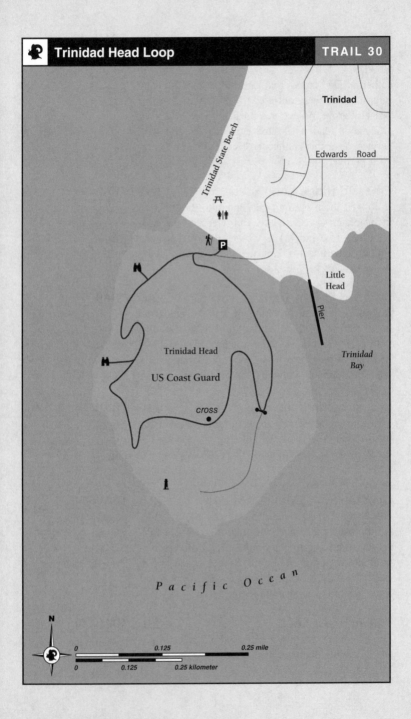

Trinidad Head Loop

TRAIL 30

Trinidad

Edwards Road

Trinidad State Beach

Little Head

Pier

Trinidad Bay

Trinidad Head

US Coast Guard

cross

Pacific Ocean

N

0   0.125   0.25 mile

0   0.125   0.25 kilometer

Trinidad Head Loop

The 358-foot-high promontory of Trinidad Head juts dramatically into the Pacific Ocean away from the forested mainland, an unobstructed aerie offering stunningly panoramic vistas of the scenic Northern California coastline. However, its exposed location ensures that the promontory receives more than its fair share of foggy days. Fortunately, the scenery is still enjoyable even when fog obscures the numerous surrounding rock outcroppings, creating a somber, mysterious mood.

On clear days, this loop provides an abundance of potential viewpoints, many of which are accompanied by park benches, with each flank offering a different perspective on the surrounding coastline. The trip also offers a bit of history, including a view of a lighthouse built in 1871 that is still operating and an old granite cross commemorating the area's discovery by the Spanish in 1775. Nearby Trinidad State Beach is a fine spot for an afterhike picnic, and the quaint seaside village of Trinidad is a great place to grab a meal.

TRAIL USE
Dayhiking, Running,
Dogs Allowed

LENGTH & TIME
1.4 miles, 1–2 hours

VERTICAL FEET
+300'/-300'

DIFFICULTY
- 1 2 **3** 4 5 +

TRAIL TYPE
Loop

START & FINISH
N41° 03.402'
W124° 08.916'

FEATURES
Views
Historic Interest
Lighthouse

FACILITIES
Resort Town

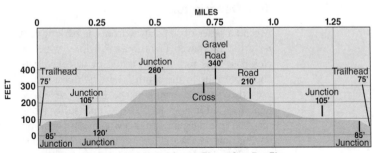

TRAIL 30 Trinidad Head Loop Elevation Profile

Best Time

The trail is open all year. Sunny days without coastal fog, most common in spring and fall, offer the best ocean views. Spring has the added bonus of a smattering of wildflowers.

Finding the Trail

Approximately 19 miles north of Eureka, leave US 101 at Exit 728 and head toward Trinidad, following Main Street into the quaint town. Soon Main Street makes a sharp left-hand curve onto Trinity Street (Stagecoach Road on the right leads to Trinidad State Beach). Proceed 0.1 mile to a T-intersection, and turn right onto Edwards Street. At a curve, Edwards Street becomes Lighthouse Road and descends toward the ocean. Look for a large dirt parking area on the right near an intersection with Bay Street on the left, which leads to the town's tiny harbor and pier.

The trailhead parking area, a secondary lot for Trinidad State Beach, has no facilities. However, near the main entrance to Trinidad State Beach are restrooms and a small picnic area with tables and fire pits. The trail begins at the southeast side of the parking area. Trinidad has several RV parks. Nearby Patrick's Point State Park (Trail 31) has three campgrounds and two group campgrounds.

Trail Description

Ascend a series of steps away from the parking area ►1 up to the paved Lighthouse Road, ►2 which is closed to foot and vehicle traffic by a locked gate about 0.4 mile to the south. The U.S. Coast Guard uses this road to maintain the lighthouse whose light was automated in 1974. Climb stiffly along the road to a hairpin turn, ►3 where you begin following single-track trail on a counterclockwise loop around the head.

Thomas H. Kuchel Visitor Center, *Redwood National Park*

Very soon you encounter the first of several viewpoints with benches. The picturesque shoreline is dotted with sea-stacks and numerous rock out-croppings; the largest rock to the north with a grove of trees on top is Pewetole Island. A short distance from the first vista point, you come to a junction ▶4 with a short spur trail leading toward the cliff edge for an unobstructed view. Back on the main trail, continue the loop around the head, climbing via a couple of switchbacks and then reaching a junction ▶5 with another spur trail, this one offering a west-ward view of Blank Rock and the expansive ocean beyond.

Views

Away from the second spur trail junction, the trail moves a bit inland and ascends a hillside. Along with the surf, you may hear barking seals, the rhythmic bellow of a foghorn, and the clanging of an offshore buoy. At the top of the climb, you reach a grass-covered clearing with a large granite cross, placed here in 1913 by a Redwood National Park & Vicinity County women's club, which replaced the original pine cross erected in 1775. The translation

Historic Interest

of the inscription originally made by explorers Bruno Heceta and Lt. Juan Francisco Bodega y Cuadra claims the territory in the name of King Charles III of Spain. The explorers named the area Trinity, as they made their discovery on the day after the Feast of the Holy Trinity, the first Sunday following Pentecost. Opposite the cross is a wooden viewing platform from which you can see the top of the short lighthouse and an old wooden water tank nearby.

The trail continues uphill past the cross, briefly following a utility line past more benches with views of the southern coastline on the way to a union with a gravel road. ►7 Follow the gravel road on a winding descent, with views of the community of Trinidad, and reach a wide turnaround ►8 with a picnic table, bench, and bearproof trashcan near the locked gate across the road to the lighthouse.

 Views

Turn left onto paved Lighthouse Road, and descend past more benches with fine views of Trinidad Bay, Little Head, and the pier. Reach the close of the loop at the junction ►9 with the single-track section, and then retrace your steps 0.2 mile to the parking area. ►10

🚶	MILESTONES	
►1	0.0	Start at trailhead
►2	0.05	Right at paved Lighthouse Road
►3	0.2	Straight at junction with single-track
►4	0.25	First spur trail junction
►5	0.5	Second spur trail junction
►6	0.7	Stone cross
►7	0.75	Merge with gravel road
►8	0.9	Left at junction with Lighthouse Road
►9	1.2	Left at junction with single-track trail
►10	1.4	End at trailhead

Agate Beach & Rim Trails

Overlooked by many visitors heading to the renowned redwood groves in the nearby parks, lovely Patrick's Point State Park offers some of the most picturesque coastal scenery on the north coast. Jutting into the Pacific, the park's 200-foot-tall bluffs offer sublime ocean views peppered with scenic sea-stacks and offshore rocks, at least when the persistent fog takes a day off.

The park offers several trails suitable for short hikes with diverse attributes. The 0.3-mile Agate Beach Trail descends 200 feet to a picturesque stretch of beach known for sweeping coastline views and beachcombing. The Rim Trail is incredibly scenic, with short laterals to viewpoints from the top of Wedding Rock, Patrick's Point, Rocky Point, and Palmer's Point—great locations for observing the diverse wildlife. Tidepooling enthusiasts should enjoy Mussel Rocks, Rocky Point, and Cannonball Beach.

Best Time

The park is open all year. Fogless days offer the best coastline views; they can occur at any time of the year but are most common in spring and fall.

Finding the Trail

Drive on US 101 to the second Patrick's Point Drive exit, 5 miles north of Trinidad. Follow Patrick's Point Drive southwest for 0.5 mile to the entrance into Patrick's Point State Park. Continue past the entrance station to a junction between the Park Entrance Road and Wedding Rock Road. For the

TRAIL USE
Dayhiking, Running

LENGTH & TIME
Agate Beach Trail:
0.6 mile, 1–2 hours
Rim Trail:
4.2 miles, 2–4 hours

VERTICAL FEET
Agate Beach Trail:
+175'/-175'
Rim Trail:
+1,000'/-1,000'

DIFFICULTY
- 1 2 **3** 4 5 +

TRAIL TYPE
Out & Back

START & FINISH
Agate Beach Trail:
N41° 08.923'
W124° 08.923'
Rim Trail:
N41° 08.441'
W124° 09.483'

FEATURES
Beach
Views
Wildlife
Historic Interest

FACILITIES
Campgrounds
Picnic Areas
Restrooms
Visitor Center
Resort Town

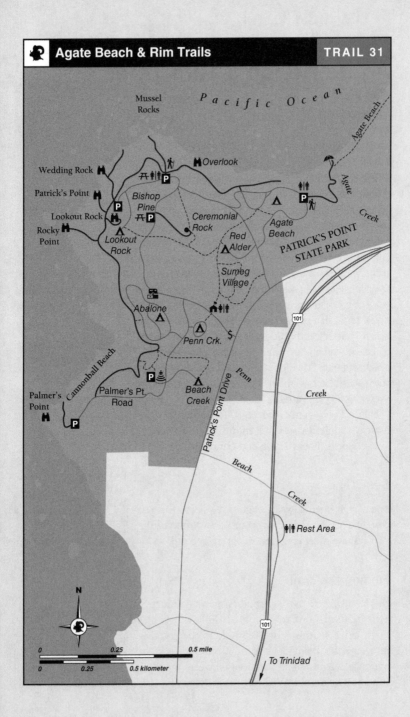

Agate Beach & Rim Trails

TRAIL 31

Mussel Rocks

Pacific Ocean

Agate Beach

Overlook

Wedding Rock

Patrick's Point

Bishop Pine

Lookout Rock

Rocky Point

Lookout Rock

Ceremonial Rock

Agate Beach

Red Alder

PATRICK'S POINT STATE PARK

Sumeg Village

Abalone

Penn Crk.

Cannonball Beach

Palmer's Pt Road

Beach Creek

Palmer's Point

Creek

Penn

Creek

Patrick's Point Drive

101

Beach

Creek

Rest Area

N

0   0.25   0.5 mile

0   0.25   0.5 kilometer

101

To Trinidad

Agate Beach Trail, continue on the Park Entrance Road on the right, and head past the campground to the parking lot.

To reach the Mussel Rocks Trailhead, drive north from the junction on Wedding Rock Road a short distance to the parking lot on the right-hand side.

The park has three campgrounds: Penn Creek, Abalone, and Agate Beach. There are also two group campgrounds: Beach Creek and Red Alder.

Trail Descriptions

Agate Beach Trail

From the parking lot, ▶1 follow a wide, gravel path on a descent across the hillside to the first switchback. Park benches are placed periodically alongside the trail, most often used for the stiff climb on the return trip. Wind downhill to a set of stairs and then across Agate Creek. Continue downhill a short distance to the beach. ▶2

Beach

The dark sand beach stretches north for miles, providing a nearly endless opportunity for extended strolls or beachcombing for agates and driftwood. The coastline to the south is impassable due to the rocky cliffs. After thoroughly enjoying the beach, retrace your steps back uphill to the parking lot. ▶3

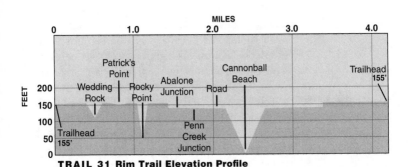

TRAIL 31 Rim Trail Elevation Profile

Rim Trail

Rim Trail hikers used to be able to cobble together a loop through the park but, due to washouts and the abandonment of other sections of trail, a hike along it must now be done as an out-and-back affair. Leaving the Mussel Rocks Trailhead, you drop down some stairs and immediately reach a four-way junction with the Rim Trail. ▶1 By continuing ahead on a sometimes steep, 0.2-mile path, you could access the mussel-covered rocks below.

Turn left (west) at the junction, and follow the Rim Trail around a picnic area, ignoring a little-used lateral heading back to the road. Reach a junction ▶2 with the Wedding Rock Trail, 0.2 mile from the Mussel Rock parking lot. The Wedding Rock parking lot to the left is oftentimes full, as the trail is perhaps the park's most popular path.

To visit Wedding Rock, turn right at the junction, and make a short descent onto a narrow ridge connecting the rock to the mainland. At the near end, the Beach Trail angles northeast down to the ocean's edge. At the far end, the trail stiffly ascends some stone stairs to viewing areas on top of Wedding Rock. Without fog, the coastline views are spectacular. In the 1930s, the park's caretaker, Viggo Anderson, built this trail and married his wife on the ancient sea-stack, a ritual repeated nowadays about 50 times a year. Retrace your steps back to the Rim Trail junction. ▶2

Views

Proceed southwest from the Wedding Rock junction, and continue 0.1 mile on the Rim Trail to the unmarked junction with the Patrick's Point Overlook Trail on the right. ▶3 To visit the overlook, turn down this trail, and follow a nearly level course through thick coastal vegetation to the top of Patrick's Point and a fine view of Wedding Rock to the north, Rocky Point to the south, and the surf crashing against a host of smaller sea-stacks and offshore rocks. After you have enjoyed the view, retrace your steps back to the junction. ▶3

Views

Fog-filtered sunlight *in Patrick's Point State Park*

Head south from the Patrick's Point junction, passing by the Lookout Rock Trail (a short climb, but vegetation obscures the view) on the left after a short distance and continue to a bridge over Ickie Ughie Creek. Walk through thick vegetation on the way to the unmarked junction ►4 with the lateral to Rocky Point on the right.

To visit the point, turn right and follow the trail through lush vegetation before a stiff descent leads across coastal prairie to aptly named Rocky Point.

Views

Wildlife

The area offers excellent views north to Wedding Rock and south to Palmer's Point. This is a great spot for tidepooling during low tide and also for watching harbor seals and a host of seabirds nearby. Return to the Rim Trail junction. ►5

Back on the Rim Trail, you contour south through a coastal forest of alders and cypress with limited views. Ignore a second trail heading toward Lookout Rock on the left and continue ahead. Reach a spot where the trail abruptly drops about 15 feet, requiring you to clamber down steeply (enough of an obstacle to deter the average tourist). The trail continues past a well-marked junction with a lateral to Abalone Campground.

Continuing ahead on the Rim Trail, you pass the western fringe of the campground, and then bend east briefly at the south end to a bridge over a seasonal swale. Shortly beyond, the trail comes alongside Penn Creek and soon passes by a second path on the left to the campground. Turning right, you cross a stout wood bridge over Penn Creek, and immediately reach a four-way junction ►6 with the Penn Creek Trail (which heads upstream before arcing south to Beach Creek Group Campground), and a trail ahead to the Campfire Center.

Turn right, remaining on the Rim Trail, and shortly come to a fenced viewpoint. From there, the trail bends back into the forest and passes by another trail on the left to the Campfire Center. Soon you cross a pair of bridges over Beach Creek and proceed through a forest of Bishop pine, Sitka spruce, and shore pine to paved Palmer's Point Road. ▶7

Turn right and follow the road southwest to the day-use parking lot at the end. Here the Palmer's Point Beach Trail begins descending toward the ocean. Follow this trail down to a junction, where the left-hand trail heads west toward a fenced viewpoint atop Palmer's Point. The right-hand path continues to descend via some stairs to rocky Cannonball Beach, ▶8 another fine spot for tide-pooling at low tide.

After enjoying the fine scenery at Cannonball Beach, retrace your steps 2.4 miles to the Mussel Rocks Trailhead parking area. ▶9

Views

Wildlife

⊀ MILESTONES

AGATE BEACH TRAIL

▶1   0.0   Start at Agate Beach Trailhead

▶2   0.3   Agate Beach

▶3   0.6   Return to trailhead

RIM TRAIL

▶1   0.0   Start at Mussel Rocks trailhead and left at Rim Trail junction

▶2   0.2   Wedding Rock junction

▶3   0.7   Patrick's Point junction

▶4   1.0   Junction with spur to Rocky Point

▶5   1.2   Right to continue on Rim Trail

▶6   1.75   Right at Penn Creek junction

▶7   2.05   Right at Palmer's Point Road

▶8   2.4   Cannonball Beach

▶9   4.2   Return to trailhead

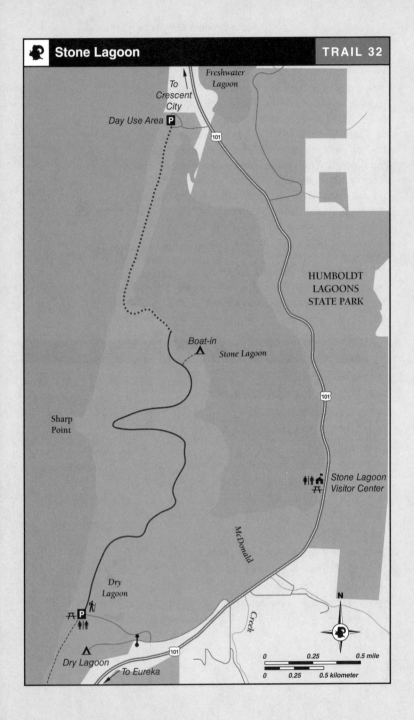

Freshwater Lagoon

To
Crescent
City

Day Use Area **P**

101

HUMBOLDT
LAGOONS
STATE PARK

Boat-in
Stone Lagoon

101

Sharp
Point

Stone Lagoon
Visitor Center

McDonald

Dry
Lagoon

Creek

P

N

Dry Lagoon

101

To Eureka

| 0 | 0.25 | 0.5 mile |
| 0 | 0.25 | 0.5 kilometer |

Stone Lagoon

Redwood National Park & Vicinity's Humboldt Lagoons State Park encompasses the largest lagoon system in the United States. This hike utilizes two stretches of beach hiking and an intervening forested section on the Sharp Point Trail to make a fine 8-mile, out-and-back hike offering stunning ocean and coastal forest scenery. Wildflower enthusiasts should find plenty to enjoy along the way as well. If a shuttle can be arranged, you can turn this trip into a 4-mile, one-way hike.

Best Time

Because winter rains can make this trail a muddy mess and may make the crossing of the narrow spit between Stone Lagoon and the ocean impossible, spring through fall are generally a more appealing time. Fog is common in this area during the summer and oftentimes in the morning at other times of the year. Spring to early summer offers the additional highlight of a fine wildflower display.

Finding the Trail

Leaving US 101 about 13 miles north of Trinidad, drive west on the access road toward Dry Lagoon Environmental Campground. Heading northbound on 101, this junction occurs where the four-lane highway narrows to two lanes (just before the Redwood Trails RV Campground on the left). Follow the access road to the campground entrance and veer right, continuing to the parking area at the end of the road near the beach.

TRAIL USE
Dayhiking, Running

LENGTH & TIME
8.0 miles, 4-6 hours

VERTICAL FEET
+250'/-250'

DIFFICULTY
- 1 **2** 3 4 5 +

TRAIL TYPE
Out & Back

START & FINISH
N41° 13.352'
W124° 06.490'
Shuttle trailhead:
N41° 15.496'
W124° 05.939'

FEATURES
Beach
Lake
Views
Wildflowers

FACILITIES
Restrooms
Picnic Area

If you're taking advantage of the shuttle option, the access road to the north trailhead is another 2.8 miles northbound on US 101.

First-come, first-served Big Lagoon County Park is on the southwest shore. Dry Lagoon Walk-In Campground offers six primitive, first-come, first-served sites (register at Patrick's Point State Park to get the lock combination). Stone Lagoon Boat-In Campground also has six primitive, first-come, first-served sites.

Trail Description

Leaving the parking area, ►1 you have two options to access the defined tread of the Sharp Point Trail 0.4 mile to the north. Either follow a sandy path that leaves the north side of the parking area near a warning sign heading through the low vegetation above the beach, or walk down to the beach and head north on wet sand toward a mowed section of trail ►2 at the base of the hillside.

Follow the Sharp Point Trail on an ascent up the hillside through lush coastal vegetation, including cow parsnip, daisies, and columbine, in the spring and early summer. Fine coastal views accompany the first stretch of trail until you enter the cover of alder and Sitka spruce forest. Continue climbing through dense foliage, and then traverse around the

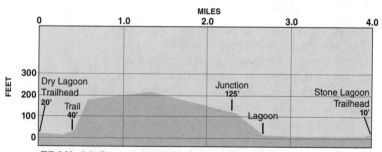

TRAIL 32 Stone Lagoon Trail Elevation Profile

Beach near Stone Lagoon

406-foot-tall hill southeast of Sharp Point. Farther on, the gently graded traverse angles back to the east and swings around the 375-foot-tall hill northeast of Sharp Point, eventually reaching a junction ▶3 with a lateral headed downhill to the environmental campground near the west shore of Stone Lagoon.

Veer left onto the less-used tread of the trail toward the ocean, which becomes steeper on the way down to the shore of Stone Lagoon. ▶4 The trail ends at the lagoon, but the way to the beach is a straight-forward cross-country amble along the shoreline.

Head north ►5 on the beach, and walk along the narrow spit separating Stone Lagoon from the ocean, reaching the Stone Lagoon Day Use Parking Area ►6 after a mile. If you didn't make shuttle arrangements, retrace your steps to the Dry Lagoon Parking Area. ►7

🚶 MILESTONES

►1	0.0	Start at Dry Lagoon Parking Area
►2	0.4	Start of Sharp Point Trail
►3	2.3	Left at junction to environmental campground
►4	2.7	Stone Lagoon and end of Sharp Point Trail
►5	2.9	Right at beach
►6	4.0	Stone Lagoon Day Use Parking Area (ending trailhead for shuttle)
►7	8.0	Return to Dry Lagoon Parking Area

Redwood Creek Trail

As the only area where dispersed backcountry camping is allowed within Redwood National Park, the Redwood Creek Trail offers the best opportunity for backpacking (the loops of the Orick Horse Trail network are better suited for equestrians). While logging affected the southwestern part of the drainage, an 8,000-acre tract on the east side represents one of the largest stands of continuous old-growth forest in the redwood parks. Nonetheless, there aren't too many huge redwoods right along the trail, at least until the Tall Trees Grove near the end, where the former number one largest coast redwood and other stately monarchs fill an alluvial flat next to the creek. The 1.3-mile Tall Trees Trail (see Trail 35) provides visitor access to this grove, which diminishes the likelihood of observing the giants in complete solitude. However, there should be fewer people here than in the groves along US 101.

The out-and-back distance of more than 16 miles will be a tad long for many dayhikers, although the trail gains less than 450 vertical feet on the way to the Tall Trees Grove. A 9.4-mile shuttle option is possible by ending at the Tall Trees Grove Trailhead but requires obtaining one of the 50 daily permits issued at the Thomas H. Kuchel Visitor Center (factor in an additional 675-foot climb from the grove to that trailhead).

Best Time

The summer season is the usual time to hike this trail, when the Park Service has installed the two seasonal bridges over Redwood Creek at 1.6 miles and 7.5

TRAIL USE
Dayhiking, Backpacking, Running

LENGTH & TIME
16.4 miles, 8–10 hours

VERTICAL FEET
+815'/-815'

DIFFICULTY
- 1 2 **3** 4 5 +

TRAIL TYPE
Out & Back

START & FINISH
N41° 17.931'
W124° 01.985'

FEATURES
Redwoods
Stream
Backcountry Camping

FACILITIES
Restrooms

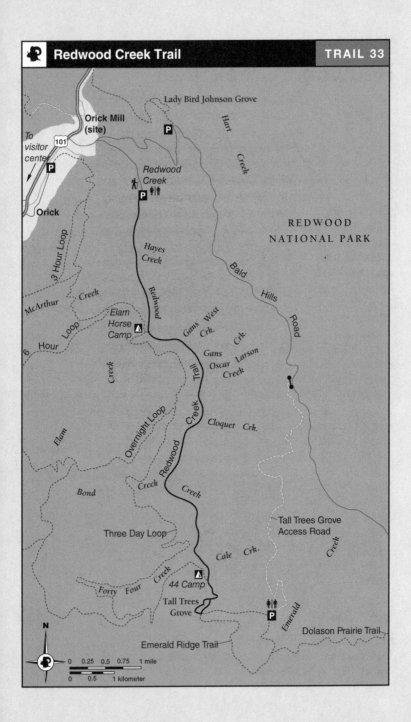

Lady Bird Johnson Grove

Orick Mill (site)

To visitor center

Orick

Redwood Creek

REDWOOD NATIONAL PARK

Hart Creek

Hayes Creek

3 Hour Loop

McArthur Creek

6 Hour Loop

Elam Horse Camp

Redwood Trail

Bald Hills Road

Gans West Crk.

Gans Crk.

Oscar Larson Creek

Creek

Overnight Loop

Redwood Creek

Cloquet Crk.

Elam

Bond Creek

Creek

Three Day Loop

Cale Crk.

Tall Trees Grove Access Road

Creek

Forty Four Creek

44 Camp

Tall Trees Grove

Emerald

Emerald Ridge Trail

Dolason Prairie Trail

N

0 0.25 0.5 0.75 1 mile

0 0.5 1 kilometer

miles. During the winter and spring, the creek runs swift and deep and oftentimes floods the trail, and the gravel bars used for campsites are underwater. Perhaps the best time is early autumn, after the bridges have been removed and before the rainy season begins, when the creek is shallow enough to ford easily and most of the tourists are long gone.

Finding the Trail

Drive north from the Thomas H. Kuchel Visitor Center (where you can get a camping permit) on US 101 for 4 miles, passing through the town of Orick to a right-hand turn onto Bald Hills Road. Proceed for 0.4 mile past the former site of the Orick Mill on the left to a right-hand turn signed for the Redwood Creek Trailhead. Continue 0.5 mile to the paved parking lot, which has a vault toilet.

The nearest developed campground is Elk Prairie in Prairie Creek Redwoods State Park.

Trail Description

A wood bridge over a seasonal swale leads away from the parking lot ►1 and onto an old logging road, the Redwood Creek Trail. Well-graded tread passes through a forest composed of Douglas firs,

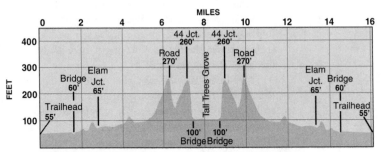

TRAIL 33 Redwood Creek Trail Elevation Profile

Seasonal Bridge *over Redwood Creek*

bigleaf maples, red alders, and some widely scattered redwoods. Its open nature allows a prolific patch of blackberry brambles to flourish alongside the trail. Late-spring visitors will have the bonus of wildflowers, including bleeding hearts, milkmaids, and giant trillium. Due to the thick vegetation, the creek mostly remains out of sight until you cross a footbridge over Gans West Creek, pass a park bench, and then come to a seasonal bridge, ▶2 1.6 miles from the trailhead. This bridge and the one farther upstream are usually in place from early June to late September, but they seem somewhat unnecessary when the shin-deep, slow-moving creek would be easily forded. Here the wide, rocky channel hints at the raging torrent Redwood Creek must be during winter and early spring. Above the banks, towering redwoods dwarf the lesser trees of the forest.

The tread narrows on the opposite side of Redwood Creek and passes through thick forest and dense trailside foliage, soon coming to a steel bridge spanning McArthur Creek. The trail sticks fairly close to Redwood Creek, allowing for filtered views of it and straightforward access to its gravel

Stream

bars. A short, steep section leads past a couple of interesting redwoods: a fire-hollowed tree and a four-trunked specimen. The trail then shifts higher above the creek, crossing several spring-fed rivulets and passing a sawed redwood stump with an old sign dating it as at least 750 years old. Farther on, just before a steel bridge, you reach a junction ▶3 with the Elam Creek Trail to Elam Horse Camp, 2.6 miles from the trailhead.

Cross Elam Creek and head upstream on the Redwood Creek Trail, where intermittent use trails cut through the edge of the forest and shortly lead to the creek. The forest scenery becomes redundant for a while, at least until you pass below a massive redwood that has fallen across the trail and then an upended specimen's roots, which provide different perspectives on these trees' massive size. Between mileposts 4 and 5, you cross several bridges over unnamed creeks and then begin to see some redwood stumps on the hillside above the trail, a stark reminder of the logging once practiced in this drainage.

Where the creek bends sharply east, you cross Bond Creek on a long, wood-rail bridge. Just past the bridge, a use trail heads sharply downhill toward the banks of Redwood Creek; camping is allowed from here to within a quarter mile of the Tall Trees Grove. Continuing, several short wood bridges lead across side streams on the way past milepost 6 and then 0.3 mile farther to a closed logging road, ▶4 3.7 miles from the Elam Trail junction.

After another 0.3 mile, you cross a bridge above picturesque, fern-lined Forty Four Creek and then continue high above Redwood Creek. Much of the route is through a dense alder thicket until it reenters more typical forest cover on the way to a junction ▶5 with the 44 Creek Loop Spur to 44 Camp.

From the junction, the trail drops 150 feet to the second seasonal bridge across Redwood Creek ▶6 and then heads through streamside foliage to an alluvial flat harboring the Tall Trees Grove and a junction ►7 with the loop through the grove, 0.6 mile from the 44 Creek Spur junction.

Turn left to make a clockwise journey through the grove, which saves the most impressive redwoods for the climax of the circuit. Shoulder-high ferns line the trail in places and hazelnut, bigleaf maples, California laurel, and red alders intermix with the tall trees. Halfway around the loop, you reach a junction ►8 with the Tall Trees Trail, which climbs about 650 feet in 1.3 miles to the parking lot (see Trail 35 for details).

🌲 **Redwoods**

Not far from the junction is the Howard Libbey Tree, which was named for the president of the Arcata Lumber Company, former owners of the land. The tree was declared the tallest living thing by a 1963 National Geographic Survey and along with the grove was influential in the eventual designation of Redwood National Park five years later. Continue to the Tall Trees junction ►9 at the close of the loop, and then retrace your steps back to the Redwood Creek Trailhead. ►10

🚶	MILESTONES	
►1	0.0	Start from Redwood Creek Trailhead
►2	1.6	Redwood Creek Bridge
►3	2.6	Straight at Elam Creek Trail
►4	6.3	Straight at closed logging road
►5	7.2	Veer left at 44 Creek Loop spur junction
►6	7.4	Redwood Creek Bridge
►7	7.6	Left at Tall Trees Loop junction
►8	7.9	Right at Tall Trees Trail junction
►9	8.2	Tall Trees Loop junction
►10	16.4	Return to Redwood Creek Trailhead

Lady Bird Johnson Grove

A knoll at the north end of Bald Hills Ridge harboring an old-growth upland redwood forest was chosen as the site for the dedication of Redwood National Park in 1969. Among the dignitaries in attendance were President Richard M. Nixon, Governor Ronald Reagan, and Lady Bird Johnson, wife of former President Lyndon Baines Johnson, who signed the bill creating the park on October 2, 1968. Nowadays, visitors can stroll along a nearly level loop through an impressive stand of tall trees. A color brochure provides interesting tidbits of botanical and historical information. Park benches offer fine places from which to relax and enjoy the forest.

TRAIL USE
Dayhiking, Handicapped Access, Child-Friendly

LENGTH & TIME
1.4 miles, 1–2 hours

VERTICAL FEET
Nominal

DIFFICULTY
- **1** 2 3 4 5 +

TRAIL TYPE
Semiloop

START & FINISH
N41° 18.223'
W124° 01.125'

FEATURES
Redwoods
Historic Interest

FACILITIES
Restrooms

Best Time

As with many of the trails within Redwood National Park, the Lady Bird Johnson Grove Trail is open all year. Summer is the busiest season, making spring and autumn fine times for a less crowded visit. Late spring provides the added bonus of blooming rhododendrons and azaleas, while bigleaf and vine maples provide autumn color. Oftentimes, when the lower valleys are shrouded in fog, the grove is at a high enough elevation (1,270 feet) to be in sunshine.

Finding the Trail

From the Thomas H. Kuchel Visitor Center, drive north on US 101 for 4 miles, passing through the town of Orick, to a right-hand turn onto Bald Hills Road. Proceed past the former site of the Orick Mill on the left and a junction with a road to the Redwood

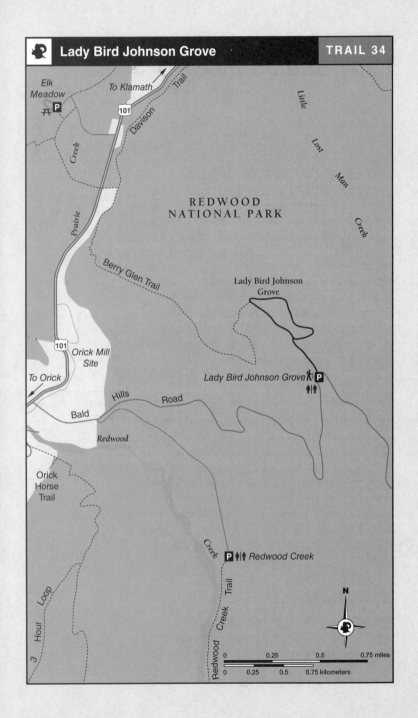

Lady Bird Johnson Grove

Elk Meadow

To Klamath

Davison Trail

101

Creek

REDWOOD
NATIONAL PARK

Little

Lost

Man

Creek

Prairie

Berry Glen Trail

Lady Bird Johnson
Grove

101

Orick Mill
Site

To Orick

Lady Bird Johnson Grove

Hills   Road

Bald

Redwood

Orick
Horse
Trail

Creek

P Redwood Creek

3 Hour Loop

Redwood Creek Trail

N

0   0.25   0.5   0.75 miles

0   0.25   0.5   0.75 kilometers

Creek Trailhead on the right, and continue on Bald Hills Road to a right-hand turn into the parking area (which has a vault toilet), 2.7 miles from US 101, just beyond where the road passes beneath a pedestrian viaduct. The parking lot fills up fast on busy summer days, so get an early start during peak season. The nearest developed campground is Elk Prairie in Prairie Creek Redwoods State Park.

Trail Description

From the west side of the parking area, ▶1 walk across the viaduct over the Bald Hills Road, and soon come to a box containing the trail brochures (with a suggested donation of a dollar in 2012). Follow the wide, gravel path through the lush vegetation common to an upland, old-growth redwood

In the *Lady Bird Johnson Grove*

Redwoods

forest, including a ground cover composed of sword fern and redwood sorrel, shaded by shrubs like evergreen huckleberry, salmonberry, red-flowering currant, azalea, and salal. Deciduous plants higher off the ground include rhododendron and tanoak, while the tips of Douglas fir, grand fir, and western hemlock strain to catch the redwoods forming the canopy. Shortly past post 3, you reach the loop junction. ▸2

Veer left and proceed clockwise around the loop on the wide surface of the old Bald Hills Road, which was replaced by the current road in the 1950s to accommodate an increase in logging traffic. About a quarter of the way around the loop, you reach a small clearing, site of the 1969 dedication of Redwood National Park, marked by a plaque and

 Historic Interest

some wood benches. Beyond the clearing, the trail proceeds to a junction ▸3 with the Berry Glen Trail, which continues along the course of the old road down toward US 101 and the Elk Meadow Day Use Area (see Trail 40).

Your trail bends to the right near the edge of an old clear-cut, leaves the old roadbed behind, and heads back toward the junction. The towering redwoods are more impressive on this side of the ridge. To your left, the terrain drops precipitously toward Little Lost Man Creek 700 feet below. Upon reaching the junction, ▸4 retrace your steps 0.3 mile back to the parking lot. ▸5

🚶 MILESTONES

▸1	0.0	Start at Lady Bird Johnson Grove Trailhead
▸2	0.3	Left at loop junction
▸3	0.6	Right at Berry Glen Trail junction
▸4	1.1	Left at loop junction
▸5	1.4	Return to Lady Bird Johnson Grove Trailhead

Tall Trees Grove

The Tall Trees Grove is one of the premier old-growth redwood groves in the park, harboring (among other distinctive specimens) the 367-foot Howard Libbey Tree, formerly the tallest tree in the world. Located on an alluvial flat alongside Redwood Creek, the grove is a good distance away from US 101, which allows for a serene ambiance in which to admire the big trees. While the peaceful cathedral of the Tall Trees Grove is the main attraction, the banks of Redwood Creek offer fine spots for enjoying a picnic lunch or taking a dip on a hot summer day. A seasonal bridge spans the creek from June to September, connecting the grove to the Redwood Creek Trail.

To minimize human impact, the Park Service limits the number of free daily permits to 50, which includes the combination to the padlock at the beginning of the Tall Trees Access Road and allows motorists to drive to the trailhead. A 0.6-mile loop circles the grove, accessible via a 1.3-mile trail that's all uphill on the return.

TRAIL USE
Dayhiking, Running
LENGTH & TIME
3.2 miles, 2–3 hours
VERTICAL FEET
+675'/-675'
DIFFICULTY
- 1 2 **3** 4 5 +
TRAIL TYPE
Semiloop
START & FINISH
N41° 12.479'
W123° 59.593'

FEATURES
Redwoods
Stream

FACILITIES
Restrooms

Best Time

The Tall Trees Grove Trail can be hiked year-round, although most hikers will want to avoid the area during rainy periods in the winter when the trail and access road are a muddy mess. Most visitors hike this popular trail during the summer, which makes fall and spring attractive times for those seeking solitude and serenity. Rhododendrons bloom in late spring, and an extensive stand of bigleaf maples near Redwood Creek provides autumn color.

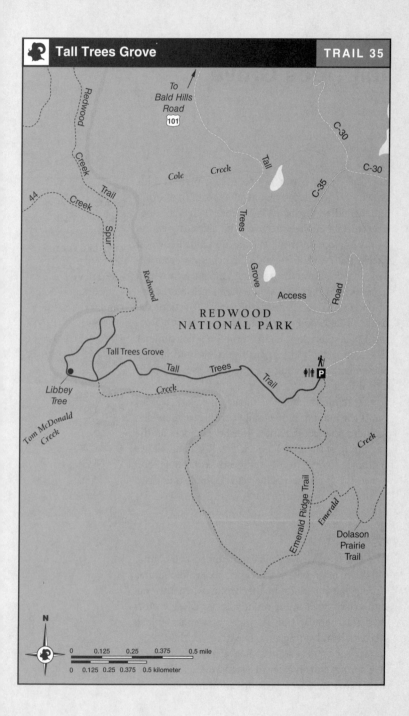

To
Bald Hills
Road
101

Redwood

Creek

Trail

44

Creek

Spur

Redwood

Cole

Creek

Tall

Trees

Grove

Access

C-30

C-30

C-35

Road

REDWOOD
NATIONAL PARK

Tall Trees Grove

Tall   Trees   Trail

Libbey
Tree

Tom McDonald
Creek

Creek

Creek

Emerald Ridge Trail

Emerald

Dolason
Prairie
Trail

N

0   0.125   0.25   0.375   0.5 mile

0   0.125 0.25 0.375   0.5 kilometer

Finding the Trail

The first stop is at the Thomas H. Kuchel Visitor Center in order to obtain a permit and the combination for the locked gate to the Tall Trees Access Road. A maximum of 50 permits are issued each day, so get an early start, especially if you are here during the busy summer season. Drive north from the visitor center on US 101 for 4 miles, passing through the town of Orick, and then turn right onto Bald Hills Road. Proceed past the former site of the Orick Mill on the left and the Redwood Creek Trailhead road on the right, and continue on Bald Hills Road for 7 miles to a right-hand turn onto the Tall Trees Access Road (0.4 mile past Redwood Overlook). Go through the gate (closing it behind you), and follow the dirt access road for 6.1 miles to the parking area and Tall Trees Grove Trailhead, which has a vault toilet.

The nearest developed campground is Elk Prairie in Prairie Creek Redwoods State Park.

Trail Description

From the trailhead, ▶1 the trail drops gently through a shady forest of redwoods and Douglas firs, with a lush understory of tanoaks, chinquapins,

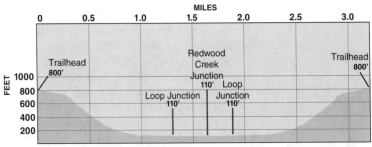

TRAIL 35 Tall Trees Grove Elevation Profile

Old-growth redwood *in the Tall Trees Grove*

rhododendrons, evergreen huckleberry, ceanothus, and ferns. After a short distance, reach the often-overlooked junction with the Emerald Ridge Trail (see Trail 36) on the left. Farther on, the trail starts to descend more steeply, winding past park benches, rest stops for weary tourists on the uphill return. Continuing downhill, you hop over a couple tiny rivulets on the way to an alluvial flat next to Redwood Creek, home of the Tall Trees Grove and the loop junction. ▶2 Nearby, a faint path (the

Redwoods

much-less-used Emerald Ridge Trail) ventures over to Redwood Creek.

Stream

Veer left at the junction, and follow a clockwise route through the Tall Trees Grove, soon encountering the Howard Libbey Tree, named for the former president of the Arcata Lumber Company, previous owner of the grove. A 1963 National Geographic Survey declared this redwood, which is taller than 367 feet, to be the world's tallest tree; it is also known as the National Geographic Society Tree. Unfortunately, the tree has suffered the consequences of popularity. Increased visitation caused trampling and compaction of the surrounding soil, interfering with its roots' ability to absorb enough water; the top 10 feet of the tree withered and finally died in 1991. Subsequently, taller trees have been discovered, with a tree named Hyperion holding the title for tallest at 379.1 feet. The park now keeps the location of such trees secret to help them avoid a fate similar to that of the Libbey Tree.

The gently graded path continues past more tall trees, reaching the junction ▶3 of the Redwood Creek Trail (see Trail 33), 0.3 mile from the loop junction. Veer to the right to remain on the loop, soon passing through a stand of moss-covered bigleaf maples. Farther away from the creek, the trail passes some more tall redwoods on the way to the close of the loop ▶4 near the Libbey Tree. From there, retrace your steps on the 1.3-mile climb back to the trailhead. ▶5

🚶	**MILESTONES**	
▶1	0.0	Start at Tall Trees Grove Trailhead
▶2	1.3	Left at loop junction
▶3	1.6	Right at Redwood Creek Trail junction
▶4	1.9	Left at loop junction
▶5	3.2	Return to trailhead

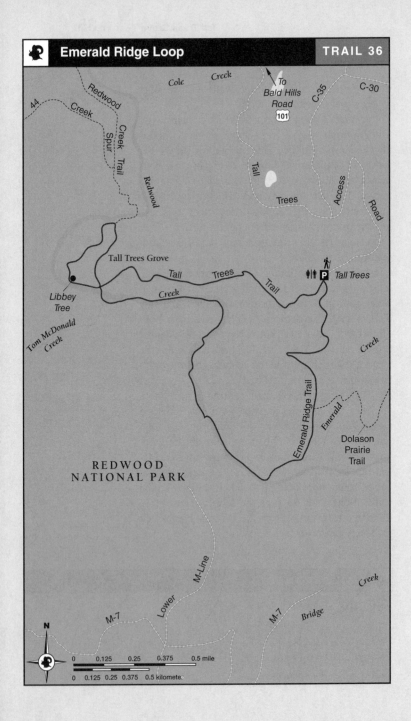

Emerald Ridge Loop

TRAIL 36

Cole Creek

To Bald Hills Road

101

C-35   C-30

Redwood   Creek   Spur   Trail

44   Creek

Redwood

Tall   Trees

Access   Road

Tall Trees Grove

Tall   Trees   Trail

Libbey Tree

Creek

Tall Trees

Tom McDonald Creek

Creek

Emerald Ridge Trail

Emerald

Dolason Prairie Trail

REDWOOD NATIONAL PARK

Lower   M-Line

Creek

M-7   M-7   Bridge

N

0   0.125   0.25   0.375   0.5 mile

0   0.125   0.25   0.375   0.5 kilomete.

Emerald Ridge Loop

For hikers looking for more of a challenge than the out-and-back, 1.3-mile Tall Trees Grove Trail and who still want to enjoy this magnificent redwood sanctuary, the Emerald Ridge Loop should fill the bill quite nicely. Almost immediately, the route veers away from the much more popular Tall Trees Grove Trail. After a solitude-filled descent on the Emerald Ridge Trail, the route follows Redwood Creek downstream via gravel bars and several fords, enters the Tall Trees Grove, and finally climbs back up to the trailhead via the Tall Trees Grove Trail. The 5-mile circuit samples several different habitats, including shady upland redwood forest below the trailheads, a bright and sunny riparian zone along Redwood Creek, and stately old-growth lowland redwoods in the Tall Trees Grove.

Best Time

The Emerald Ridge Loop should only be attempted when stream levels allow hikers to safely ford

TRAIL USE
Dayhiking, Running

LENGTH & TIME
5.2 miles, 3–5 hours

VERTICAL FEET
+700'/-700'

DIFFICULTY
- 1 2 3 **4** 5 +

TRAIL TYPE
Loop

START & FINISH
N41° 12.479'
W123° 59.593'

FEATURES
Redwoods
Wildflowers
Stream
Swimming

FACILITIES
Restrooms

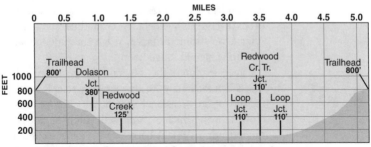

TRAIL 36 Emerald Ridge Loop Elevation Profile

Redwood Creek, which is generally between May and October.

Finding the Trail

The first stop is at the Thomas H. Kuchel Visitor Center in order to obtain a permit and the combination for the locked gate to the Tall Trees Access Road. A maximum of 50 permits are issued each day, so get an early start, especially if you are here during the busy summer season.

Drive north from the visitor center on US 101 for 4 miles, passing through the town of Orick, and then turn right onto Bald Hills Road. Proceed past the former site of the Orick Mill on the left and the Redwood Creek Trailhead road on the right, and continue on Bald Hills Road for 7 miles to a right-hand turn onto the Tall Trees Access Road (0.4 mile past Redwood Overlook). Go through the gate (closing it behind you), and follow the dirt access road for 6.1 miles to the parking area and Tall Trees Grove Trailhead, which has a vault toilet.

The nearest developed campground is Elk Prairie in Prairie Creek Redwoods State Park.

Trail Description

From the trailhead, ▶1 the trail drops gently through a shady forest of redwoods and Douglas firs, with a lush understory of tanoaks, chinquapins, rhododendrons, evergreen huckleberry, ceanothus, and ferns. After a very short distance, reach the junction ▶2 with the Emerald Ridge Loop.

Veer left onto the Emerald Ridge Loop and descend moderately to moderately steeply with the aid of an occasional switchback through old-growth forest, which is composed mainly of tanoak, rhododendron, huckleberry, and widely scattered redwoods. After a 0.9-mile descent, reach a junction

with the Dolason Prairie Trail. ►3 Proceed ahead on
the right-hand trail, and continue dropping toward
the bottom of the canyon through a slightly darker
forest, reaching the north bank of Redwood Creek
►4 after 0.4 mile.

Stream

Turning right, you begin the journey down the
wide, gravel channel of Redwood Creek. Unless
a blanket of fog hangs over the stream, the bright
and sunny canyon should contrast sharply with
the dark and shady forest. The going may be slow,
as you negotiate the gravel streambed and ford the
creek a half dozen times. Not far from where you
left the trail is a fine swimming hole, well suited for
a refreshing dip on a hot summer day. After following the winding creek for 1.5 miles, the tops of the
Tall Trees Grove's mighty redwoods come into view,
heralding the approach to the last ford of the creek.
Keep on the lookout for an orange marker signaling
the short lateral that leads from the creek to the Tall
Trees Grove Loop, ►5 1.7 miles from the Emerald
Ridge Loop.

Swimming

Unless you've already visited the Tall Trees
Grove and have no desire for a repeat performance,
bend left at the loop junction and follow a clockwise
route through the grove, soon encountering the
Howard Libbey Tree, named for the former president of the Arcata Lumber Company, the previous
landowner. A 1963 National Geographic Survey
declared this redwood, which is taller than 367 feet,
to be the world's tallest tree; it is also known as the
National Geographic Society Tree. Unfortunately,
the tree has suffered the consequences of popularity.
Increased visitation caused trampling and compaction of the surrounding soil, interfering with its
roots' ability to absorb enough water; the top 10
feet of the tree withered and finally died in 1991.
Subsequently, taller trees have been discovered,
with a tree named Hyperion holding the title for tallest at 379.1 feet. The park now keeps the location of

Redwoods

Emerald Creek Bridge

such trees secret to help them avoid a fate similar to that of the Libbey Tree.

The gently graded path continues past more tall trees, reaching the junction ▶6 of the Redwood Creek Trail (see Trail 33), 0.3 mile from the loop junction. Veer to the right to remain on the loop, soon passing through a stand of moss-covered big-leaf maples. Farther away from the creek, the trail passes some more tall redwoods on the way to the close of the loop ▶7 near the Libbey Tree.

Now you must regain all the elevation you've lost, as the trail makes a stiff, winding climb through shady forest up toward the Tall Trees Grove Trailhead. The grade eases just before you reach the Emerald Ridge junction. ▶8 From there, retrace your steps the short distance to the parking area. ▶9

🚶	**MILESTONES**	
▶1	0.0	Start at Tall Trees Grove Trailhead
▶2	0.05	Left at Emerald Ridge Loop junction
▶3	0.9	Right at Dolason Prairie Trail junction
▶4	1.3	Right at Redwood Creek
▶5	3.2	Left at Tall Trees Grove Loop
▶6	3.5	Right at Redwood Creek Trail junction
▶7	3.8	Left at Tall Trees Grove Loop
▶8	5.15	Straight at Emerald Ridge Loop junction
▶9	5.2	Return to Tall Trees Grove Trailhead

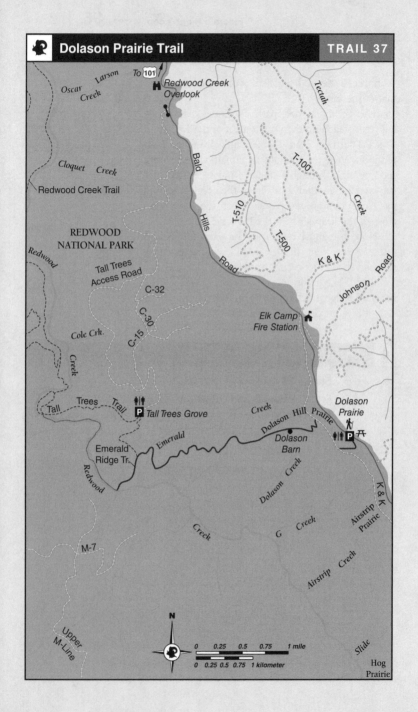

To 101

Redwood Creek
Overlook

Larson

Oscar
Creek

Tectah

Cloquet Creek

Redwood Creek Trail

T-100

Bald

T-510

Creek

REDWOOD
NATIONAL PARK

Hills

T-500

K & K

Redwood

Tall Trees
Access Road

C-32

Road

Johnson

Road

Cole Crk.

C-30

C-15

Creek

Elk Camp
Fire Station

Dolason
Prairie

Trees

Trail

Tall

Creek

Tall Trees Grove

Emerald

Dolason Hill Prairie

Dolason
Barn

Emerald
Ridge Tr.

Redwood

Dolason Creek

K & K

Creek

G Creek

Airstrip
Prairie

M-7

Airstrip Creek

N

Upper
M-Line

Slide

Hog
Prairie

0   0.25   0.5   0.75   1 mile

0   0.25 0.5 0.75 1 kilometer

Dolason Prairie Trail

Aside from not reaching the coastline, the Dolason Prairie Trail offers the most comprehensive example of the Redwood National Park ecosystem. The trail begins at 2,400 feet near the spine of the Bald Hills, a lengthy ridge carpeted mostly with grass-covered prairie, offering sweeping views of the Redwood Creek Watershed. Red-tailed hawks patrol the skies, and coyotes wander the prairie itself, which sheep once grazed. You may see elk feeding on the lush grasses in spring and early summer and hear rutting males bugling in autumn. Intermixed with the prairie are groves of Douglas firs and oaks. Below the prairie, you descend through a bright, upland redwood forest and then a darker, lowland redwood forest, before reaching the usually sunny corridor of Redwood Creek.

Hikers uninterested in a trip with a nearly 5-mile, 2,500-foot climb back to the Dolason Prairie Trailhead can arrange for a shuttle at the Tall Trees Grove Trailhead, or start there and reverse the description from the Emerald Ridge junction.

TRAIL USE
Dayhiking, Running

LENGTH & TIME
10.4 miles, 5–7 hours

VERTICAL FEET
+2,500'/-2,500'

DIFFICULTY
- 1 2 **3** 4 5 +

TRAIL TYPE
Out & Back

START & FINISH
41° 12.367'N, 123° 57.283'W

FEATURES
Stream
Wildflowers
Views
Historic Interest

FACILITIES
Picnic Area
Restrooms

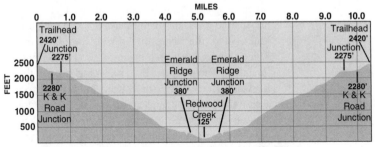

TRAIL 37 Dolason Prairie Trail Elevation Profile

Best Time

This hike can be done at any time of the year, except in the winter when the Bald Hills are occasionally covered with snow. Spring offers vibrantly colored wildflowers, but it is also when ticks are most common. Summers up on the exposed Bald Hills can be hot, and views of the lower valleys are often obstructed by fog. Autumn, prior to the rainy season, usually offers mild and clear weather.

Finding the Trail

From the Thomas H. Kuchel Visitor Center, drive north on US 101 for 4 miles, passing through the town of Orick, and then turn right onto Bald Hills Road. Proceed past the former site of the Orick Mill (at 0.3 mile), the turnoff to the Redwood Creek Trailhead (at 0.4 mile), the Lady Bird Johnson Grove parking lot (at 2.7 miles), and the Tall Trees Access Road (at 7 miles) on the way to a right-hand turn into the parking area, 11.3 miles from US 101. The parking area has a vault toilet and a couple of picnic tables. The nearest developed campground is Elk Prairie in Prairie Creek Redwoods State Park.

Trail Description

The trail leaves the parking area, ▶1 crosses a strip of open, grass-covered prairie, enters a grove of fire-scarred trees, and then breaks out into the open again. Soon, the route merges with the old K and K logging road ▶2 and makes a level, 0.35-mile traverse, complemented by a sweeping vista of the Redwood Creek Watershed. Keen eyes will detect a scar from a massive clear-cut on the far side of the canyon, a scene that would have been much more widespread without the eventual protection afforded this area by its national park status.

 Views

The historic Dolason Barn

Just before the road enters the trees, single-track trail ▶3 heads downhill into a mixed forest of Douglas firs, California bays, and tanoaks, crossing a couple of small streams shaded by bigleaf maples. Eventually the path breaks out onto grass-covered prairie again, where spring visitors will be treated to splashes of color from a variety of wildflowers, including checker lily, bush lupine, and baby blue eyes. Later in the season, California poppies, red maids, and harvest brodiaea grace the slopes. By midsummer, most of the flowers have faded and the grasses have dried, taking on the characteristic hue of the Golden State.

Wildflowers

The old Dolason Barn, on the National Register of Historic Places, sits in the middle of this waist-high-grass field. The former sheep barn was built in 1914 and named for 1860s rancher James Donaldson. (The name has become corrupted over time, resulting in the area's current moniker of "Dolason.") Signs next to the trail on the uphill and downhill sides of the barn provide a bit of historical insight. The old barn backdropped by the watershed is one of the park's many picture-postcard scenes.

Historic Interest

Beyond the barn, continue downslope on a mild to moderate grade, eventually coming under the shade of a forest of gray-barked Douglas firs and grand firs, where the trail starts to descend more steeply. After a while, you emerge from the trees once more for one last opportunity to enjoy the open prairie and sweeping views of Redwood Canyon. Beyond this last clearing, the trail enters an upland redwood forest, where the trees with the red bark stand much taller than their neighboring western hemlocks. The initially sparse ground cover becomes lusher as you descend, with ferns and then redwood sorrel lining the winding path.

 Views

After several switchbacks, the trail makes a descending traverse into the Emerald Creek drainage and eventually reaches a bridge across the stream. A quarter-mile climb leads to a junction ▶4 with the Emerald Ridge Trail, 4.5 miles from the trailhead. (If you made shuttle arrangements, turn right at this junction and go 0.9 mile to the Tall Trees Grove Trailhead).

Stream

Turn left and drop toward the bottom of Redwood Canyon through a slightly darker forest, reaching the north bank of usually bright and sunny Redwood Creek ▶5 after 0.4 mile. Once you've thoroughly enjoyed the creek, the hard work is all before you on the 4.9-mile, 2,500-foot climb back to the trailhead. ▶6

MILESTONES

▶1	0.0	Start at Dolason Prairie Trailhead
▶2	0.4	Right at road junction
▶3	0.7	Left at single-track trail junction
▶4	4.8	Left at Emerald Ridge junction
▶5	5.2	Redwood Creek
▶6	10.4	End at Dolason Prairie Trailhead

Lyons Ranch Loop

When fog drapes the lowlands, the 2,000-foot higher Bald Hills offer a reasonable hope of leaving the gloom behind in exchange for clear and sunny skies. The Lyons Ranch Trail follows the course of old roads back into history, when three generations of the Lyons family raised sheep on broad patches of lush prairie grasses. A less than 2-mile hike leads to Home Place, where the main Lyons home once stood. Only a barn and a couple of bunkhouses remain, along with a sheep shed a couple of miles away. History is not the only draw here, as widespread views of the Redwood Canyon Watershed and surrounding terrain provide stunning scenery. About as far away as you could get from the major tourists centers of the park, the Lyons Ranch Loop has a decidedly remote feel.

Best Time

This hike can be done at any time of the year, except in the winter when the Bald Hills are occasionally covered with snow. Spring offers vibrantly colored wildflowers, but it is also when ticks are most common. Summers up on the exposed Bald Hills can be hot, and views of the lower valleys are often obstructed by fog. Autumn, before the rainy season begins, usually offers mild and clear weather.

Finding the Trail

From the Thomas H. Kuchel Visitor Center, drive north on US 101 for 4 miles, passing through the town of Orick, and then turn right onto Bald Hills

TRAIL USE
Dayhiking, Running
LENGTH & TIME
4.5 miles, 2–4 hours
VERTICAL FEET
+750'/-750'
DIFFICULTY
- 1 2 **3** 4 5 +
TRAIL TYPE
Semiloop
START & FINISH
N41° 08.358'
W123° 51.603'

FEATURES
Stream
Wildflowers
Views
Historic Interest

FACILITIES
Picnic Area
Restrooms

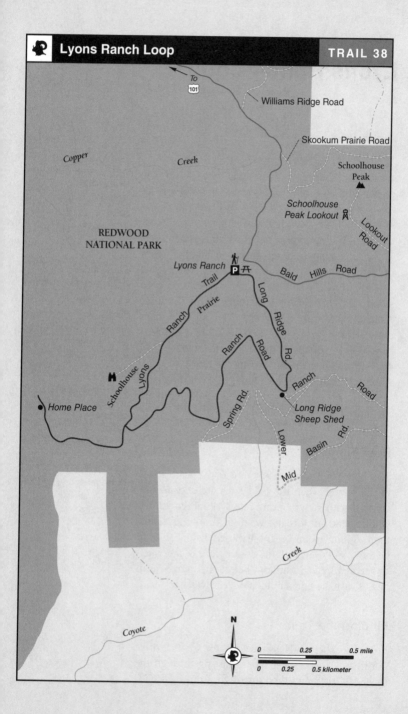

Lyons Ranch Loop

TRAIL 38

To 101

Williams Ridge Road

Skookum Prairie Road

Schoolhouse Peak

Copper *Creek*

Schoolhouse Peak Lookout

Lookout Road

REDWOOD NATIONAL PARK

Lyons Ranch

P

Bald Hills Road

Long Ridge Road

Trail

Ranch

Prairie

Schoolhouse

Lyons

Ranch

Ranch

Road

Rd.

Ranch Road

• *Home Place*

Spring Rd.

Long Ridge Sheep Shed

Lower

Basin Rd.

Mid

Creek

N

Coyote

0   0.25   0.5 mile

0   0.25   0.5 kilometer

Road. Proceed past the former site of the Orick Mill (0.3 mile), the turnoff to the Redwood Creek Trailhead (at 0.4 mile), the Lady Bird Johnson Grove parking lot (at 2.7 miles), the Tall Trees Access Road (at 7 miles), and the Dolason Prairie Trailhead (at 11.3 miles) on the way to a right-hand turn onto the short, dirt road leading to the parking area, 17 miles from US 101.

The nearest developed campground is Elk Prairie in Prairie Creek Redwoods State Park.

Trail Description

Initially, the Lyons Ranch Trail ▸1 follows an old road along a ridge across the open, view-packed, grass-covered slope of Schoolhouse Prairie, immediately reaching a junction with Long Ridge Road ▸2 on the left (the return route). Continuing ahead, the Lyons Ranch Trail eventually curves and starts to drop into an open forest of Oregon oaks, which allows filtered views of the surrounding terrain. Ignore a less-used road on the right leading to a weather station on the ridge, as your road slices down its southeast flank. Past the oaks, where the views fully open up again, you reach a junction ▸3 with Ranch Road on the left, 1.2 miles from the trailhead.

Views

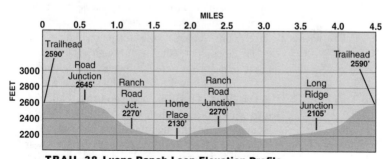

TRAIL 38 Lyons Ranch Loop Elevation Profile

View of *fog-filled Redwood Creek drainage from the old Lyons Ranch Road*

 Historic Interest

The Lyons Ranch Trail continues ahead on an arcing descent around the ridge, reaching Home Place ▶4 after 0.6 mile. Although the area was the center of activity for the Lyons family, only a few signs remain: a barn, two bunkhouses, the shell of an outhouse, an orchard, a cemetery, and some scattered debris. A picnic table on a patch of grass offers a fine lunch spot. After a thorough visit of Home Place, retrace your steps 0.6 mile to Ranch Road. ▶5

If you're pressed for time, the shortest route to the trailhead is back the way you came. Otherwise, turn right onto Ranch Road, and make a slightly rising traverse through viewless oak woodland, descend to a faint road, and then climb back toward the trailhead. On the ascent, you cross a tributary of

Coyote Creek and then work your way over to the old Long Ridge Sheep Shed, set picturesquely in a serene, grassy field. Reach a junction ▶6 with Long Ridge Road near the shed and turn left.

Historic Interest

The Long Ridge Road attacks the prairie-covered slope with a vengeance on a nearly-mile-long, 500-foot ascent. If the possible sighting of soaring red-tailed hawks or some grazing deer don't spur you onward, the views of the watershed and surrounding terrain should inspire you. At the top of the climb, the road merges with the Lyons Ranch Trail close to the trailhead. ▶7

Views

🚶	**MILESTONES**	
▶1	0.0	Start at Lyons Ranch Trailhead
▶2	0.05	Straight at Long Ridge Road
▶3	1.2	Straight at Ranch Road
▶4	1.8	Home Place
▶5	2.4	Right at Ranch Road
▶6	3.7	Left at Long Ridge Road
▶7	4.5	Return to Lyons Ranch Trailhead

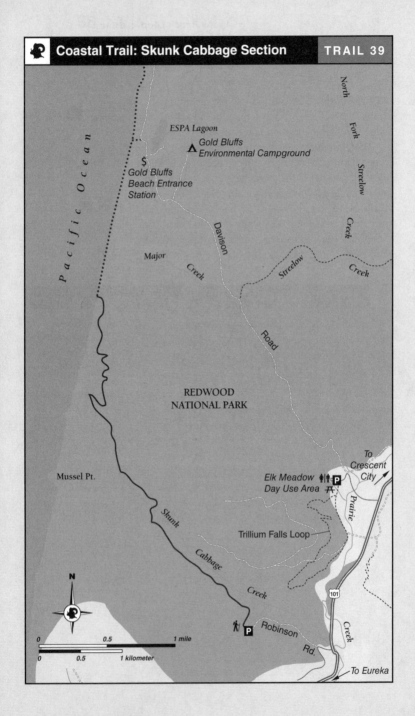

Coastal Trail: Skunk Cabbage Section

TRAIL 39

Pacific Ocean

ESPA Lagoon

Gold Bluffs
Environmental Campground

Gold Bluffs
Beach Entrance
Station

North Fork Streelow Creek

Major Creek

Davison

Streelow Creek

Streelow Creek

Road

REDWOOD
NATIONAL PARK

To
Crescent
City

Elk Meadow
Day Use Area

Mussel Pt.

Trillium Falls Loop

Prairie

Skunk

Cabbage

Creek

101

Robinson
Rd.

N

Creek

To Eureka

0   0.5   1 mile
0   0.5   1 kilometer

Coastal Trail: Skunk Cabbage Section

A seldom-used section of the California Coastal Trail in Redwood National Park beckons hikers to explore a lush coastal forest and a usually deserted strip of sandy beach. The first part is a pleasant stroll through lush forest, highlighted in spring and early summer by a profusion of blooming skunk cabbage. Beyond, the trail climbs stiffly up a coastal bluff and then plunges downhill just as steeply to a scenic and often-times empty beach that is more than enough reward. If you would like to make shuttle arrangements, you could park a second car along Davison Road near where it meets the beach (north of the featured trail).

TRAIL USE
Dayhiking, Running
LENGTH & TIME
8.0 miles, 4–5 hours
VERTICAL FEET
+440'/-440'
DIFFICULTY
- 1 2 3 **4** 5 +
TRAIL TYPE
Out & Back
START & FINISH
N41° 18.482'
W124° 03.381'

FEATURES
Stream
Beach
Wildflowers
Flora
Views
Secluded
Steep

FACILITIES
Restrooms

Best Time

Although the trail can be hiked year-round, the wildflowers along Skunk Cabbage Creek, including the prolific namesake plant, are at their peak in May and June.

Finding the Trail

Turn west from US 101 onto Robinson Road, 0.4 mile north of Bald Hills Road and 1.2 miles south of Davison Road, at a sign marked "Coastal Trail, Skunk Cabbage Section." Proceed 0.1 mile, where a private section of paved road bends uphill to the left. Continue ahead on gravel road for another 0.6 mile to the parking area, which has a vault toilet.

The nearest developed campground is Elk Prairie in Prairie Creek Redwoods State Park.

Trail Description

Walk away from the trailhead ▶1 along the course of an old logging road into second-growth forest of Sitka spruce, western hemlock, and redwood, immediately passing high above Skunk Cabbage Creek, which flows through an old culvert. Turning northwest, you follow the old roadbed well above the alder-shaded creek on gently graded tread with minor ups and downs. After a half mile or so, the forest parts enough to allow a view down to the boggy stream, where countless skunk cabbage plants carpet the floor of the canyon. When they are in full bloom, the sight is extraordinary.

❋ **Wildflowers**

The trail crosses several side streams, most on short, wood bridges, and many of these watercourses also harbor skunk cabbage (but not in the same massive swaths as the main channel). The lush ground cover alongside the trail includes wildflowers, such as false lily-of-the-valley, redwood sorrel, bleeding heart, clintonia, piggyback, and trillium. After a set of steps leads down to a bridge, the trail narrows to single track. Eventually it drops onto the floor of Skunk Cabbage Creek canyon and crosses the main branch on a wood railed bridge, 1.3 miles from the trailhead.

Beyond Skunk Cabbage Creek, the trail climbs mildly to moderately up the north side of the canyon,

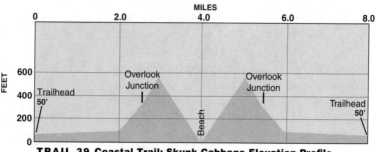

TRAIL 39 Coastal Trail: Skunk Cabbage Elevation Profile

On the Coastal Trail

crossing a few more short bridges over boggy areas. The trail turns into the side canyon of a usually flowing tributary, crosses it on a wood rail bridge, and then climbs more steeply with the aid of four switchbacks. As you exit the canyon, the distant roar of the crashing surf replaces the sound of the gurgling stream. Farther up the hillside, reach a signed junction with a very short lateral on the left to an overlook, 2.5 miles from the trailhead. ►2 The overlook has an old wood bench with a narrow but picturesque view of the ocean. For those who might not be enthralled with the stiff climb to the top of the bluff ahead and the stiff but even longer climb

Views 🔭

back from the beach, the overlook is an excellent turnaround point.

Away from the junction, the trail doubles back and climbs stiffly up the hillside via a trio of switchbacks to the top of a bluff, where you begin an equally stiff descent down the other side. Initially, the trail angles steeply across the hillside, but somewhere near the midpoint it starts winding down into a stream canyon. Partial ocean views through breaks in the foliage and the increasing sound of the surf propel you onward before a final stretch of short-legged switchbacks lead onto the beach, 4.0 miles from the trailhead. ▸3

 Beach

Without any easy access, this section of pristine coastline may be your private playground, a fine, scenic spot for a picnic lunch, where driftwood logs should provide reasonably comfortable places to sit and watch the crashing waves. If you have made shuttle arrangements, you could continue north along the beach for 1.2 miles to where Davison Road reaches the coast. Otherwise, after a thorough exploration of the beach, retrace your steps back to the trailhead. ▸4

MILESTONES

▸1	0.0	Start at trailhead
▸2	2.5	Overlook junction
▸3	4.0	Reach the beach
▸4	8.0	Return to trailhead

Trillium Falls Loop

The lovely Trillium Falls Trail begins at the Elk Meadow Day Use Area, set in a restored clearing where the Arcata Redwood Company once operated a sawmill. The great deal of effort expended in the restoration of the meadow and neighboring wetlands has been well rewarded by an influx of wildlife, most notably the resident elk herd. Consequently, the area is quite popular, especially during the busy summer tourist season. With convenient access from US 101, this relatively new trail past a pretty waterfall and through stately redwood groves has also become a very popular hiking path.

Best Time

This trail is open year-round. Spring and early summer adds wildflowers to this attractive loop, although during the height of summer, the area can feel crowded. Autumn is quite pleasant before the rainy season begins.

Finding the Trail

From the Thomas H. Kuchel Visitor Center, drive north on US 101 for 4.6 miles, passing through the town of Orick, to a left-hand turn onto Davison Road. Follow the road across Elk Meadow to the day-use parking area on the left, which has vault toilets and picnic tables.

The nearest developed campground is Elk Prairie in Prairie Creek Redwoods State Park.

TRAIL USE
Dayhiking, Running, Child-Friendly

LENGTH & TIME
2.6 miles, 1½–2 hours

VERTICAL FEET
+450'/-450'

DIFFICULTY
- 1 **2** 3 4 5 +

TRAIL TYPE
Loop

START & FINISH
N41° 19.341'
W124° 02.672'

FEATURES
Stream
Waterfall
Wildflowers
Redwoods
Wildlife

FACILITIES
Picnic Area
Restrooms

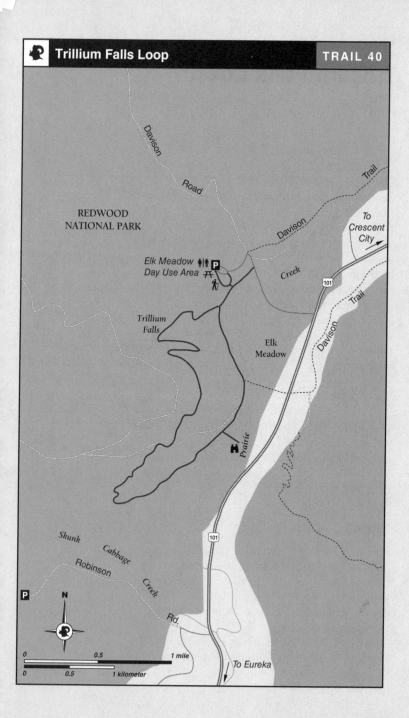

REDWOOD
NATIONAL PARK

Davison
Road

Davison

Trail

Creek

To
Crescent
City

Elk Meadow
Day Use Area

101

Trillium
Falls

Elk
Meadow

Davison

Trail

Prairie

101

Skunk

Cabbage

Robinson

Creek

P

N

Rd.

0   0.5   1 mile
0   0.5   1 kilometer

To Eureka

Trail Description

From the parking lot, ▶1 descend shortly on a paved
path to a signed junction at an old roadbed, ▶2 turn
right and walk along the edge of Elk Meadow to
where the dirt, single-track Trillium Falls Trail veers
uphill to the right. ▶3 Follow it across a brushy
hillside, and then enter the shade from a mixed redwood forest. Aided by switchbacks, the fern-lined
trail ascends a drainage, crosses a couple of wood
bridges over seasonal swales, and then reaches a
steel bridge immediately downstream from lovely
Trillium Falls. ▶4

Redwoods 🌲

Waterfall ▮▮

Beyond the falls, the trail continues to climb,
switchbacking occasionally through dense forest.
Along the way you pass several commemorative
signs and benches dedicating redwood groves to
individuals, families, or groups. The climbing ends
about a mile into the hike.

Now the trail begins a nearly uninterrupted
descent back to Elk Meadow. After you cross an
old logging road, the redwoods become more
impressive. Unfortunately, as is the case with many
redwood groves, the sense of seclusion you would
otherwise feel amid the tall trees is tainted somewhat by the muted sound of traffic on US 101.
The winding descent continues, with occasional

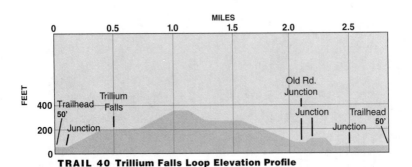

TRAIL 40 Trillium Falls Loop Elevation Profile

switchbacks and bridged crossings of trickling side streams on the way to where the trail merges with an old road. ▶5

The road descends steeply to a junction ▶6 with a short path on the right heading to a viewing platform above Elk Meadow, where you may spy members of the resident elk herd. Beyond the junction, a gently graded section of road roughly paralleling Prairie Creek leads through alders back to the Trillium Falls Trail junction ▶7 and then to the junction ▶8 of the short path back to the Elk Meadow Day Use Area. ▶9

Wildlife

Stream

🚶 MILESTONES

▶1	0.0	Start at Elk Meadow Day Use Trailhead
▶2	0.05	Right at old roadbed
▶3	0.1	Right Trillium Falls Trail junction
▶4	0.5	Trillium Falls
▶5	2.1	Trail merges with old road
▶6	2.2	Straight at path to viewing platform
▶7	2.5	Straight at Trillium Falls Trail junction
▶8	2.55	Left at junction
▶9	2.6	Return to Elk Meadows Day Use Area Trailhead

Opposite *Trillium Falls*

CHAPTER 5

Prairie Creek

Prairie Creek

S imilar to Humboldt Redwoods, Prairie Creek Redwoods State Park is bisected by a major waterway bordered by impressive redwoods and accessed by a scenic highway. The banks of Prairie Creek harbor a lush old-growth redwood forest, and the Newton B. Drury Parkway provides easy tourist access to these wonders. Unlike its neighbor to the south, Prairie Creek has a better network of trails and a scenic strip of coastline. The centerpiece of the park, Elk Prairie has picnic areas, campgrounds, and a visitor center and is home to a resident population of Roosevelt elk. Away from Elk Prairie, the park rarely feels crowded.

Permits

Permits are not required for any of these trips. There is no entrance fee except for access to Gold Bluffs Beach via Davison Road.

Maps

By far, the best map covering Prairie Creek Redwoods State Park and vicinity is the 1:25,000-scale map *Redwood National and State Parks North,* published by Redwood Hikes Press. The accurate, detailed, full-color, topographic map shows both trails with mileages and the location of footbridges and memorial redwood grove signs and benches.

Overleaf and opposite: *Roosevelt Elk in Prairie Creek Redwoods State Park*

Prairie Creek

TRAIL	DIFFICULTY	LENGTH	TYPE	USES & ACCESS	TERRAIN	NATURE	FEATURES
41	2	1.6	Loop	Dayhiking, Running	Beach, Stream, Redwoods	Flora	Camping, Picnic Area
42	3	7.5	Loop	Dayhiking, Running	Beach, Stream, Redwoods	Flora	Camping, Picnic Area
43	2	3.0	Loop	Dayhiking, Running, Child-Friendly	Stream, Redwoods	Wildflowers	Camping, Picnic Area
44	3	3.6	Loop	Dayhiking, Running	Stream, Redwoods	Wildflowers	
45	3	5.9	Loop	Dayhiking, Running	Stream, Redwoods		Camping, Picnic Area
46	3	3.5	Loop	Dayhiking, Running	Stream, Redwoods	Wildflowers	
47	4	4.2	Out & Back	Dayhiking, Running, Biking	Beach, Stream, Redwoods	Wildlife	Lighthouse

USES & ACCESS	TYPE	TERRAIN	NATURE	FEATURES
🏃 Dayhiking	Loop	Mountain	Flora	Views
Backpacking	Semiloop	Beach	Wildflowers	Camping
Running	Out & Back	Lake	Wildlife	Picnic Area
Biking	Shuttle	Stream		Swimming
Dogs Allowed		Waterfall		Secluded
Handicapped Access	DIFFICULTY	Redwoods		Steep
Child-Friendly	- 1 2 3 4 5 +	Pygmy Forest		Historic Interest
	less more			Resort town
				Lighthouse

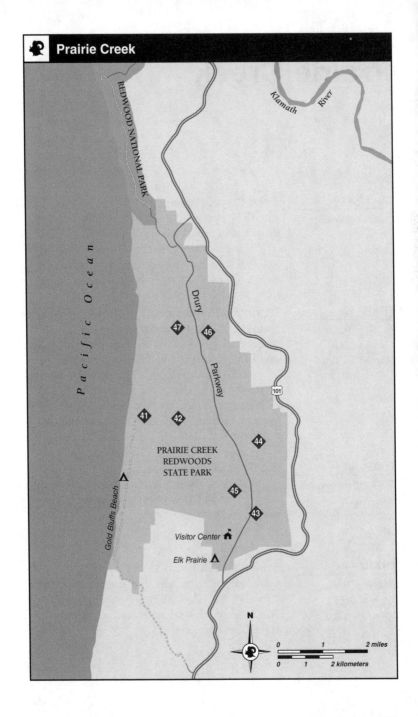

Prairie Creek

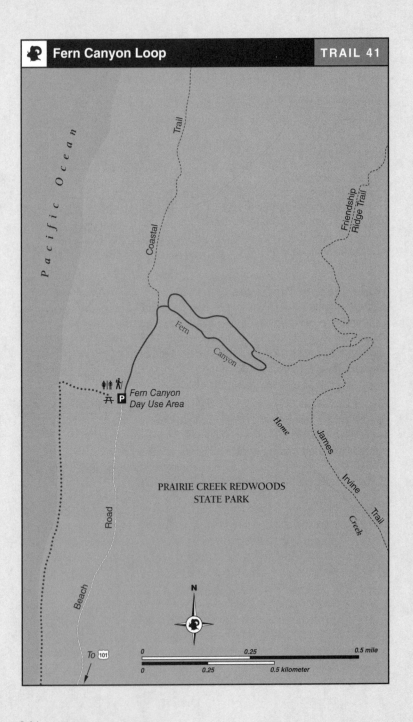

Fern Canyon Loop

TRAIL 41

Pacific Ocean

Coastal Trail

Friendship Ridge Trail

Fern Canyon

Fern Canyon
Day Use Area

Home

James

Irvine Trail

Creek

PRAIRIE CREEK REDWOODS
STATE PARK

Beach Road

To 101

N

0   0.25   0.5 mile

0   0.25   0.5 kilometer

Fern Canyon Loop

The short Fern Canyon Loop exposes visitors to a wide range of highlights, including ocean beach, a lush stream canyon, and the park's namesake highlight, the coast redwood. The 40-foot-tall canyon walls of Home Creek were formed in the 1800s by the destructive practice of hydraulic mining. Nature has done much to heal those wounds by carpeting the vertical walls with a solid mat of ferns, creating a stunning visual delight. Starting near the beach, the loop soon winds upstream through this magical gorge and then climbs above the canyon to return through a brief stretch of redwood and then spruce forest.

TRAIL USE
Dayhiking, Running

LENGTH & TIME
1.6 miles, 2 hours

VERTICAL FEET
+175'/-175'

DIFFICULTY
- 1 **2** 3 4 5 +

TRAIL TYPE
Loop

START & FINISH
N41° 26.162'
W124°03.567'

FEATURES
Stream
Beach
Redwoods
Flora

FACILITIES
Campground
Picnic Area
Restroom

Best Time

Although the Fern Canyon Trail is technically open all year, during the rainy season, the access road may be impassable to many vehicles at the creek crossings above Gold Bluffs Beach. Also, because the numerous plank bridges used for stream crossings in Fern Canyon are only in place during summer, hikers should expect wet fords the rest of the year. Foggy conditions are often prevalent in summer, especially in the morning, less so during spring and fall.

Finding the Trail

From the Thomas H. Kuchel Visitor Center, drive north on US 101 for 4.6 miles, passing through the town of Orick, to a left-hand turn onto Davison Road. Follow the road across Elk Meadow past the left-hand road into the day-use parking area (which has vault toilets and picnic tables) to the end of the

Fern Canyon, *Prairie Creek Redwoods State Park*

asphalt. Follow the narrow dirt road through a dark and gloomy section of forest, which opens up on the approach to the coast.

Reach the Gold Bluffs Beach Etrance Station, where you'll have to pay a fee ($8 in 2012) unless you have a national park or state park pass. From there, the road parallels Gold Bluffs Beach and passes a day-use parking area and campground on the way to the Fern Canyon Trailhead parking area at the end of the road. The road crosses a pair of streams that may be impassable when the water is high.

Trail Description

From the trailhead, ▶1 follow a section of the Coastal Trail through alders for 0.2 mile to Home Creek, immediately downstream from the mouth of Fern Canyon. On the far side of the creek is a junction ▶2 between the continuation of the north-bound Coastal Trail and the right-hand James Irvine Trail headed uphill (the return route). Rather than proceed on either of these trails, turn upstream and follow the gravel streambed into Fern Canyon.

Stream

Flora

Follow a nearly level course over the gravel into a steep-walled gorge draped with ferns, which is a radical departure from the typical V-shaped, steeply dropping canyon of the Northern California coast. Fern Canyon feels similar to a Columbia River Gorge side canyon. Along with the most common five-finger fern, this area hosts several other varieties, including bladder, bracken, California wood, deer, lady, leather, licorice, sword, and woodwardia. From June to September, planks are installed for the numerous crossings of Home Creek on the way up the serpentine canyon. Farther on, the walls rise from the creek bed even higher, topping out at more than 60 feet at their highest point.

The enchanting journey eventually comes to an end after about a half mile, where upstream the canyon assumes a more typical demeanor. From there, a signed path makes a steep but brief winding climb up the left-hand hillside to a junction ▶3 with the James Irvine Trail.

Turn left and follow dirt tread back down toward the beach, crossing several bridges and boardwalks on the way through predominantly Sitka spruce forest. At the bottom of the descent, you reach the Coastal Trail junction. ▶4 Turn left and retrace your steps 0.2 mile to the parking lot. ▶5

🚶	**MILESTONES**	
▶1	0.0	Start at Fern Canyon Trailhead
▶2	0.2	Right at Fern Canyon and Coastal Trail junction
▶3	0.8	Left at James Irvine Trail junction
▶4	1.4	Left at Fern Canyon and Coastal Trail junction
▶5	1.6	Return to Fern Canyon Trailhead

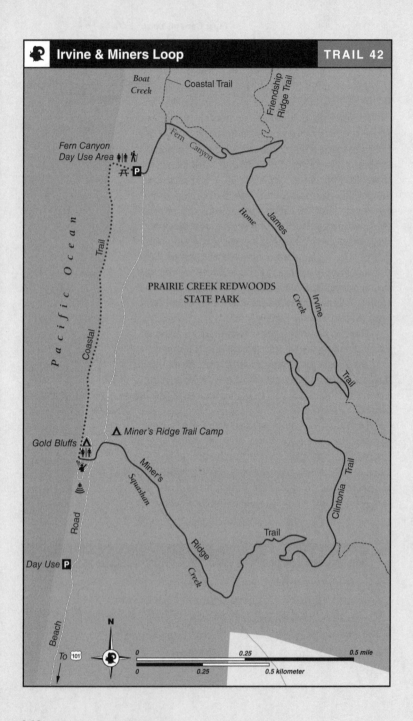

Irvine & Miners Loop

TRAIL 42

Boat Creek

Coastal Trail

Friendship Ridge Trail

Fern Canyon

Fern Canyon Day Use Area

Coastal Trail

Home Creek

James

Irvine

PRAIRIE CREEK REDWOODS STATE PARK

Pacific Ocean

Trail

Miner's Ridge Trail Camp

Gold Bluffs

Miner's

Squashan

Ridge

Creek

Trail

Clintonia Trail

Day Use

Road

Beach

To 101

N

| 0 | 0.25 | 0.5 mile |
| 0 | 0.25 | 0.5 kilometer |

Irvine & Miners Loop

One of the park's more diverse hikes, the Irvine & Miners Loop offers stunning canyon, forest, and seaside scenery. Beginning near Gold Bluffs Beach, the circuit soon heads into the enchanted surroundings of lushly vegetated Fern Canyon, followed by an extended romp through old-growth redwood forest. Heading toward the coast, the trail follows Squashan Creek through second-growth forest, and then a mile-plus-long stroll along a usually deserted stretch of beach leads back to the trailhead.

Best Time

Although the trail is open all year, access along Gold Bluffs Beach Road will determine whether or not you can reach the trailhead. When the road is muddy and the creeks it crosses are running full, most passenger cars won't be able to make the journey. Since summer is the busiest season, late spring or early fall are good options for solitude seekers.

TRAIL USE
Dayhiking, Running

LENGTH & TIME
7.5 miles, 3½–5 hours

VERTICAL FEET
+1,350'/-1,350'

DIFFICULTY
- 1 2 **3** 4 5 +

TRAIL TYPE
Loop

START & FINISH
N41° 26.162'
W124° 03.567'

FEATURES
Beach
Stream
Redwoods
Flora

FACILITIES
Campground
Picnic Area
Restroom

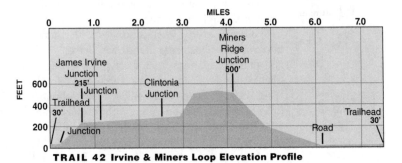

TRAIL 42 Irvine & Miners Loop Elevation Profile

Finding the Trail

From the Thomas H. Kuchel Visitor Center, drive north on US 101 for 4.6 miles, passing through the town of Orick, to a left-hand turn onto Davison Road. Follow the road across Elk Meadow past the left-hand road into the day-use parking area (which has vault toilets and picnic tables) to the end of the asphalt. Follow the narrow dirt road through a dark and gloomy section of forest, which opens up on the approach to the coast.

Reach the park entrance station, where you'll have to pay a fee ($8 in 2012) unless you have a national park or state park pass. From there, the road parallels Gold Bluffs Beach and passes a day-use parking area and campground on the way to the Fern Canyon Trailhead parking area at the end of the road. The road crosses a pair of streams that may be impassable when the water is high.

Trail Description

From the trailhead, ▶1 follow a section of the Coastal Trail through alders for 0.2 mile to Home Creek, immediately downstream from the mouth of Fern Canyon. On the far side of the creek is a junction ▶2 between the continuation of the north-bound Coastal Trail and the right-hand James Irvine Trail headed uphill. Rather than proceed on either of these trails, turn upstream and follow the gravel streambed into Fern Canyon.

▶ Stream

▶ Flora

Follow a nearly level course over the gravel into a steep-walled gorge draped with ferns, which is a radical departure from the typical V-shaped, steeply dropping canyon of the Northern California coast. Fern Canyon feels similar to a Columbia River Gorge side canyon. Along with the most common five-finger fern, this area hosts several other varieties, including bladder, bracken, California wood, deer, lady, leather, licorice, sword, and

Twin-trunked redwood *in Prairie Creek Redwoods State Park*

woodwardia. From June to September, planks are installed for the numerous crossings of Home Creek on the way up the serpentine canyon. Farther on, the walls rise from the creek bed even higher, topping out at more than 60 feet at their highest point. The enchanting journey eventually comes to an end after about a half mile, where upstream the canyon assumes a more typical demeanor. From there, a signed path makes a steep but brief winding climb up the left-hand hillside to a junction ▶3 with the James Irvine Trail.

Redwoods

Turning right from the junction, the James Irvine Trail ascends through old-growth redwood forest to a wood railed bridge and a junction ▶4 a short way beyond with the Friendship Ridge Trail on the left. Continue ahead on the James Irvine Trail to a railed bridge over a tributary of Home Creek; a short picturesque waterfall spills down a rock face above the bridge. Beyond the stream, the trail turns southwest on a brief, moderate climb, followed by a moderate descent alongside the main branch of Home Creek. The trail follows the diminishing creek upstream for the better part of a mile, crossing side streams on plank and rail bridges. At 1.4 miles from the Friendship Ridge Trail, reach a junction ▶5 with the Clintonia Trail.

Redwoods

Turn right onto the Clintonia Trail, and ascend a path lined with redwood sorrel and ferns through old-growth redwood forest, passing by the classic redwood features of downed giants, nurse logs, and incredibly tall trees. The grade eases where the trail gains Miners Ridge and turns southeast. Farther on, between signs for the Strawn and Wayburn Groves, you pass a closed road on the right leading downhill to another memorial redwood grove. Continue through magnificent redwood forest, passing another closed road on the right, to a junction ▶6 with the Miners Ridge Trail.

Stream

Continue ahead, now on the coast-bound section of the Miners Ridge Trail, passing through a lush, dark stand of old-growth forest. The trail makes a winding descent to Squashan Creek, leaves the old growth behind, and then heads down the maple-lined stream, crossing several bridges over side streams. As you approach the coast, the sound of the surf increases, the air becomes strikingly cooler, and the single-track trail merges with an old roadbed. After awhile, you pass a water tank and by an overgrown path to the Miners Ridge Hikers' Camp (recently closed due to the state budget crisis). Continue down the road and past a closed gate to Gold Bluffs Beach Road. ▶7

Turn left onto the road, and walk about 100 yards to the campground. Pass through it onto the beach, ▶8 and head north, preferably on wet sand, which is easier to walk on than dry sand. You will most likely have the beach to yourself for the next mile—the seclusion combines with the stunning coastal scenery to create very enjoyable hiking.

Beach

After 1.2 miles along the beach, you will be near the parking lot; however, the thick vegetation obscures it. During fair weather, the presence of other people should help you find the right path back to the trailhead. Otherwise, keep your eyes peeled for a pair of indentations in the bluffs, where Home Creek and then Boat Creek make their way toward the ocean. The route to the parking lot ▶9 is 0.2 mile south of Fern Canyon. If you reach Home Creek, you're too far north.

⚡ MILESTONES

▶1	0.0	Start at Fern Canyon Trailhead
▶2	0.2	Right at Fern Canyon junction
▶3	0.8	Right at James Irvine Trail junction
▶4	1.1	Straight at Friendship Ridge Trail junction
▶5	2.5	Right at Clintonia Trail junction
▶6	4.1	Straight at Miners Ridge Trail junction
▶7	6.1	Left at Gold Bluffs Beach Road
▶8	6.2	Head north on beach
▶9	7.5	Return to Fern Canyon Trailhead

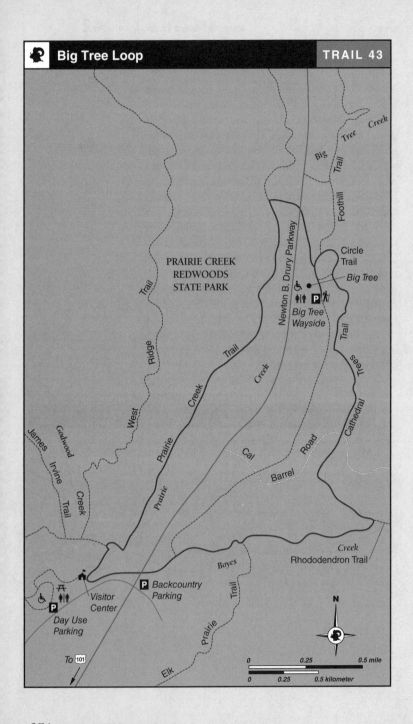

Big Tree Loop

TRAIL 43

PRAIRIE CREEK
REDWOODS
STATE PARK

Big Tree Creek

Big Tree Trail

Foothill Trail

Newton B. Drury Parkway

Circle Trail

Big Tree

Big Tree Wayside

Trail

Ridge Trail

Creek Trail

West

Godwood Creek

James Irvine Trail

Prairie Creek Trail

Cathedral Trees Trail

Prairie

Cal

Barrel

Road

Creek

Rhododendron Trail

Visitor Center

Backcountry Parking

Boyes Trail

Day Use Parking

Prairie Trail

N

To 101

Elk

0   0.25   0.5 mile
0   0.25   0.5 kilometer

Big Tree Loop

Most visitors to Prairie Creek Redwoods State Park stop at the Big Tree Wayside and stroll to the base of the enormous tree, which can cause some congestion during the peak summer season. The accompanying traffic noise combined with the tree's popularity makes for a less than ideal way to admire and appreciate this coast redwood icon. However, you can escape most of the crowds by taking a longer loop, even though you won't be able to completely avoid the sound of traffic. Beginning at the Big Tree, the loop follows a section of the Circle Loop, heads south through lowland redwood groves, and returns via a trail through more stately redwoods along lushly lined Prairie Creek.

Best Time

The trail is open all year, except when winter storms temporarily close Newton B. Drury Parkway. Visitor use is highest during summer, which makes spring or fall a fine time to hike this easy loop.

Finding the Trail

From the south, take Exit 753 from US 101 onto Newton B. Drury Parkway. The trailhead is on the east shoulder of the parkway at milepost 127.96, 0.8 mile north of the intersection with the access road to the visitor center and Elk Prairie Campground.

Trail Description

After departing from the trailhead ▶1 and paying homage to the massively large Big Tree, head north

TRAIL USE
Dayhiking, Running, Child-Friendly

LENGTH & TIME
3.0 miles, 1½–2 hours

VERTICAL FEET
+200'/-200'

DIFFICULTY
- 1 **2** 3 4 5 +

TRAIL TYPE
Loop

START & FINISH
N41° 22.470'
W124° 00.813'

FEATURES
Stream
Wildflowers
Redwoods

FACILITIES
Campground
Picnic Area
Restroom
Visitor Center

on the wide path of the 0.3-mile Circle Trail. Passing numerous tall trees, you soon come to a junction ▶2 of the Foothill Trail heading north. Veer right to continue on the Circle Trail, crossing a wood bridge over a seasonal swale and passing through a cut in a massive downed redwood. The trail arcs around to the south on the way to a junction ▶3 with the Cathedral Trees Trail.

Redwoods 🌲

Turn left, leaving the Circle Trail and most of the tourists behind, to follow the Cathedral Trees Trail on a short climb up the east slope of Prairie Creek canyon. Near the top, you pass a pair of upended giants that provide an interesting view of their root structure. Farther on is an old burned redwood, with new trees growing out of burls a fair distance above the ground. Pass a seep lined with skunk cabbage, and soon come to a crossing of Cal Barrel Road. Pick up single-track trail again on the far side, and travel past more-impressive redwood specimens to a junction ▶4 with the Rhododendron Trail, 0.8 mile from the Circle Trail junction.

Turn right and head west along lushly lined Boyes Creek for 0.3 mile to another junction, ▶5 this one with the Elk Prairie Trail heading south. Continue ahead, following Boyes Creek downstream toward a union with Prairie Creek. The trail emerges from the dark forest momentarily at the north edge of Elk Prairie. Back in the trees, you reach a junction ▶6 with the Foothill Trail on the right. Proceeding ahead, you soon cross a railed bridge over Boyes Creek, descend briefly through some alders, and then pass through a concrete culvert beneath Drury Parkway. Climb shortly to the edge of the campground access road, and follow it toward the visitor center. ▶7

Stream

From the north side of the visitor center, head northeast on the Nature Trail across a long, wood bridge over Boyes Creek, and proceed to a junction

Opposite *Big Tree*

Redwoods

▶8 with the Prairie Creek Trail heading north-northeast. Turn right and follow the trail upstream along the west bank of Prairie Creek through old-growth forest. Continue through magnificent redwood forest, crossing bridges over a seasonal stream, Prairie Creek, and another seasonal stream. Farther on, just after another bridge, is a junction ▶9 with a lateral heading east toward the parkway.

Turn right onto the lateral, cross the parkway, and then follow the path south-southeast back to the Big Tree Wayside Parking Area. ▶10

MILESTONES

▶1	0.0	Start at Big Tree Wayside Parking Area
▶2	0.1	Right at Foothill Trail junction
▶3	0.25	Left at Cathedral Trees Trail junction
▶4	1.05	Right at Rhododendron Trail junction
▶5	1.35	Straight at Elk Prairie Trail junction
▶6	1.55	Straight at Foothill Trail junction
▶7	1.75	Visitor center
▶8	1.8	Right at Prairie Creek Trail junction
▶9	2.8	Right at lateral junction
▶10	3.0	Return to the parking area

Brown Creek Loop

The Browns Creek Loop, which offers plenty of diversity in 3.6 miles, is one of the better routes in Prairie Creek Redwoods State Park. After an easy stroll through pleasant forest, the South Fork Trail climbs into a serene upland forest to meet the Rhododendron Trail. A pleasant descent then continues through upland redwoods past numerous showy rhododendrons, which are in full bloom in late spring. When you reach Brown Creek, the namesake trail heads downstream and visits some magnificent old-growth redwoods. Separated by a ridge from Newton B. Drury Parkway, the trail is not plagued by the sounds of automobile traffic. You are more apt to hear the ocean from its upper elevations than any man-made noise.

TRAIL USE
Dayhiking, Running
LENGTH & TIME
3.6 miles, 2–3 hours
VERTICAL FEET
+550'/-550'
DIFFICULTY
- 1 2 **3** 4 5 +
TRAIL TYPE
Loop
START & FINISH
N41° 23.253'
W124° 01.015'

FEATURES
Redwoods
Stream
Wildflowers

FACILITIES
None

Best Time

The trail is open all year, except when winter storms temporarily close the parkway. The rhododendrons, along with other seasonal wildflowers, are usually at their peak in late spring.

Finding the Trail

Take Exit 753 from US 101, and follow Drury Parkway 2.9 miles north, past the Big Tree Wayside, to a pullout on the east side of the road near a sign for the South Fork Trail. The nearest developed campground is Elk Prairie near the visitor center.

Trail Description

From the parkway, ▶1 follow the South Fork Trail beneath tall old-growth redwoods and to the south

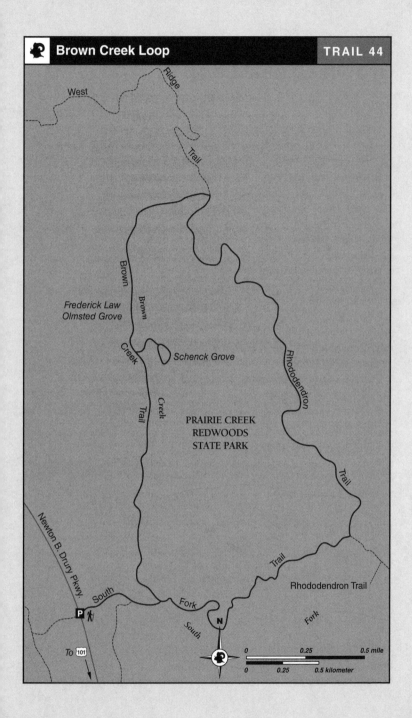

West

Ridge

Trail

Brown

Brown

Frederick Law
Olmsted Grove

Creek

Schenck Grove

Rhododendron

Creek

PRAIRIE CREEK
REDWOODS
STATE PARK

Trail

Trail

Trail

Rhododendron Trail

Newton B. Drury Pkwy.

South

Fork

South

Fork

N

To 101

| 0 | 0.25 | 0.5 mile |
| 0 | 0.25 | 0.5 kilometer |

of Brown Creek, reaching a junction ▶2 with the Foothill Trail on the right signed "Big Tree." Continue ahead past spring wildflowers, shortly reaching a bridge over South Fork Creek and another junction on the far side, ▶3 where the loop begins.

Wildflowers

Continue ahead, soon starting a steep, switch-backing climb up the hillside into redwood uplands. Fortunately, the ascent eases farther up the slope. As you climb, the redwoods become less impressive. Nevertheless, the forest is still serene and pleasant on the way to a junction ▶4 with the Rhododendron Trail well below the ridgecrest.

Redwoods

Turn left at the well-signed junction, and follow a section of the Rhododendron Trail, which switchbacks twice and then descends across the forested hillside. Pass an old redwood bench, cross a picturesque, trickling side stream, and continue downslope into an increasingly impressive redwood forest. Despite being less than a mile from US 101, you cannot noticeably hear traffic noise; however, you can hear the faint, distant roar of the ocean in this quiet stretch. After crossing another rivulet on a rail-less footbridge, the descent becomes steeper on the way to a steel bridge across Brown Creek and a junction ▶5 with the Brown Creek Trail and West Ridge Trail.

Stream

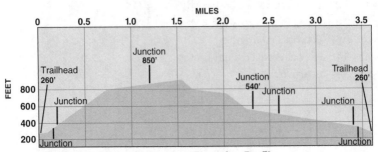

TRAIL 44 Brown Creek Loop Elevation Profile

Turning left at the junction, you follow Brown Creek downstream through a delightful section of old-growth redwood forest, soon descending steps to a wood railed bridge over an attractive side stream and then ascending more steps on the far side. Beyond four short, rail-less bridges, the trail draws closer to Brown Creek and the redwoods become more statuesque.

You soon reach the Fredrick Law Olmsted grove and continue downstream to the Carl Alwin Schenck Grove, named for the founder of the Biltmore School of Forestry, the first such school in the United States. Here a side trail ►6 on the left leads across a bridge over Brown Creek and then wanders through the grove, passing six concrete monuments linked to a giant redwood.

Away from the Schenck Grove, the trail follows Brown Creek through more old-growth forest, eventually reaching the junction ►7 with the South Fork Trail at the close of the loop. From there, retrace your steps 0.2 mile to the trailhead, ►8 passing the Foothill Trail junction along the way.

🚶	MILESTONES	
►1	0.0	Start at South Fork Trailhead
►2	0.15	Straight at Foothill Trail junction
►3	0.2	Right at Brown Creek Trail junction
►4	1.2	Left at Rhododendron Trail junction
►5	2.3	Left at Brown Creek Trail junction
►6	2.6	Schenck Grove junction
►7	3.4	Right at South Fork Trail junction
►8	3.6	Return to trailhead

West Ridge & Prairie Creek Loop

This highly scenic loop combines a delightful ridge-line ramble through straight, tall redwoods with the most scenic stretch of the Prairie Creek Trail. After a brief walk through an attractive old-growth grove along Godwood Creek, the trail climbs stiffly up a hillside to the apex of West Ridge and then heads north through serene forest, where you may hear the distant roar of the ocean. The section along Prairie Creek is lined with uncommonly lush flora, perfectly complementing some of its tallest red-woods; the only drawback is intermittent road noise from the nearby parkway.

Best Time

The trail is open all year, except when winter storms temporarily close Drury Parkway. Although summer is the busiest season, the steep climb up the West Ridge Trail discourages most tourists. However, expect to see plenty of traffic on the Prairie Creek section. Spring, when wildflowers are blooming, and autumn, when the deciduous foliage along the creek is turning color, are excellent times for a visit.

Finding the Trail

Take Exit 753 from US 101, and follow Newton B. Drury Parkway north a mile to the far end of Elk Prairie and a left-hand turn onto the access road for the visitor center and campground. Drive past the visitor center to the long-term parking area near the restrooms. The well-marked trail begins on the north side of the visitor center.

TRAIL USE
Dayhiking, Running
LENGTH & TIME
5.9 miles, 3–5 hours
VERTICAL FEET
+750'/-750'
DIFFICULTY
- 1 2 **3** 4 5 +
TRAIL TYPE
Loop
START & FINISH
N41° 21.822'
W124° 01.404'

FEATURES
Stream
Redwoods

FACILITIES
Visitor Center
Restrooms
Picnic Area
Campground

283

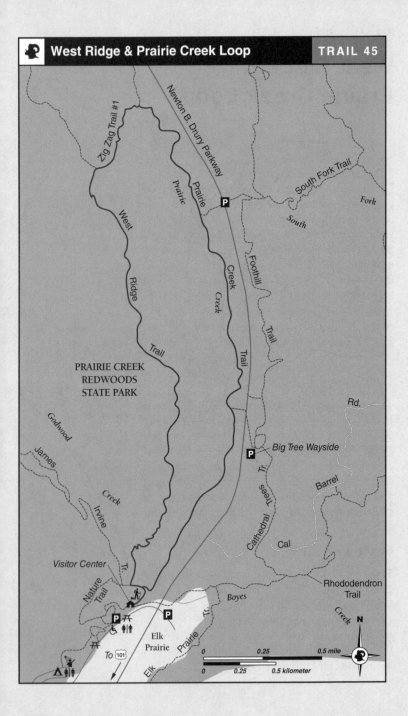

PRAIRIE CREEK
REDWOODS
STATE PARK

Newton B. Drury Parkway

Zig Zag Trail #1

West

Ridge

Trail

Prairie

Prairie

Creek

Creek

Trail

South Fork Trail

South

Fork

Foothill

Trail

Rd.

Big Tree Wayside

Barrel

Cal

Cathedral

Trees

Tr.

Godwood

James

Creek

Irvine

Tr.

Visitor Center

Nature

Trail

Boyes

Tr.

Elk
Prairie

Prairie

Elk

Rhododendron
Trail

Creek

N

0   0.25   0.5 mile

0   0.25   0.5 kilometer

To 101

Trail Description

From the visitor center parking lot, ▶1 follow the right-hand trail to a bridge over lovely Prairie Creek and then wind around to a junction ▶2 with the Prairie Creek Trail headed north (your return route). Bear left at the junction, and walk a short distance to the next junction, ▶3 this one with the West Ridge Trail.

Turn right onto the broad track of the fern-lined West Ridge Trail, and stroll easily through impressive redwoods along Godwood Creek to a wood bench, where the path bends sharply right and begins a steep, switchbacking climb up the nose of the ridge. Initially, the views of the tall trees below are quite stirring, but the trees diminish in stature as you progress up the slope. The grade eases where the trail gains the crest, and then it follows the undulating ridge northward, with the faint but discernible roar of the ocean. Spring wildflowers along the way include western trillium, Columbia windflower, and Douglas iris, as well as the occasional blooms of rhododendron. The ridge also harbors a fine stand of big trees. You ramble along the ridgecrest for about 1.5 miles, and just after passing through a sawed-out redwood, you come to a junction ▶4 with Zig Zag Trail #1.

Redwoods

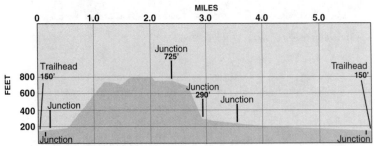

TRAIL 45 West Ridge & Prairie Creek Loop Elevation Profile

Upland redwood forest *along the West Ridge Trail*

Turn right at the junction, and start the appropriately zigzagging, steep descent toward Prairie Creek. The forest becomes more impressive as you descend to the bottom of the canyon, reaching a junction ▶5 with the Prairie Creek Trail after 0.5 mile, but you are likely to hear passing cars on Drury Parkway.

Follow Prairie Creek through a stand of huge redwoods, and soon cross a railed bridge to the east bank. The trail passes through lush riparian foliage, including blackberry brambles, thimbleberry, ferns, and vine maple, while a healthy swath of red alder and bigleaf maple shades the creek. Just after crossing an angled bridge over Brown Creek, you reach a junction ▶6 with a short lateral to the parkway.

Stream

Continue ahead at the junction, passing more groves of stately redwoods alternating with pockets of shady maples and open areas on the way to a bridge over a seasonal stream and a bridge over Big Tree Creek. Just after the creek is a junction with another lateral heading east to the parkway.

With 1.2 miles to go, continue ahead on the Prairie Creek Trail, shortly crossing a bridge over a seasonal swale and passing a park bench near a bend in the creek. Farther on, an angled bridge crosses Prairie Creek, and the trail continues downstream along the east bank. After another bridge over a steep side canyon, you pass through cuts in a pair of massive downed redwoods, pass another park bench, and soon come to the close of the loop at the junction ▶7 with the Nature Trail.

Turn left at the junction, and retrace your steps to the visitor center. ▶8

🚶 **MILESTONES**

▶1	0.0	Start at visitor center trailhead
▶2	0.1	Left at Prairie Creek Trail junction
▶3	0.2	Right at West Ridge Trail junction
▶4	2.4	Right at Zig Zag Trail #1 junction
▶5	2.9	Right at Prairie Creek Trail junction
▶6	3.6	Straight at lateral junction
▶7	5.8	Left at junction
▶8	5.9	Return to visitor center

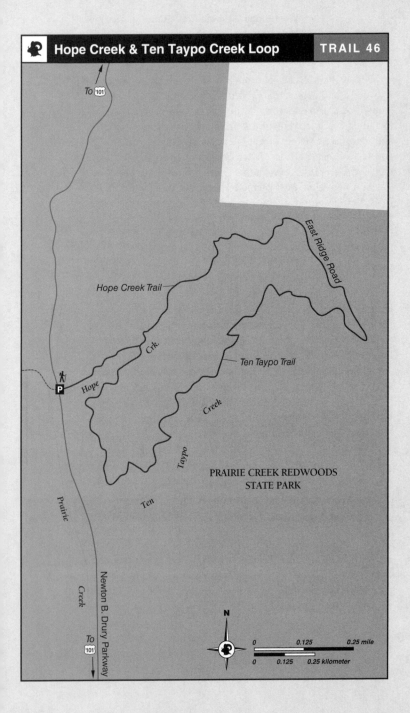

To 101

Hope Creek Trail

East Ridge Road

Crk.

Ten Taypo Trail

Hope

Creek

Taypo

PRAIRIE CREEK REDWOODS
STATE PARK

Ten

Prairie

Newton B. Drury Parkway

Creek

To 101

N

| 0 | 0.125 | 0.25 mile |

| 0 | 0.125 | 0.25 kilometer |

Hope Creek &
Ten Taypo Creek Loop

This loop trail climbs up the drainage of Hope Creek, follows a section of the old East Ridge Road along a ridgecrest, and then drops down the drainage of Ten Taypo Creek before arcing back to Hope Creek. It passes through diverse stretches of both lowland and upland redwood forest. The stiff climb limits the number of visitors, which may be advantageous for anyone looking for seclusion in Prairie Creek Redwoods State Park.

Best Time

The trail is open all year, except when winter storms temporarily close Newton B. Drury Parkway. Late spring and early summer offer the added bonus of seasonal wildflowers, including the blossoms of rhododendron.

Finding the Trail

Follow the Newton B. Drury Parkway to milepost 132.74, 2.5 miles from Exit 765 from US 101, and

TRAIL USE
Dayhiking, Running

LENGTH & TIME
3.5 miles, 2 hours

VERTICAL FEET
+700'/-700'

DIFFICULTY
- 1 2 **3** 4 5 +

TRAIL TYPE
Loop

START & FINISH
N41° 26.024'
W124° 02.311'

FEATURES
Stream
Redwoods
Wildflowers

FACILITIES
None

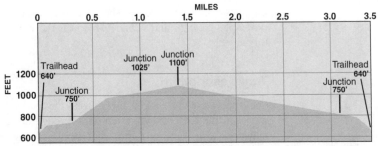

TRAIL 46 Hope & Ten Taypo Loop Elevation Profile

A "Goosepen" redwood

park your vehicle on the east shoulder. The nearest developed campground is Elk Prairie near the visitor center.

Trail Description

Redwoods

Wildflowers

The trail ▶1 climbs stiffly away from the parkway with the aid of short switchbacks through tall redwoods towering over a lush understory of ferns and shrubs, including rhododendron and azalea. The grade eventually eases, at least momentarily, on the way to the loop junction. ►2

Turn left onto the Hope Creek Trail, climbing above the namesake stream and passing through the trunk of a still living, hollowed-out redwood. The climb continues to the top of a ridge, where you veer right onto the former East Ridge Road. ►3

After a short climb, the road drops into a saddle and then swings around a hillside before resuming the ascent. The redwoods here are quite striking and have a particularly dense understory. Shortly beyond a sign for the Hooker Grove, the grade eases and continues southeast to a junction ►4 with the Ten Taypo Trail.

The Ten Taypo Trail follows a winding descent back toward Prairie Creek through redwood forest with a ground cover of rhododendron and huckleberry. Starting high above the drainage, the trail eventually nears Ten Taypo Creek before bending north and then west around the nose of a ridge into the lush canyon of Hope Creek. Cross the creek on an angled wood bridge, and immediately reach the end of the loop. ►5 From there, retrace your steps 0.3 mile to the trailhead. ►6

MILESTONES

►1	0.0	Start at trailhead
►2	0.3	Left at loop junction
►3	1.0	Right at former East Ridge Road
►4	1.4	Right at Ten Taypo Trail junction
►5	3.1	Left at loop junction
►6	3.5	Return to trailhead

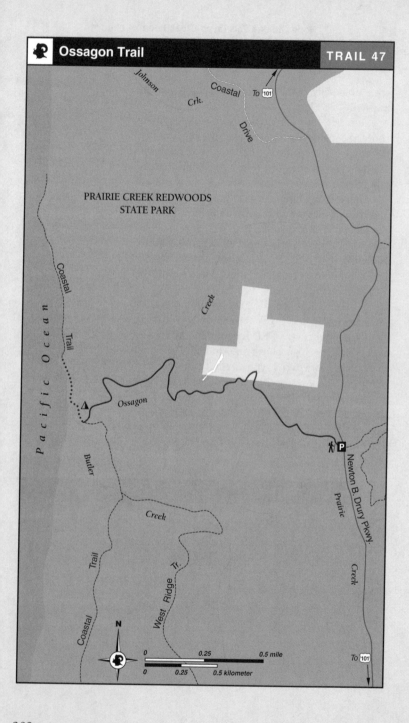

PRAIRIE CREEK REDWOODS
STATE PARK

Johnson

Crk.

Coastal

Drive

To 101

Pacific Ocean

Coastal

Trail

Creek

Ossagon

Butler

Creek

West Ridge Tr.

Coastal

Trail

Newton B. Drury Pkwy

Prairie

Creek

To 101

N

0   0.25   0.5 mile

0   0.25   0.5 kilometer

Ossagon Trail

The Ossagon Trail offers a variety of scenery over the course of only a couple of miles. Beginning in impressive old-growth redwood forest, the route drops through second-growth forest on the way toward the coast, crossing lushly lined Ossagon Creek twice on the way. A herd of elk can often be seen near the mouth of the creek. Just beyond is a stretch of secluded beach accented by a cluster of dramatic-looking rocks. Although the trail is relatively short, make sure you save enough energy for the mostly uphill trip back to the car.

Best Time

During the rainy season, the area on the way to the beach is prone to flooding, and the rest of the trail can be a muddy mess. Anytime from late spring through early fall should offer pleasant hiking conditions.

TRAIL USE
Dayhiking, Running, Biking

LENGTH & TIME
4.2 miles, 2–3 hours

VERTICAL FEET
+725'/-725'

DIFFICULTY
- 1 2 3 **4** 5 +

TRAIL TYPE
Out & Back

START & FINISH
N41° 26.024'
W124° 02.311'

FEATURES
Beach
Stream
Redwoods
Wildlife
Steep

FACILITIES
None

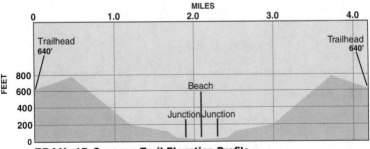

TRAIL 47 Ossagon Trail Elevation Profile

Tangle of ferns *along the trail*

Finding the Trail

Follow the Newton B. Drury Parkway to milepost 132.74, 2.5 miles from Exit 765 from US 101, and park your vehicle on the west shoulder. The nearest public campground is north of the trailhead in Redwood National Park. Free, first-come, first-served Flint Ridge Walk-In Campground has 11 sites (without water). There are several private RV campgrounds along the Klamath River.

Trail Description

Redwoods

The trail leaves the edge of the parkway, ►1 immediately crosses nascent Prairie Creek, and climbs through an outstanding old-growth redwood forest above a shallow ravine filled with lush vegetation, including deer fern and salmonberry. After 0.2 mile, you reach the crest of a ridge.

Soon you begin a lengthy, moderate descent toward the coast, leaving the old-growth redwoods behind. Journeys along this trail often begin in sunshine but eventually drop into persistent fog on the way toward the beach. Even without fog, you'll certainly notice the cooler coastal air and the distant sound of the surf. Proceed through mixed forest, predominantly second-growth spruce lined by red alder. The route now follows the old Ossagon Road, which carried automobile traffic until the 1960s. After crossing plank bridges over a seasonal swale, the trail bends north and reaches a bridged crossing of alder-lined Ossagon Creek. As you arc across the hillside above the creek, thick vegetation starts to crowd the trail. After a switchback, you cross back over Ossagon Creek on a wood railed bridge and reach a flat near Ossagon Creek Trail Camp. The flat's dense foliage blocks views of the coast, as you soon reach a junction ▶2 with the Coastal Trail. Elk often roam this flat and the marshy area nearby.

Wildlife

Turn right at the junction, cross a seasonal bridge over a marshy area, and then reach sand dunes. ▶3 A short way farther, the trail leads onto the usually deserted and picturesque beach. Heading north, you soon reach Ossagon Creek where it enters the Pacific. Just beyond is a cluster of scenic rocks.

Beach

After fully enjoying the beach, retrace your steps back to the trailhead. ▶4

🚶 MILESTONES

▶1	0.0	Start at trailhead
▶2	1.9	Right at Coastal Trail junction
▶3	2.1	Reach the beach at Ossagon Creek
▶4	4.2	Return to trailhead

CHAPTER 6

Del Norte Coast Redwoods

Del Norte Coast Redwoods

S imilar to the other redwood parks along the North Coast, the steep topography of Del Norte Coast Redwoods State Park provides many picture-postcard scenes. Unlike its neighbors, the park's most impressive redwood groves are not positioned alongside a major waterway, but they instead grow on the steep hillside above the ocean. Persistent fog along this stretch of coastline nourishes the tall trees, oftentimes adding a touch of ethereal mystery.

Most of the prime hiking trails within the narrow park are relatively short and coastal, either traversing the hillsides above the ocean or starting from US 101 and descending to the beach. Consequently, ocean views are abundant.

Permits

Permits are not required for any of these trips. The park does not charge an entrance fee.

Maps

By far, the best map covering Del Norte Coast Redwoods State Park and vicinity is the 1:25,000-scale map *Redwood National and State Parks North,* published by Redwood Hikes Press. The accurate, detailed, full-color, topographic map shows trails with mileages and the location of footbridges and memorial redwood grove signs and benches.

Overleaf and opposite: *Ocean view*

Del Norte Coast Redwoods

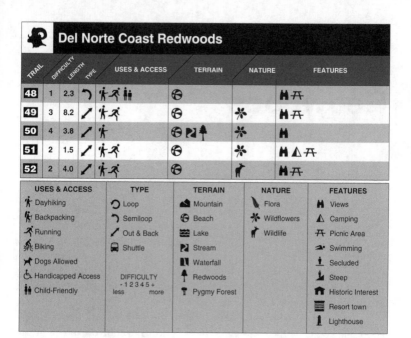

TRAIL	DIFFICULTY	LENGTH	TYPE	USES & ACCESS	TERRAIN	NATURE	FEATURES
48	1	2.3	↱	🚶 🏃 👫	🌐		⌂ 🪑
49	3	8.2	⟋	🚶 🏃	🌐	✳	⌂ 🪑
50	4	3.8	⟋	🚶	🌐 📲 🌲	✳	⌂
51	2	1.5	⟋	🚶 🏃	🌐	✳	⌂ ⚠ 🪑
52	2	4.0	⟋	🚶 🏃	🌐	🦌	⌂ 🪑

USES & ACCESS	TYPE	TERRAIN	NATURE	FEATURES
🚶 Dayhiking	↺ Loop	⛰ Mountain	🌿 Flora	⌂ Views
🎒 Backpacking	↱ Semiloop	🌐 Beach	✳ Wildflowers	⚠ Camping
🏃 Running	⟋ Out & Back	🌊 Lake	🦌 Wildlife	🪑 Picnic Area
🚲 Biking	🚌 Shuttle	📲 Stream		⤳ Swimming
🐕 Dogs Allowed		💦 Waterfall		⬍ Secluded
♿ Handicapped Access	DIFFICULTY	🌲 Redwoods		⬍ Steep
👫 Child-Friendly	- 1 2 3 4 5 +	🌱 Pygmy Forest		🏠 Historic Interest
	less more			▦ Resort town
				🏮 Lighthouse

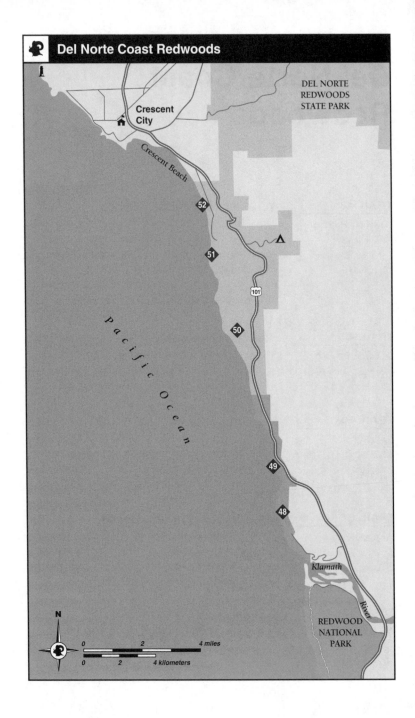

Del Norte Coast Redwoods

Crescent City

Crescent Beach

52

51

101

50

Pacific Ocean

49

48

Klamath

River

DEL NORTE
REDWOODS
STATE PARK

REDWOOD
NATIONAL
PARK

N

0   2   4 miles

0   2   4 kilometers

Del Norte Coast Redwoods

Yurok Loop & Hidden Beach

The Yurok Loop, in an outlying section of Redwood National Park, visits an area once inhabited by a tribe of Native Americans, although almost all evidence of their presence has disappeared over the years. The striking scenery includes beautiful ocean vistas and patches of dense coastal foliage. By adding the out-and-back trip to Hidden Beach, hikers can access a remote stretch of sandy beach and ocean surf backdropped by picturesque sea-stacks.

Best Time

The trail is open all year. However, hiking it during and immediately after winter storms can be wet and miserable. Wildflowers add splashes of color to the hillsides in spring and early summer.

Finding the Trail

About 14 miles south of Crescent City and 5 miles north of the town of Klamath, leave US 101 at the signed turnoff for Lagoon Creek Picnic Area, which is at the north end of Lagoon Pond and just south of False Klamath Cove. The nearest public campground is south of the trailhead within a section of Redwood National Park. Free, first-come, first-served Flint Ridge Walk-In Campground has 11 sites (without water). There are several private RV campgrounds along the Klamath River. To the north of the trailhead within Del Norte Coast Redwoods State Park is Mill Creek Campground.

TRAIL USE
Dayhiking, Running, Child-Friendly

LENGTH & TIME
2.3 miles, 1–2 hours

VERTICAL FEET
+200'/-200'

DIFFICULTY
- **1** 2 3 4 5 +

TRAIL TYPE
Semiloop

START & FINISH
N41° 35.698'
W124° 06'050'

FEATURES
Beach
Views

FACILITIES
Restrooms
Picnic Area

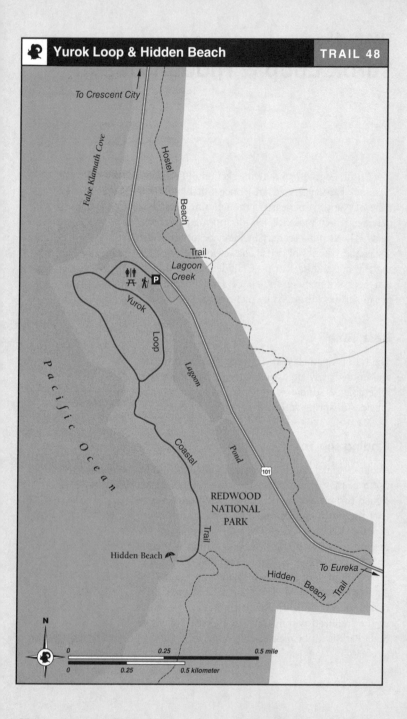

Yurok Loop & Hidden Beach

TRAIL 48

To Crescent City

False Klamath Cove

Hostel

Beach

Trail

Lagoon
Creek

P

Yurok

Loop

Lagoon

Coastal

Pond

Pacific Ocean

101

REDWOOD
NATIONAL
PARK

Trail

Hidden Beach

To Eureka

Hidden Beach Trail

N

0   0.25   0.5 mile

0   0.25   0.5 kilometer

Trail Description

Head away from the northwest side of the parking lot
►1 on a wide track into a stand of mixed forest to a
►2 Y-junction, where the northbound Coastal Trail
veers off to the right. Continue ahead on the left-hand
trail, soon crossing a wood railed bridge over the outlet from Lagoon Pond. Following an old roadbed, the
trail passes through open terrain, which was the site
of an old Yurok village, but no trace of the settlement
exists. Soon you reach a second junction, ►3 with the
beginning of the Yurok Loop.

Take the right-hand path, and dive into a tunnel of coastal vegetation until you break out into
the open to a fine view of the ocean, highlighted by
several sea-stacks. A park bench nearby invites passersby to linger and enjoy the stunning view. Beyond,
the trail moves into viewless forest and continues
southeast to a junction ►4 between the Coastal Trail
continuing southbound and the Yurok Loop circling
back toward the trailhead (your return route).

Views

Proceed ahead on the Coastal Trail, with fine
views of the beach and the ocean. Pass a short lateral
on the right leading down to a camping area beneath
a grove of spruce. At 0.5 mile from the previous
junction, you reach a junction ►5 with the trail to
Hidden Beach.

Turn right and make a short, steep descent to a
pile of driftwood, followed by a stretch of boulders
and finally the sand of Hidden Beach. ►6 The beach
is blessed with fine views of the ocean punctuated
by a smattering of sea-stacks, and because it is about
0.5 mile from the closest road, you may have the
area all to yourself.

Beach

After thoroughly enjoying Hidden Beach, retrace
your steps back to the junction with the Coastal Trail,
turn left, ►7 and head back 0.5 mile to the junction
►8 with the Yurok Loop. Turning right onto the
Yurok Loop, the trail bounces up and down before
smoothing out along the northwest bank of Lagoon

Hidden Beach

Pond. The alder-filled forest is thick enough to block any views of the lily-pad-covered lagoon. After 0.4 mile, you close the loop section at the junction, ▶9 turn right, and turn right again at the next junction, ▶10 soon returning to the trailhead. ▶11

🚶 MILESTONES

▶1	0.0	Start at trailhead
▶2	0.05	Straight at northbound Coastal Trail junction
▶3	0.1	Right at Yurok Loop junction
▶4	0.7	Straight at Yurok Loop junction
▶5	1.2	Right at Hidden Beach junction
▶6	1.25	Reach Hidden Beach
▶7	1.3	Left at Coastal Trail junction
▶8	1.8	Right at Yurok Loop junction
▶9	2.2	Right at junction
▶10	2.25	Right at northbound Coastal Trail junction
▶11	2.3	Return to trailhead

Klamath Overlook

This seldom-traveled, 4-mile section of the Coastal Trail provides periodic coast vistas from spruce-covered bluffs. The Klamath Overlook, an aerie 200 feet above the ocean, offers a stunning view of the Klamath River's entry into the Pacific Ocean. The area's lack of development makes the trail feel similar to the Lost Coast (see Trails 13 and 15).

Best Time

The trail is open all year. However, hiking it during and immediately after winter storms can be wet and miserable. Wildflowers add splashes of color to the hillsides in spring and early summer.

Finding the Trail

About 14 miles south of Crescent City and 5 miles north of the town of Klamath, leave US 101 at the signed turnoff for Lagoon Creek Picnic Area, which is at the north end of Lagoon Pond and just south of False Klamath Cove. The nearest public campground is south of the trailhead within a section of Redwood National Park. Free, first-come, first-served Flint Ridge Walk-In Campground has 11 sites (without water). There are several private RV campgrounds along the Klamath River. To the north of the trailhead within Del Norte Coast Redwoods State Park is Mill Creek Campground.

TRAIL USE
Dayhiking, Running

LENGTH & TIME
8.2 miles, 4–6 hours

VERTICAL FEET
+1,450'/-1,450'

DIFFICULTY
- 1 2 **3** 4 5 +

TRAIL TYPE
Out & Back

START & FINISH
N41° 35.698'
W124° 06'050'

FEATURES
Beach
Wildflowers
Views

FACILITIES
Restrooms
Picnic Area

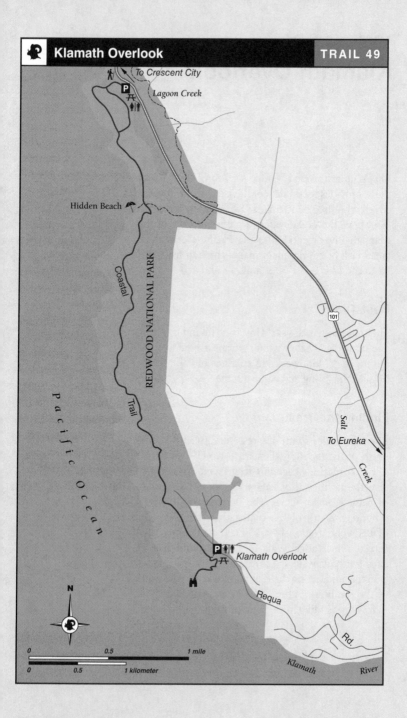

Klamath Overlook

TRAIL 49

To Crescent City

Lagoon Creek

Hidden Beach

Coastal

REDWOOD NATIONAL PARK

Trail

Pacific Ocean

101

To Eureka

Salt

Creek

Klamath Overlook

Requa

Rd.

Klamath River

N

0   0.5   1 mile

0   0.5   1 kilometer

Trail Description

Head away from the northwest side of the parking lot ▶1 on a wide track into a stand of mixed forest to a ▶2 Y-junction, where the northbound Coastal Trail veers off to the right. Continue ahead on the left-hand trail, soon crossing a wood railed bridge over the outlet from Lagoon Pond. Following an old roadbed, the trail passes through open terrain, which was the site of an old Yurok village, but no trace of the settlement exists. Soon you reach a second junction, ▶3 with the beginning of the Yurok Loop.

Take the right-hand path, and dive into a tunnel of coastal vegetation until you break out into the open to a fine view of the ocean, highlighted by several sea-stacks. A park bench nearby invites passersby to linger and enjoy the stunning view. Beyond, the trail moves into viewless forest and continues southeast to a junction ▶4 between the Coastal Trail continuing southbound and the Yurok Loop circling back toward the trailhead.

Views

Proceed ahead on the Coastal Trail, with fine views of the beach and the ocean. Pass a short lateral on the right leading down to a camping area beneath a grove of spruce. Eventually, you reach a junction ▶5 with the short path down to Hidden Beach. If you're not in a hurry, turn right on a steep descent leading to a pile of driftwood, followed by

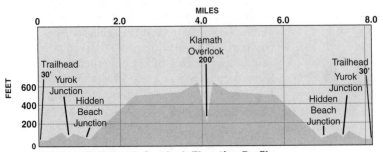

TRAIL 49 Klamath Overlook Elevation Profile

View from *a section of the Coastal Trail*

a stretch of boulders, and then the sand of Hidden Beach. The beach is blessed with good views of the ocean punctuated by a smattering of sea-stacks, and because it is about 0.5 mile from the closest road, you may have the area all to yourself.

Continuing straight ahead from the Hidden Beach junction, the Coastal Trail makes a steady ascent along the old roadbed through lush foliage. The dense, tall forest obscures ocean views, but the sound of the surf is complemented by the occasional barks of harbor seals. Farther on, the grade undulates across the forested hillside on a general traverse, where the trees part just enough to provide very brief, intermittent views of the ocean. Around 2 miles from the Hidden Beach junction, you reach a fenced overlook with a fine view of the coastline. The traverse continues well above the ocean, veering back under forest cover and crossing a couple of tiny streams before breaking out into the open again on the way to a junction with the lateral to the Klamath Overlook. ▶6

Views

Leave the Coastal Trail, and turn right at the junction, winding down the slope through lush foliage, including numerous blackberry brambles and a smattering of wildflowers in spring and early summer. The steady descent leads down to a fenced area ►7 atop a promontory, with an excellent view of the mouth of the Klamath River and the ocean. A park bench provides a place to sit and enjoy the vista.

Wildflowers

If you have arranged for a shuttle, retrace your steps back to the junction, and then head northeast a short distance to the Klamath Overlook parking lot. Otherwise, retrace your steps 4.1 miles to the Lagoon Creek Trailhead. ►8 By taking the right-hand section of the Yurok Loop on the way back, you can shave off 0.3 mile; however, its scenery is inferior.

MILESTONES

►1	0.0	Start at trailhead
►2	0.05	Straight at northbound Coastal Trail junction
►3	0.1	Right at Yurok Loop junction
►4	0.7	Straight at Yurok Loop junction
►5	1.2	Straight at Hidden Beach junction
►6	3.9	Right at Klamath Overlook junction
►7	4.1	Klamath Overlook
►8	8.2	Return to trailhead

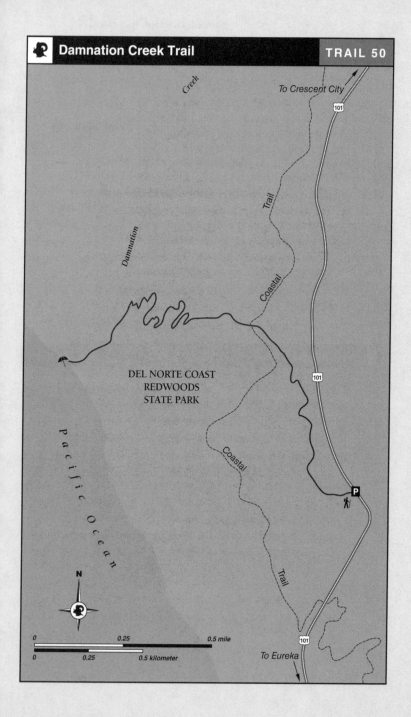

DEL NORTE COAST
REDWOODS
STATE PARK

Pacific Ocean

Damnation

Creek

To Crescent City

To Eureka

Trail

Coastal

Coastal

Trail

N

| 0 | | 0.25 | | 0.5 mile |
| 0 | | 0.25 | | 0.5 kilometer |

Damnation Creek Trail

The relatively short Damnation Creek Trail offers visitors a diverse sampling of beautiful coastal scenery. The route begins in an impressive stand of stately old-growth redwood forest, diminished in magnificence only by the sound of passing cars on US 101. After a stroll through the tall trees, the trail starts an uninterrupted descent to the coast, passing through serene redwood and then spruce forest. A steep descent along verdant Damnation Creek leads the final distance to a rugged, rocky cove at the ocean's edge. Hikers must save plenty of energy for the mostly uphill return trip.

TRAIL USE
Dayhiking

LENGTH & TIME
3.8 miles, 2–3 hours

VERTICAL FEET
+1,200'/-1,200'

DIFFICULTY
- 1 2 3 **4** 5 +

TRAIL TYPE
Out & Back

START & FINISH
N41° 38.895'
W124° 06.801'

Best Time

This is a fine hike at any time of year, except during and after winter storms.

Finding the Trail

The trailhead, located near mile marker 16 on US 101, can be hard to find. A dirt pullout on the west

FEATURES
Beach
Stream
Redwoods
Views
Wildflowers

FACILITIES
None

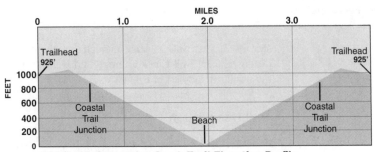

TRAIL 50 Damnation Creek Trail Elevation Profile

Fog-draped forest *on the Damnation Creek Trail*

side of the highway is large enough for about a dozen vehicles. Mill Creek Campground is north of the trailhead and east of US 101.

Trail Description

Initially, the Damnation Creek Trail rises mildly away from the highway ▶1 through an impressive grove of old-growth redwood forest. Redwood sorrel and ferns line the path, while rhododendron and tall huckleberry dot the forest floor. The area is often shrouded in fog, particularly in summer when a persistent marine layer hovers over the coastline, creating a rather primeval feel to the forest. The trail soon crests the journey's high point and then begins a moderate descent toward the coast. Eventually, the distant sound of the surf replaces the hum of vehicles on the highway. At 0.6 mile from the trailhead is a junction ►**2** with the Coastal Trail.

Continue ahead, remaining on the Damnation Creek Trail, soon veering onto an old roadbed briefly and then returning to single-track tread. Farther on, switchbacks aid the descent, as the forest transitions from redwood to spruce. After a while, the trail comes alongside Damnation Creek and heads downstream. Watch your footing along this stretch; the trail gets steeper and the tread is quite slick in places when wet. After crossing a pair of side streams on wood bridges, the forest opens up to coastal scrub on top of a bluff, which allows excellent views of the coast.

Follow a set of steps down to the creek, and then clamber over boulders onto the narrow, rocky beach. ►**3** Despite the stunning scenery, without any sand, the small cove doesn't lend itself to a lingering visit, although during very low tides it has some tidepools. When the time has come, retrace your steps back to the trailhead. ►**4**

Redwoods

Wildflowers

Stream

Views

Beach

🚶	**MILESTONES**	
►1	0.0	Start at trailhead
►2	0.6	Straight at Coastal Trail junction
►3	1.9	Beach
►4	3.8	Return to trailhead

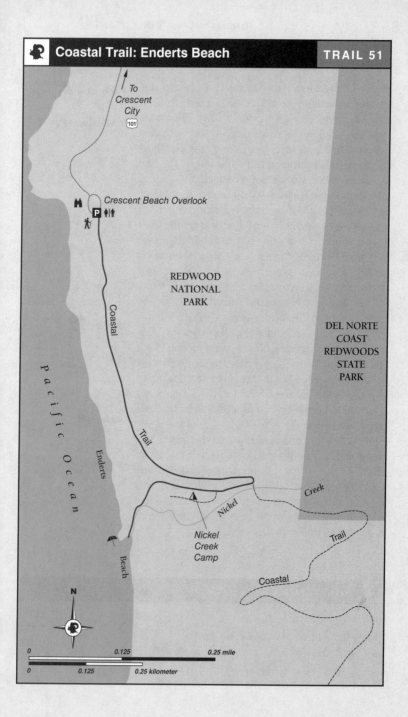

To
Crescent
City
[101]

Crescent Beach Overlook

P

REDWOOD
NATIONAL
PARK

DEL NORTE
COAST
REDWOODS
STATE
PARK

Coastal

P a c i f i c   O c e a n

Trail

Enderts

Creek

Nickel

Nickel
Creek
Camp

Beach

Coastal

Trail

N

| 0 | 0.125 | 0.25 mile |
| 0 | 0.125 | 0.25 kilometer |

Coastal Trail: Enderts Beach

A short stretch of the Coastal Trail, in an outlying section of Redwood National Park, leads to a picturesque sandy beach. Along the way are stunning coastal views and colorful wildflowers in spring and early summer.

Best Time

Although the trail is open all year, the ideal time for this trip is in spring or early summer, when skies are clear and wildflowers are blooming.

Finding the Trail

Immediately south of Crescent City, leave US 101 at Enderts Beach Road, and continue to the end at the parking lot for the Crescent Beach Overlook. Mill Creek Campground is north of the trailhead and east of US 101.

Trail Description

Pass through an opening ▶1 in a split rail fence, and follow the gravel surface of an old road, enjoying views of the ocean from Crescent City in the north to your destination of Enderts Beach immediately ahead. The lush trailside vegetation includes blackberry brambles, with the fruit ripening in late summer. Enter a stand of spruce forest, reaching an interpretive sign and a park bench nearby. Spring wildflowers include cow parsnip and daisy. Reach a junction near Nickel Creek, ▶2

TRAIL USE
Dayhiking, Running
LENGTH & TIME
1.5 miles, 1–2 hours
VERTICAL FEET
+175'/-175'
DIFFICULTY
- 1 **2** 3 4 5 +
TRAIL TYPE
Out & Back
START & FINISH
N41° 42.411'
W124° 08.602'

FEATURES
Beach
Wildflowers
Views
Backcountry Camping

FACILITIES
Restrooms
Picnic Area
Overlook

Views

Wildflowers

View of *Crescent City from Enderts Beach*

where the Coastal Trail continues ahead and the trail to the beach goes right.

Heading downhill, the trail passes a pit toilet and a lateral to sites at Nickel Creek Camp. Proceed ahead to where another interpretive sign provides information about tidepools, and then descend steeply to the sandy beach. ▶3 When you're ready, retrace your steps to the trailhead. ▶4

 Beach

🚶	**MILESTONES**	
▶1	0.0	Start at trailhead
▶2	0.5	Right at junction
▶3	0.75	Enderts Beach
▶4	1.5	Return to trailhead

Coastal Trail: Crescent Beach

This section of the California Coastal Trail (in an outlying section of Redwood National Park) begins at a sandy beach and ends at an overlook with a fine coastal view. Along the way, you pass through lush coastal vegetation well watered by several small rivulets. Picnic areas at the beginning and end offer the opportunity for combining the hike with a picnic lunch—a fine way to spend a few hours on the North Coast.

Best Time

Although the trail is open all year, wet, muddy conditions during the rainy winter season may deter the average hiker. Summer skies are often veiled with a blanket of fog, which may give days in spring and fall a better shot at clear and sunny weather. Spring and early summer offer colorful wildflowers.

Finding the Trail

Immediately south of Crescent City, leave US 101 at Enderts Beach Road, and continue 0.5 mile to a right-hand turn for the Crescent Beach Picnic Area. Follow this road to the end and park as space allows. The nearest public campground is Mill Creek Campground. Crescent City has a few RV parks and several motels.

Trail Description

From the parking area, ▶1 walk back up the picnic area access road a short distance to the start of the

TRAIL USE
Dayhiking, Running

LENGTH & TIME
4.0 miles, 2–3 hours

VERTICAL FEET
+225'/-225'

DIFFICULTY
- 1 **2** 3 4 5 +

TRAIL TYPE
Out & Back

START & FINISH
N41° 42.637'
W124° 09.124

FEATURES
Beach
Wildlife
Views

FACILITIES
Restrooms
Picnic Area
Overlook

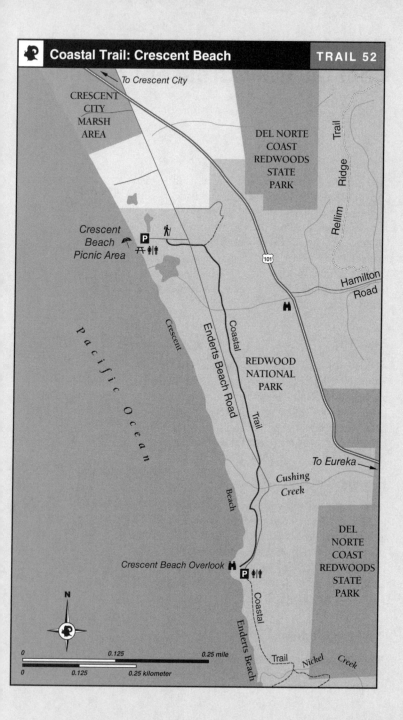

Coastal Trail: Crescent Beach

TRAIL 52

To Crescent City

CRESCENT CITY MARSH AREA

DEL NORTE COAST REDWOODS STATE PARK

Rellim Ridge Trail

Crescent Beach Picnic Area

P

Hamilton Road

101

Pacific Ocean

Crescent

Enderts Beach Road

Coastal

Trail

REDWOOD NATIONAL PARK

To Eureka

Cushing Creek

Beach

DEL NORTE COAST REDWOODS STATE PARK

Crescent Beach Overlook

P

N

Coastal

Enderts Beach

Trail

Nickel Creek

| 0 | 0.125 | 0.25 mile |
| 0 | 0.125 | 0.25 kilometer |

Ocean view *from the Crescent Beach Trail*

trail on the right-hand side. With the ever-present sound of the crashing surf as your companion, head across grasslands to a crossing of Enderts Beach Road, and continue east for a while to a T-junction ▶2 with a path from the old Enderts Beach House. You may see a herd of elk in the vicinity, but if you don't, signs of their presence will likely be scattered across the grassy field.

Wildlife

Turn right at the junction, and bear south across a mowed section of coastal grasses, soon crossing a short plank bridge over the first of many tiny streams to come. Enter a tunnel of moss-covered alders, breaking briefly back out into the open near the bridged crossing of Hamilton Creek. Continue southbound, crossing four more bridges over thin streams and emerging from the dense vegetation on the way to a crossing of Enderts Beach Road.

Pick up the trail on the far side, and drop shortly to an area with an old picnic table near a bridged crossing of picturesque Cushing Creek. From there, climb wood rail steps and soon begin climbing toward the overlook, crossing one more bridge along the way. Soon the vegetation parts enough to allow a good view of the coast, a precursor to the grand vista awaiting at the overlook. The steep topography then forces the trail onto the road, which you walk up to the open, grass-covered top of the bluff at the Crescent Beach Overlook. ►3 The expansive view stretches south along the coast for several miles and also north along Crescent Beach to Crescent City. Interpretive signs identify some of the visible significant landmarks, as well as information about sea-stacks and whale watching.

H Views

After enjoying the overlook, retrace your steps back to the trailhead. ►4 To extend the hike, you could follow the Coastal Trail from the lower end of the parking lot toward Enderts Beach (see Trail 51).

🏃	MILESTONES	
►1	0.0	Start at Crescent Beach Picnic Area
►2	0.4	Right at junction
►3	2.0	Klamath Overlook
►4	4.0	Return to picnic area

Opposite *Enderts Beach*

Jedediah Smith Redwoods

Jedediah Smith Redwoods

Jedediah Smith Redwoods State Park is the farthest north redwood park in California, which limits its number of tourists compared to some of the parks farther south. Jed Smith is also perhaps the most pristine of the Redwood Coast national and state parks and offers some of the best redwood scenery as well. Unfortunately for hikers, trails, especially ones that enter the magnificent redwood backcountry, are rather scarce. Most of the area's hiking trails are short and close to highways and roads, with the Boy Scout Trail the lone exception. Additionally, the location of the largest trees, including the Del Norte Titan and the Grove of Titans, is kept secret to minimize environmental degradation.

Permits

Permits are not required for any of these trips. The park does not charge an entrance fee.

Maps

By far, the best map covering Del Norte Coast Redwoods State Park and vicinity is the 1:25,000-scale map *Redwood National and State Parks North*, published by Redwood Hikes Press. The accurate, detailed, full-color, topographic map shows trails with mileages and the location of footbridges and memorial redwood grove signs and benches.

Overleaf and opposite: *Redwood forest, Jedediah Smith Redwoods State Park*

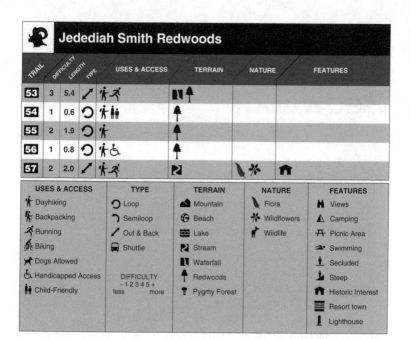

Jedediah Smith Redwoods

TRAIL	DIFFICULTY	LENGTH	TYPE	USES & ACCESS	TERRAIN	NATURE	FEATURES
53	3	5.4	↗	🚶🏃	◗▮🌲		
54	1	0.6	↻	🚶👫	🌲		
55	2	1.9	↻	🚶	🌲		
56	1	0.8	↻	🚶♿	🌲		
57	2	2.0	↗	🚶🏃	⤵	🍃✳	🏠

USES & ACCESS	TYPE	TERRAIN	NATURE	FEATURES
🚶 Dayhiking	↻ Loop	◣ Mountain	🍃 Flora	🔭 Views
🎒 Backpacking	↱ Semiloop	🏖 Beach	✳ Wildflowers	⛰ Camping
🏃 Running	↗ Out & Back	🌊 Lake	🦌 Wildlife	⛩ Picnic Area
🚴 Biking	🚌 Shuttle	⤵ Stream		⤴ Swimming
🐕 Dogs Allowed		◗▮ Waterfall		⬇ Secluded
♿ Handicapped Access	DIFFICULTY	🌲 Redwoods		⬇ Steep
👫 Child-Friendly	- 1 2 3 4 5 +	⚘ Pygmy Forest		🏠 Historic Interest
	less more			▦ Resort town
				⬇ Lighthouse

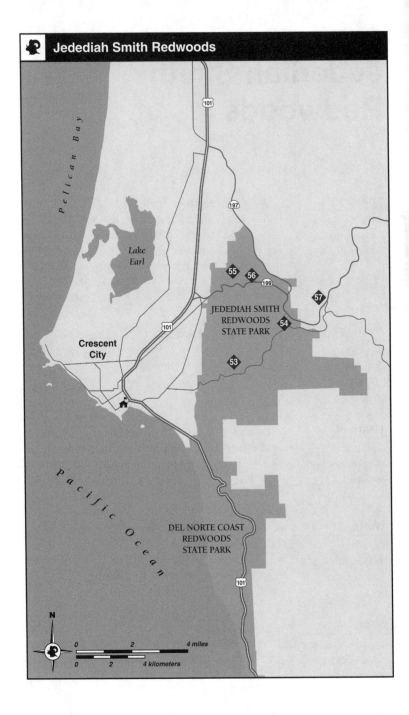

Pelican Bay

Lake Earl

Crescent City

JEDEDIAH SMITH
REDWOODS
STATE PARK

Pacific Ocean

DEL NORTE COAST
REDWOODS
STATE PARK

N

0   2   4 miles

0   2   4 kilometers

Jedediah Smith Redwoods

Boy Scout Tree Trail

Given its distance from the megapopulation centers of Northern California compared to the more popular redwood parks farther south, you would think that Jedediah Smith Redwoods State Park would experience fewer visitors. But the Boy Scout Tree Trail seems to defy convention, as the small parking area is often full on summer weekends. The only trail to enter the heart of the park's backcountry traverses through attractive groves of old-growth redwoods on the way to an immense coastal sequoia and a scenic waterfall. The trail's distance from the highway allows visitors the opportunity to enjoy the redwoods the way they should be enjoyed—in peace and quiet.

Best Time

The trail can be hiked at any time during the year, although rainy spells in winter make the tread muddy and unappealing. The waterfall is typically at a dramatic zenith in early spring.

Finding the Trail

From US 101 in Crescent City, head east on Elk River Road for 1 mile, and turn right onto Howland Hill Road. Follow this road for 2.7 miles to the trailhead parking area, which is 0.2 mile past the Nickerson Ranch Trailhead. Alongside the road, there is enough parking for about a half dozen vehicles.

Trail Description

A gently graded trail ▶1 leads away from the road into old-growth redwood forest, soon crossing a

TRAIL USE
Dayhiking, Running

LENGTH & TIME
5.4 miles, 4–7 hours

VERTICAL FEET
+750'/-750'

DIFFICULTY
- 1 2 **3** 4 5 +

TRAIL TYPE
Out & Back

START & FINISH
N41° 46.138'
W124° 06.587'

FEATURES
Waterfall
Redwoods

FACILITIES
None

Redwoods

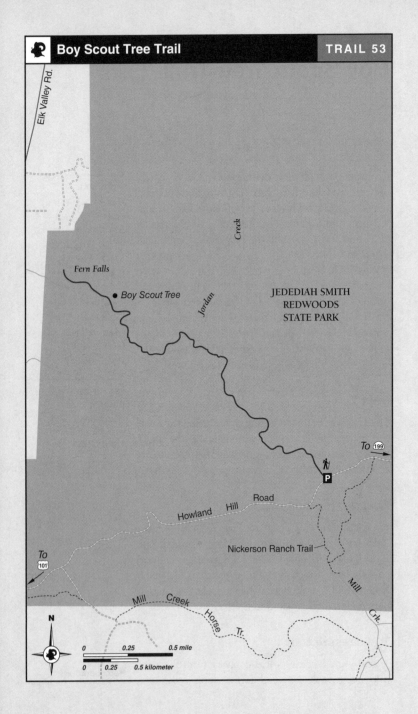

Elk Valley Rd.

Creek

Fern Falls

● Boy Scout Tree

Jordan

JEDEDIAH SMITH
REDWOODS
STATE PARK

To 199

P

Howland   Hill   Road

To
101

Nickerson Ranch Trail

Mill

Mill   Creek

Horse   Tr.

Crk.

N

0   0.25   0.5 mile
0   0.25   0.5 kilometer

Rhododendron and redwoods *on the Boy Scout Tree Trail*

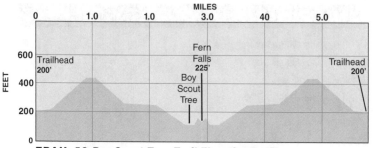

TRAIL 53 Boy Scout Tree Trail Elevation Profile

wood rail bridge over a sluggish stream. Climb stiffly before the grade eases again, and a couple of massive downed redwoods provide classic examples of plant succession in the redwood forest. A lengthy descent leads to a set of steps down to a bridged crossing of Jordan Creek. Tackle a short climb, and then follow a rolling traverse through the forest. Soon, a couple of short-legged switchbacks guide you down to a short bridge over a side stream and then around the nose of a ridge above the creek. Follow the creek downstream, and then veer into a side drainage and cross another bridge. Beyond the bridge, work your way back into the main channel, and reach an unmarked junction ►2 with the short lateral to the Boy Scout Tree on the right.

Two short paths scale the steep hillside up to the twin-trunked giant of a redwood. The right-hand path switchbacks across the slope, which must be the original trail, while a use trail on the left climbs straight up the steep hillside.

Waterfall

Continue ahead (northwest) from the junction, soon crossing two more bridges and rounding a hillside on the way to Fern Falls. ►3 Reach the base of the falls, which spills down black rock bordered by moss and ferns—a most picturesque sight. Nearby, tall old-growth redwoods stand guard.

After enjoying the falls, retrace your steps to the trailhead. ►4

🚶	MILESTONES	
►1	0.0	Start at trailhead
►2	2.5	Boy Scout Tree
►3	2.7	Fern Falls
►4	5.4	Return to trailhead

Stout Grove Loop

Barely long enough to be considered a hike, the Stout Grove Loop harbors some of the most photogenic old-growth redwoods in any of the Redwood Coast national or state parks. Therefore, the grove should not be missed.

Best Time

Like most trails in the redwood parks, the Stout Grove Loop is usually open all year, although the access road and trail may be a mess during and after heavy rainstorms. Summer season, when the lighting is best in late afternoon, sees the most visitors. Spring and fall, when visitation is lighter, are excellent seasons to enjoy the grove.

Finding the Trail

The easiest way to reach the grove in summer is to walk over the seasonal footbridge across the Smith River from the south end of Jedediah Smith Campground and turn left (southeast) toward the Stout Grove. At other times of the year, from US 101 in Crescent City, you can head east on Elk River Road for 1 mile, and turn right onto Howland Hill Road. Follow it 4.6 miles (passing the trailhead for the Boy Scout Tree at 2.7 miles) to the Stout Grove turnoff.

Most drivers will instead opt to take CA 199 eastbound from the junction with US 101 just north of Crescent City and follow the highway 6.7 miles to a junction with the South Fork Road. Turn right at the junction, cross a bridge over the Smith River, and then cross a second bridge over the South

TRAIL USE
Dayhiking,
Child-Friendly

LENGTH & TIME
0.6 mile, ½–1 hour

VERTICAL FEET
+50'/-50'

DIFFICULTY
- **1** 2 3 4 5 +

TRAIL TYPE
Loop

START & FINISH
N41° 47.367'
W124° 05.073'

FEATURES
Redwoods

FACILITIES
Restrooms

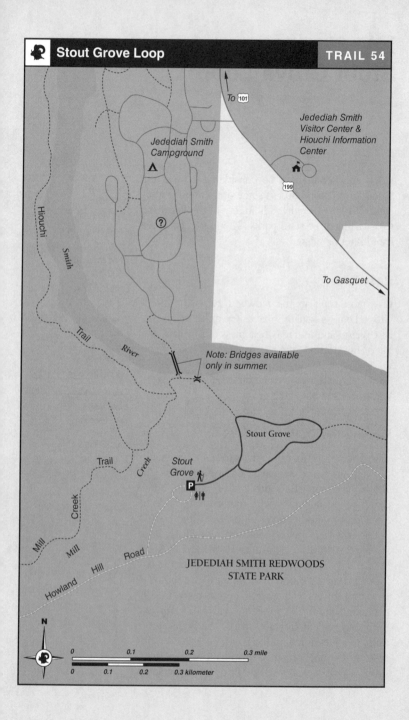

Stout Grove Loop

TRAIL 54

Jedediah Smith
Visitor Center &
Hiouchi Information
Center

To 101

199

To Gasquet

Jedediah Smith
Campground

Hiouchi

Smith

Trail

River

Note: Bridges available
only in summer.

Stout Grove

Stout
Grove

P

Trail

Creek

Creek

Mill

Mill

Howland Hill Road

JEDEDIAH SMITH REDWOODS
STATE PARK

N

| 0 | 0.1 | 0.2 | 0.3 mile |

| 0 | 0.1 | 0.2 | 0.3 kilometer |

Fork. Turn right at the intersection on the far side of the South Fork Bridge onto Douglas Park Drive, which becomes Howland Hill Road at the end of the pavement. Continue on dirt road past the Little Bald Hills Trailhead, and turn right onto the short access road to the small Stout Grove parking area, 2.4 miles from intersection.

The park has one campground, which is just off of CA 199 across from the visitor center. Hiouchi Hamlet RV Park is a private facility near the town of Hiouchi. Crescent City has a few RV parks and several motels.

Admirers *in the Stout Grove*

Trail Description

From the parking lot, ▶1 descend a short section of paved road to the start of the loop. ▶2 Turn right, following signed directions to the Hiouchi Trail, and begin a counterclockwise circuit through the old-growth grove. Periodic flooding from the nearby Smith River has kept this flat free of a shrubby understory, allowing the tall and straight redwoods to rise unobstructed above a lush carpet of redwood sorrel and ferns. Just after a memorial bench is a junction ▶3 with the River Trail headed east.

🌲 **Redwoods**

Turn left to remain on the loop, following the course of the unseen river downstream. Soon you reach a junction ▶4 with a lateral on the right leading down to seasonal bridges over Mill Creek and Smith River, which connects to the Mill Creek and Hiouchi Trails, as well as Jedediah Smith Campground.

Turn left at the junction, and head back toward the close of the loop. On the way is the Stout Tree, by far the tallest redwood in the grove. At the next junction, ▶5 turn right and retrace your steps up the paved road to the parking lot. ▶6

🚶	**MILESTONES**	
▶1	0.0	Start at trailhead
▶2	0.1	Left at loop junction
▶3	0.25	Left at River Trail junction
▶4	0.4	Left at lateral junction
▶5	0.5	Right at loop junction
▶6	0.6	Return to trailhead

Leiffer & Ellsworth Loops

As the northernmost trails in the redwood parks, the Leiffer and Ellsworth Loops don't receive the volume of tourists common to some of the groves farther south. A fair distance away from CA 199, the area is less prone to traffic noise than some of those groves as well. While you may not see any spectacular giants with correspondingly statuesque names, these old-growth redwoods are quite impressive in their own right.

Best Time

The trail is open all year.

Finding the Trail

From US 101 north of Crescent City, follow CA 199 east for 2.8 miles to a left-hand turn onto Walker Road. Proceed up the road, which soon turns to gravel after a bridge over Clarks Creek. At 0.6 mile from the highway is a small parking area on the left marked by a small sign for the Leiffer Trail, across the road from a larger sign for the Adams Grove. The park has one campground, which is just off of CA 199 across from the visitor center. Hiouchi Hamlet RV Park is a private facility near the town of Hiouchi. Crescent City has a few RV parks and several motels.

Trail Description

From the trailhead, ▶1 follow the wide track of the former road into redwood forest, soon crossing a

TRAIL USE
Dayhiking

LENGTH & TIME
1.9 miles, 1–2 hours

VERTICAL FEET
+325'/-325'

DIFFICULTY
- 1 **2** 3 4 5 +

TRAIL TYPE
Loop

START & FINISH
N41° 49.165'
W124° 06.637'

FEATURES
Redwoods

FACILITIES
None

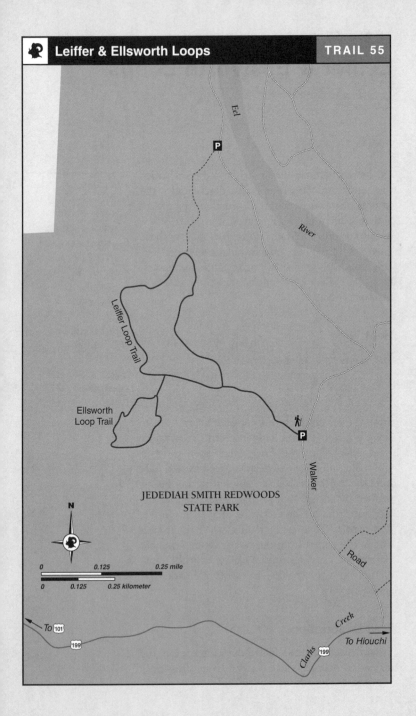

Eel

River

Leiffer Loop Trail

Ellsworth
Loop Trail

JEDEDIAH SMITH REDWOODS
STATE PARK

N

0   0.125   0.25 mile
0   0.125   0.25 kilometer

Walker

Road

To 101

199

Creek

Clarks

199

To Hiouchi

wood rail bridge and a boardwalk before reaching a junction ►**2** with the Leiffer Loop.

Turn left at the junction, and arc around to the northwest on the way to a junction ►**3** with the Ellsworth Loop Trail near a redwood bench.

Turning left, walk a very short distance to the start of the loop, and bear left to follow a clockwise circuit through the forest. The trail climbs rather stiffly up the hillside, from where you have a good view of the towering redwoods on the flat below. A couple of benches offer the opportunity to rest and enjoy the serenity of the forest. Just after you pass through a pair of fire-charred but still living redwoods, an equally stiff descent winds down the hillside and returns to the end of the loop. From there, retrace your steps a very short distance back to the junction ►**4** with the Leiffer Loop.

At the Ellsworth and Leiffer Loops junction, veer to the left to continue the clockwise circuit on the Leiffer Loop. After passing another memorial bench, the trail climbs moderately for a stretch, followed by a sometimes steep, winding descent on the way to the junction with the lateral to the north trailhead. ►**5**

Taking the right-hand path, the route heads south back to the end of the loop at the first junction. ►**6** From there, retrace your steps 0.2 mile to the trailhead. ►**7**

Redwoods 🌲

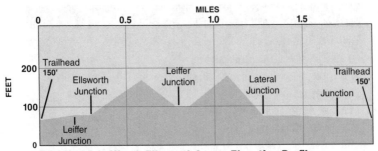

TRAIL 55 Leiffer & Ellsworth Loops Elevation Profile

Sign in Ellsworth Grove

🚶	**MILESTONES**	
►1	0.0	Start at trailhead
►2	0.2	Left at Leiffer Loop junction
►3	0.3	Left at Ellsworth Loop junction
►4	0.8	Left at Leiffer junction
►5	1.2	Right at lateral junction
►6	1.7	Left at junction
►7	1.9	Return to trailhead

Simpson-Reed & Peterson Loop

Combining these two short loops creates an easy stroll through a picturesque redwood grove suitable for just about anyone. The old-growth redwood forest is quite lush, with a particularly dense and varied understory, including moss-covered hemlocks and a number of deciduous varieties somewhat unusual for a typical redwood forest. Interpretive signs along the Simpson-Reed section provide a good introduction to the history and ecology of the redwood forest. The grove is directly north of CA 199, but the dense foliage seems to be fairly effective at muffling some of the traffic noise.

Best Time

The trail is open all year. Autumn can be quite colorful when the leaves of the hazels and maples are turning.

Finding the Trail

From US 101 north of Crescent City, follow CA 199 east for 2.8 miles to a left-hand turn onto Walker Road. The trailhead parking area is a very short distance up the road on the right side. The park has one campground, which is just off of CA 199 across from the visitor center. Hiouchi Hamlet RV Park is a private facility near the town of Hiouchi. Crescent City has a few RV parks and several motels.

TRAIL USE
Dayhiking, Handicapped Access
LENGTH & TIME
0.8 mile, ½–1 hour
VERTICAL FEET
Nominal
DIFFICULTY
- **1** 2 3 4 5 +
TRAIL TYPE
Loop
START & FINISH
N41° 48.745'
W124° 06.548'

FEATURES
Redwoods

FACILITIES
None

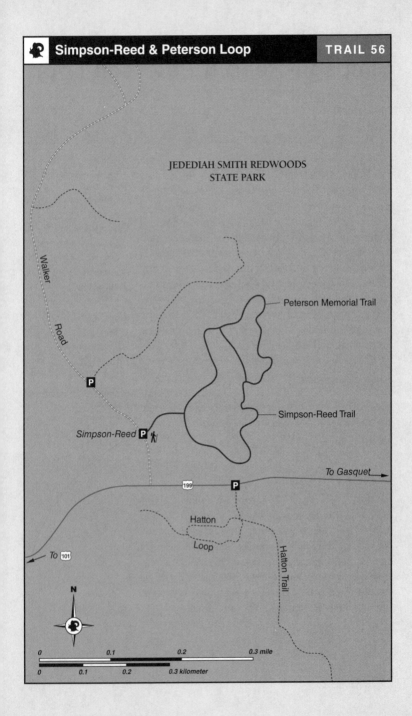

Simpson-Reed & Peterson Loop

TRAIL 56

JEDEDIAH SMITH REDWOODS
STATE PARK

Walker

Road

Peterson Memorial Trail

Simpson-Reed Trail

Simpson-Reed

To Gasquet

199

Hatton

Loop

To 101

Hatton Trail

N

0   0.1   0.2   0.3 mile
0   0.1   0.2   0.3 kilometer

Charred redwood *on the Simpson-Reed Trail*

Trail Description

Walk away from the parking area ▶1 on a flat, wide, graveled section of wheelchair-accessible tread lined with ferns, passing the bases of a pair of upended redwoods on the way to the loop junction. ▶2

 Redwoods

Turn left and follow a clockwise circuit through the old-growth redwood forest, immediately reaching the first of several interpretive signs to come. Travel alongside a massive downed redwood, and continue past some upright monarchs to a three-way junction ▶3 just beyond a memorial bench.

If you are pressed for time, take the path straight ahead to follow the Simpson-Reed Trail back to the trailhead. Otherwise, veer left onto the Peterson Memorial Trail. Cross a bridge over a small stream, and follow it for a while before the trail bends away into the forest. The route arcs back to the south, crosses two more bridges over seasonal swales, and comes to the next junction ▶4 with the Simpson-Reed Trail.

Continuing south, you follow the Simpson-Reed Trail back toward the trailhead, passing more interpretive signs along the way. Eventually, you reach the first junction, ▶5 turn left, and walk shortly back to the parking area. ▶6

🚶	MILESTONES	
▶1	0.0	Start at trailhead
▶2	0.1	Left at junction
▶3	0.3	Left at junction
▶4	0.5	Left at junction
▶5	0.7	Left at junction
▶6	0.8	Return to trailhead

Myrtle Creek Trail

Lying at the boundary of two distinct soil types and positioned halfway between the cool coastal zone and the warmer interior forest, the Myrtle Creek Botanical Area has received one of four special botanical designations within the Smith River Watershed. While the botanical area contains nearly 2,000 acres and ranges in elevation between 200 and 1,400 feet, the Myrtle Creek Trail is a 1-mile romp through the lower elevations above the namesake creek. The trail packs a lot of interest and diversity, including second-growth redwood forest and mixed evergreen forest, into a small package. Interpretive signs provide extensive insights into the human and natural history of this unique environment.

Best Time

Its biologic diversity and low elevation makes the mile-long trek along Myrtle Creek suitable for any time of year, although late spring provides the added bonus of blooming rhododendrons and trailside wildflowers.

Finding the Trail

From the US 101 and CA 199 junction north of Crescent City, head eastbound on CA 199 for 6.7 miles to a parking area on the right-hand shoulder (2.0 miles beyond the Hiouchi Visitor Center for Jedediah Smith Redwoods State Park and immediately prior to the South Fork Road turnoff toward Stout Grove, Trail 54). The trail begins by a small

TRAIL USE
Dayhiking, Running
LENGTH & TIME
2.0 miles, 1–2 hours
VERTICAL FEET
+350'/-350'
DIFFICULTY
- 1 **2** 3 4 5 +
TRAIL TYPE
Out & Back
START & FINISH
N41° 48.121'
W124° 03.272'

FEATURES
Stream
Flora
Wildflowers
Historic Interest

FACILITIES
None

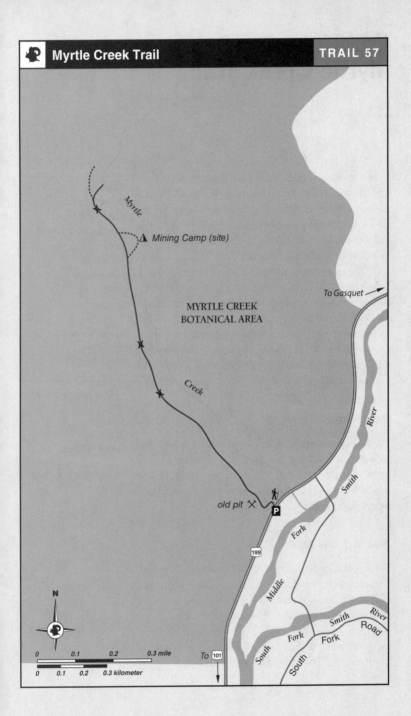

Myrtle Creek Trail

TRAIL 57

Myrtle

▲ *Mining Camp (site)*

MYRTLE CREEK
BOTANICAL AREA

Creek

To Gasquet →

Smith

River

old pit ✕

P

199

Fork

Middle

N

| 0 | 0.1 | 0.2 | 0.3 mile |

| 0 | 0.1 | 0.2 | 0.3 kilometer |

To 101

South Fork

Smith Fork River Road

South

sign on the opposite side of the highway. The park
has one campground, which is just off of CA 199
across from the visitor center. Hiouchi Hamlet RV
Park is a private facility near the town of Hiouchi.
Crescent City has a few RV parks and several motels.

Trail Description

The trail begins near a small sign marked "Myrtle
Creek Trail 1E01" ▶1 and immediately starts climbing up the hillside past a sign about the area's
unique botanical and historical significance. Nearby
is a post with the first of 15 interpretive signs,
beyond which the trail switchbacks and ascends
deeper into the trees. Proceed upstream, passing
through second-growth redwood forest, with associates of Douglas fir, tanoak, evergreen huckleberry,
and Pacific rhododendron. Springtime visitors are
treated to a wide variety of colorful wildflowers. A
short, moderate climb leads alongside the remnants
of an old ditch used for hydraulic mining during the
turn of the 20th century. Here the grade eases for
the remainder of the journey.

Proceed upstream, well above Myrtle Creek on
gently graded tread next to the old ditch, passing
several interpretive signs related to the old mining
days and this drainage's diverse vegetation. About
0.25 mile up the canyon, the serpentine soils support a different type of foliage, which is highlighted
on some of the interpretive signs. A seep farther on
supports some rare plants, including the California
pitcher plant. Near interpretive sign 10, a faint side
trail drops down to a flat next to the river, where
the miners established a camp. That trail continues
through the camp and climbs back up the hillside
to rejoin the main trail a short distance upstream.

Continuing on the Myrtle Creek Trail, three
bridges span tributary creeks, as you continue
upstream. Just past interpretive sign 15, the trail

Stream

descends steeply to the banks of beautiful Myrtle Creek, ►2 a fine spot to grab a bite or to simply enjoy the surroundings. When the time has come, retrace your steps back to the trailhead. ►3

🚶	**MILESTONES**	

►1	0.0	Start at trailhead
►2	1.0	Trails end at Myrtle Creek
►3	2.0	Return to trailhead

Opposite *Myrtle Creek*

Appendix 1

Top-Rated Trails

Chapter 1: Mendocino
Trail 3: Fern Canyon & Pygmy Forest Loop
Trail 4: Chapman Point & Spring Ranch Headlands
Trail 8: Russian Gulch Loop
Trail 9: Point Cabrillo Light Station

Chapter 2: King Range & Sinkyone Wilderness
Trail 13: Lost Coast Trail: North Section
Trail 14: Lightning Trail to King Peak
Trail 15: Lost Coast Trail: South Section

Chapter 3: Humboldt
Trail 19: Founders Grove & Mahan Loop
Trail 20: Rockefeller Grove Loop
Trail 21: Big Tree Loop
Trail 22: Big Tree & Homestead Loop
Trail 23: Bull Creek Flats & Big Tree Loop
Trail 26: Grieg, French & Bell Groves Loop
Trail 27: Drury-Chaney Loop
Trail 28: Cheatham Grove

Chapter 4: Redwood National Park & Vicinity
Trail 30: Trinidad Head Loop
Trail 31: Agate Beach & Rim Trails
Trail 35: Tall Trees Grove
Trail 36: Emerald Ridge Loop
Trail 37: Dolason Prairie Trail
Trail 40: Trillium Falls Loop

Appendix 2

Campgrounds & RV Parks

Chapter 1: Mendocino

Hendy Woods State Park

Azalea Campground
Wildcat Campground

Van Damme State Park

Van Damme Campground
Environmental Campground

Russian Gulch State Park

Russian Gulch Campground

Caspar

Caspar Beach RV Park

Jackson State Demonstration Forest

Dunlap Campground

Fort Bragg

Pomo RV Park and Campground
Fort Bragg Leisure Time RV Park

MacKerricher State Park

East Pine
West Pine
Cleone
Surfwood

Westport

Westport Beach RV and Camping
Westport-Union Landing State Beach

Chapter 2: King Range & Sinkyone Wilderness

Mattole

Mattole Campground (BLM)

A.W. Way County Park

Honeydew

Honeydew Creek (BLM)

Shelter Cove Area

Tolkan (BLM)

Horse Mountain (BLM)

Nadelos (BLM)

Wailaki (BLM)

Shelter Cove Campground and Deli

Sinkyone Wilderness State Park

Orchard Creek Campground

Usal Campground

Chapter 3: Humboldt

Meyers Flat

Giant Redwoods RV and Camp

Humboldt Redwoods State Park

Hidden Springs Campground

Burlington Campground

Albee Creek Campground

Grizzly Creek Redwoods State Park

Grizzly Creek Campground

Chapter 4: Redwood National Park & Vicinity

Trinidad

Hidden Creek

Emerald Forest

Midway RV Park

View Crest Lodge, Cottages, and Campground

Sylvan Harbor RV Park and Cabins

Sounds of the Sea RV Park

Patrick's Point State Park

Penn Creek
Abalone
Agate Beach
Humboldt Lagoons State Park
Big Lagoon County Park
Dry Lagoon Walk-In
Stone Lagoon Boat-In

Chapter 5: Prairie Creek

Prairie Creek Redwoods State Park

Elk Prairie Campground
Gold Bluffs Beach Campground

Klamath River

Terwer Park
Steelhead Lodge
Klamath's Camper Corral
Camp Marigold
Chinook RV Resort
Mystic Forest RV Park

Redwood National Park

Flint Ridge Walk-in

Chapter 6: Del Norte Coast Redwoods

Mill Creek Campground

Chapter 7: Jedediah Smith Redwoods

Crescent City

Sunset Harbor RV Park
Village Camper Inn RV Park
Bayside RV Park
Crescent City Redwoods KOA

Jedediah Smith Redwoods State Park

Jedediah Smith Campground

Hiouchi

Hiouchi Hamlet RV Resort

Appendix 3

Hotels, Lodges, Motels & Resorts

The magnificent scenery of Northern California's Redwood Coast is a long journey from any major metropolitan area, which makes the region a destination rather than something to see along the way to somewhere else. Consequently, it offers a vast array of lodging options for a broad spectrum of travelers, from primitive tent camping to upscale resorts and bed-and-breakfasts. Attempting to list all of the lodging facilities and keep them up to date would be a part-time job. Therefore, this appendix makes only general comments about each area. Except for Mendocino County, the best resources for finding lodging in a particular area may be your favorite online travel site.

Mendocino County

Mendocino County has long been a highly regarded destination for romantic getaways. The resort communities of Albion, Little River, and Mendocino cater to tourists, and lodging tends to be pricey. Fort Bragg has several motels for the more price-conscious traveler. Check out **mendocino.com/ mendocino-hotels** for more information.

The Lost Coast

Garberville, the largest town on US 101 near the road to Shelter Cove, has a handful of motels. The quaint resort community of Shelter Cove has several lodging properties.

Humboldt Redwoods State Park & Humboldt County

The few tiny communities peppering this state park along the Avenue of the Giants offer limited lodging opportunities. To the south, Garberville has a handful of motels. To the north, Fortuna, Eureka, and Arcata have many lodging options.

Redwood National Park

The Eureka and Arcata area, with its many lodging options, is many a travelers' springboard to adventures in the far Northern California national and state parks. Farther north, the tiny resort community of Trinidad offers numerous inns and campgrounds.

Prairie Creek Redwoods State Park

Just north of Redwood National Park, Prairie Creek Redwoods State Park relies on the same lodging options in the Eureka and Arcata area and Trinidad. The small Klamath River community to the north has a couple of motels, a bed-and-breakfast, a historic inn, and a few RV campgrounds. Crescent City farther north has several motels.

Del Norte Coast Redwoods & Jedediah Smith Redwoods

The town of Crescent City, which has several motels, serves both these state parks.

Appendix 4

Major Organizations

Friends of the Dunes
PO Box 186
Arcata, CA 95518
707-444-1397; email: info@freindsofthedunes.org
friendsofthedunes.org

Mendocino Coast Audubon Society
PO Box 2297
Fort Bragg, CA 95437
mendocinocoastaudubon.org

Mendocino Land Trust
PO Box 1094
Mendocino, CA 95460
707-962-0470; email: admin@mendocinolandtrust.org
mendocinolandtrust.org

Redwood Parks Association
1111 Second Street
Crescent City, CA 95531
707-464-9150
redwoodparksassociation.org

Save the Redwoods League
114 Sansome Street, Suite 1200
San Francisco, CA 94104
415-362-2352; email: info@savetheredwoods.org
savetheredwoods.org

Sierra Club-Redwood Chapter
PO Box 466
Santa Rosa, CA 95402
707-544-7651
redwood.sierraclub.org

Appendix 5

Useful Resources

Backpacking & Hiking
Beffort, Brian. *Joy of Backpacking*. Berkeley, CA: Wilderness Press, 2007.

Guidebooks
Brett, Dan. *Hiking the Redwood Coast*. Guilford, CT: Globe Pequot Press, 2004.

Freeze, Dennis F. *Mendocino Outdoors*. 3rd ed. Alameda, CA: Monolith Press, 2008.

Lorentzen, Robert S. *The Hiker's Hip Pocket Guide to the Humboldt Coast*. Mendocino, CA: Bored Feet Press, 1993.

———. *The Hiker's Hip Pocket Guide to the Mendocino Coast*. Mendocino, CA: Bored Feet Press, 1998.

McKinney, John. *California's Coastal Parks, A Day Hiker's Guide*. Berkeley, CA: Wilderness Press, 2005.

Rohde, Jerry, and Gisela Rohde. *Best Short Hikes in Redwood National and State Parks*. Seattle: The Mountaineers Books, 2004.

History & Literature
Widlick, Richard. *Trouble in the Forest: California's Redwood Timber Wars*. Minneapolis: University of Minnesota Press, 2009.

Natural History
Noss, Reed F., ed. *The Redwood Forest*. Washington, D.C.: Island Press, 2000.

Topographic Maps

California's Lost Coast. 3rd ed. Birmingham, AL: Wilderness Press, 2004.

Humboldt Redwoods State Park. Campbell, CA: Redwood Hikes Press, 2011.

King Range National Conservation Area. Bureau of Land Management. Medford, OR: Allan Cartography, 2005.

Redwood National and State Parks. Evergreen, CO: National Geographic Society, 1992.

Redwood National and State Parks North. Campbell, CA: Redwood Hikes Press, 2010.

Redwood National and State Parks South. Campbell, CA: Redwood Hikes Press, 2011.

Index